1

Priests, Prophets, Politicians, People and Protests

By
David R Amies

Priests, Prophets, Politicians, People and Protests

By
David R Amies

Priests, Prophets, Politicians, People and Protests

David R Amies

Ost.J, BA, MBBS(Hons), FRCS(Edin) FRCOph

Formerly Consultant in Ophthalmology, Medical Branch, Royal Air Force,
Senior Specialist, Royal Darwin Hospital, Northern Territory, Australia,
Senior Lecturer, UNSW and Head of Campus, Rural Clinical School,
Coffs Harbour, NSW, Australia

Dedication

To my wife, Patricia, with love

Acknowledgements

Linda Wasylciw helped me greatly with the mechanics of actual publication.
Jack Wynters provided very useful advice on points of style
To both of them, many thanks.

Table of Contents

Chapter Three – Politics

Chapter Four – People

Chapter Five – Protests

Bon mot

'I studied deeply in the philosophies and the
religions
but cheerfulness kept breaking through.'
(Leonard Cohen, singer-song writer and poet.)

Foreword by Pamela Soroczynski

David Amies has written the essays that comprise this book on the basis of the worldwide life experience gained in his eighty years of living. He has applied an excellent education and his significant intellect to this life experience, and so formed opinions on issues of personal and social interest that, because he likes words, he has committed to writing. Whether one agrees or disagrees with his opinions, one will find stimulation in reading them, and involvement in the points of view that he proposes so strongly.

However, one of the most interesting aspects of David's essays is the self-assurance and certainty that he has in the points of view that he espouses. I first encountered this self-assurance when young. My paternal grandfather's relatives came from the same region of England as David and they, also, spoke and wrote with the self-assurance and certainty that is characteristic of his writing. Of course, this could be a fluke. It could, on the other hand, be a character trait of those who were raised and educated in twentieth century England. As I was considering this idea, it seemed to me to be also possible that self-assurance and certainty could, be characteristics of the English as a people. Clearly, there is no doubt, that over five hundred years, the English developed a vast and worldwide empire. More than just a mastery of navigation and the sea, as well as the profit motive, must have been needed to establish and maintain this success.

In the words of "the Guardian Weekly" of 20-26th March, 2015, "For a century, the East India Company conquered, subjugated and plundered vast tracts of south Asia." But, as we all know, the company of Englishmen who undertook this operation was not large. The men of the East India Company, the men who took possession of Canada, South Africa,

Australia and New Zealand, and all the other possessions that made up the British Empire were never numerous. It is the opinion of this writer, that two characteristics, among others, which these Englishmen must have possessed, were self-assurance and certainty. And it is also my opinion that my friend, David, is heir to this strong and characteristic legacy.

It is, therefore, with a sense of privilege that I have undertaken to write the foreword of his vivid and involving book. The certainty of the points of view expressed have, for me, provided a window into the heads and hearts of the Englishmen who have come, before me, from my father's side of my family. Until I read this book, the forebears whom I never knew were just names, or, in some cases, photographs. Now I feel that I would have understood them, been able to relate to them, and hopefully, would have felt the respect for them that I feel for my friend, David.

This book also has the significant virtue of providing a reader with a happy opportunity to flick, skip and re-read paragraphs, or essays, at will, and never be left with a lapse in the thread of a story, plot or conclusion. The serendipitous fact that David has included, in one book, essays which have been written in various places, over many years, has given his readers freedom to select topics which appeal to them at the moment, or to discard their choice, whenever they feel like it, with no loss of continuity. And I believe that, for modern readers, this will be a welcome and happy opportunity, indeed.

On the basis of all of the above, I heartily recommend it as something they will both thoroughly enjoy and want to keep. David's opinions are carefully thought out, based on his wide experience and education, well written and firmly expressed as only an heir to what appears, to me, to be an English tradition, can express them.

Introduction

In 2006 I began to post a blog on which I published odds and ends that had caught my eye during the previous weeks. At the beginning of this enterprise, I had no idea how long I would carry on with the task or how it would turn out. I found that I enjoyed the labour of taking some topic or other and constructing a piece of coherent prose about it. So, it carried on for much longer than I had considered likely when I began.

I drew attention to my stuff by sending a group email to people that I hoped would be interested. Thus about eighty friends, relatives and acquaintances were informed of my regular updates. I never asked them whether they wanted such intrusions in their inboxes and none ever told me to take a running jump at myself. Indeed, a few wrote to tell me how much they had enjoyed them. After a few years, one or two of the regular recipients suggested that I should collect them and put them out in book form; hence this volume:

Priests, Prophets, Politicians, People and Protests.

Exactly how many essays I have written since I began the blog, I am unable to determine. I did not keep copies, relying instead on being able to recover each one from the web. My reliance looks as if it was misplaced for some have gone astray. However, I gathered up over two hundred and culled and grouped them. It turns out that I have written most often about religion, followed by politics. Articles on current affairs, education, economics and health make up the rest. Those, who know me, realise that I am critical of organised religion and am an unbeliever. They will also tell you that I have no very firm political affiliation for I consider that good ideas emanate from Left, Right and Centre of the political spectrum. No segment has a monopoly.

I am uncertain where my pre-occupation with religious affairs has come from for I have never subscribed to any faith or belonged to any church. Matters concerning religion have been greatly in the news in the last two decades, especially those to do with Islam. There will be many who argue that a group of jihadis blowing up a crowded market place in Pakistan is hardly a religious matter. But when they scream, 'God is great,' as they pull the pins of their suicide vests and thereby kill dozens of innocent women and children, I have problems with not regarding such activities as having a religious motivation. So, when you read through the essays in Chapter Three – Religion, do not think that you will find much about the minutiae of theology. I deal with the political causes and effects of this kind of 'religious' activity in the twenty-first century.

This is not the kind of book that one will read from cover to cover in a day or so. It is best thought of as something to be found on the bedside table that can be dipped into for ten minutes or so before composing oneself for sleep. The articles are not arranged in chronological order but in a way that I thought coherent.

Now, a few words of explanation and justification. I have employed British spelling. I prefer *coloured* to *colored*. And my preference is for *civilised* rather than *civilized*. I am confused by *3/18/2007*; *18/3/2007* seems to me to be more logical. People will tell me that I live in North America and should adopt the customs thereof. As most of my readers are Canadian, English and Australian, they will be comfortable with my preferred style. The book has been proofread at least three times and each time little glitches have been found. If any remain, I beg forgiveness. Perhaps the most difficult task encountered in writing this book was composing a suitable title. I tried many but discarded them as unsatisfactory. Whether the final choice is ideal I leave to the reader to decide. Having settled upon it, I noticed that it had five elements. The first outline of the book had five chapters with headings like Health, Politics and so on. Very late on, I abandoned these headings and substituted the elements of the title. Consequently, some of the topics in chapters are rather arbitrarily placed. Please overlook this breech in logic.

Lastly, the last two pieces are connected fragments of whimsy. Generally speaking, I am not a retailer of jokes but I could not resist these two!

Chapter One – Priests

A letter to a Catholic Bishop

Lethbridge, Sunday, September 28 2008

Dear Bishop Henry,

I write to protest at your malign influence on the Calgary Catholic School Board in the Gardasil affair. As you know the Alberta Government had decided to make this vaccination available to all school girls in Grade Five free of charge and you have managed to subvert this admirable public health measure on so-called moral grounds.

Permit me to give you a simple lesson on female sexual health, a topic you will know little about because of the warped life you lead due to your self-imposed celibacy. The Gardasil vaccine is a very effective and safe preventative against the human papilloma virus (HPV). HPV causes genital warts in females and these lead, in many cases to cancer of the cervix, or in lay terms, the neck of the womb. Many women die an excruciating death from this cancer. Gardasil given at the right time in a girl's life, can remove that threat. The vaccination can save the lives of 45 women each year in Alberta, thousands of lives across Canada and hundreds of thousands of lives world wide. HPV is spread through sexual intercourse. Your Church and its blinkered doctrines have come up with spurious reasons to deny this protection to girls attending Catholic schools in Calgary. Apparently you fear that the removal of the threat of womb cancer will lead to promiscuity! The ignorance and arrogance behind this reasoning is breathtaking. Parents of children who send their children to Catholic schools often publicly emphasise the extra moral dimension that is imparted to pupils at such schools. If this is important to them, it is highly likely that they will provide good quality information to their daughters and explain to them the perils of frequent, casual, unprotected, sexual contact. If the teachings of your Church are working, they should have built in safeguards against the very thing that troubles you. Lastly, to fear that young girls who have received this vaccination, will immediately throw discretion and modesty to the winds and open their legs to all and sundry is patronising and insulting.

Bishop, you are a fool and moreover, a dangerous one. Shame on you.

Cordially,
David R. Amies

Atheism and belief in God

(First published on 05/10/2008)

Mr Kevin Hart has written an earnest article, in the latest Australian Review of Books, in which he takes to task several authors who have written books promoting atheism. He is a professed Catholic convert, who prays several times a day and attends mass every Sunday. He goes with his wife to synagogue fairly often for she is Jewish. He is also a professor of theology.

This guy puts his cards on the table and makes no bones about it. His main beef with the recent clutch of atheist authors, who have published such books as 'Why god is not great' (Christopher Hutchins) and 'The god delusion' (Richard Dawkins), is that they try to prove or disprove the existence of God by scientific means. Hart says that you are not going to find God in a test tube. He claims that to attempt to reveal things about god using rational means misses the point. God is beyond reality according to him. God is perfect. If you try to add something or someone to god, you do not change anything because perfection plus something else still adds up to mere perfection. God is behind, over and through everything that there is. Using the feeble instrument of the human mind is the wrong way to discover any of the truths about God. Hart maintains that God is also 'behind being.' So arguments about his existence are meaningless because the use of such words as to be or to exist do not apply. So, with a couple of linguistic devices, an entity that is beyond reality and behind being has been set up that can only be approached through the instrument of faith. Belief in God is what is required for understanding and nearness to him, her or it.

If one accepts this argument, further discussion is futile for the object of discussion has been placed beyond the reach of analysis, criticism and reason. Game over. In a way, some kind of agreement can be reached between two conflicting camps. Believers of Kevin Hart's ilk accept the perfection and the existence of God and atheists do not. Neither side can really produce proofs for God's existence or otherwise, but the burden of proof rests with rests with those who propose the existence of God. Atheists maintain that there is no very good reason to suppose that there is a first cause or a creator. They can apply the argument that to posit a god asks more questions than it answers. Who caused the first cause? Who created the creator? To propose a creator of an entity that could create the universe, as we know it, seems to be an unlikely enterprise. Mr Hart's kind of believer recommends that we do not trouble our pretty little heads about such profound affairs and just believe. I have no objection to people going about thinking that there is a supernatural being that created and initiated the universe. Personally, I think they are nuts. My quarrel lies with their vocal supporters who aggregate themselves into religious groupings. These folk hold that certain books are holy and magic. They claim that they contain the word of God and must be hallowed, respected, taken at face value and followed to the letter. A glance at the Bible or the Koran will reveal some fairly horrifying dictates. Both are full of exhortations to murder, rape and bloodshed. Religious hierarchies, usually made up of people well versed in the scriptures, presume to control the conduct of their fellows, especially the females, and seek to lay down the law about modes of dress, what's edible, and how everyone should behave. Furthermore, such people also claim that moral behaviour is impossible without belief in a deity. Much strife has taken place over the years in the name of religion. The religions of the book claim that their special deity is merciful but not all believers behave in especially kindly ways.

Perhaps their greatest crime is to presume that any children born to them are Catholic, Muslim, Christian and so on. By this presumption, they oblige their young to believe certain things and to behave in certain ways long before they are able to make up their own minds. Catholic children are not Catholic: they are children whose parents happen to be Catholic. Similarly, with Muslim children and so on. Exposure of children to religious dogma before they are ready and able to work these matters out for themselves is a common form of societally approved child abuse. A world in which there were people who were believers but not religious and other people who were unbelievers and also not religious would be a fine place in which to live. Each group could go about its business and accept the other camp for what they were and agree to differ.

Religious people, who insist that I wear special underwear and avoid certain sorts of meat, are a pain. I have no intention of telling them what to do about such matters. Let them keep their views to themselves and not seek to obtain special privileges or to expect special respect for their beliefs. Religious people, who did not preach, proselytise or demand respect for their views would be easy to tolerate. Choosing to cling to bizarre beliefs in the supernatural would be their own business. My regarding such beliefs as nonsensical would be mine as long as I do not seek to rub their noses in it.

Enda Kenney

(First published in July 2011)

Amid the excitement of the Arab Spring, the fall of Dictator Gaddafi and the Global Financial Crisis part two, the bravery of the Irish Taoiseach (prime minister), Enda Kenny, has gone largely unnoticed. Following the release of the Cloyne Report on July 13 dealing with child abuse in that diocese, he made a speech in the Irish parliament in which he excoriated the Vatican, its officials and its culture. He decried its unwillingness to come to terms with the child abuse scandals around the World and its refusal to acknowledge its responsibility for these outrages. He called the Vatican dysfunctional and elitist and more interested in upholding the Church's power and reputation than dealing with the rape and torture of children perpetrated in Ireland by several of its functionaries. He went on to say that, *'The Cloyne Report excavates the dysfunction, disconnection, elitism, the narcissism that dominate the culture of the Vatican to this day. The rape and torture of children were downplayed or 'managed' to uphold instead, the primacy of the institution, its power, standing and 'reputation'. Far from listening to evidence of humiliation and betrayal with St Benedict's 'ear of the heart'... the Vatican's reaction was to parse and analyse it with the gimlet eye of a canon lawyer.'*

Language like this has never been used before by an Irish politician. Ireland has always bowed the head and bent the knee submissively where the Roman Catholic Church and its leaders have been concerned. The Vatican reacted with anger and withdrew its nuncio or ambassador as a mark of its displeasure. Things have changed for not forty years ago, Eamon de Valera was photographed on his knees kissing the ring of the Papal Nuncio.

Scandal after scandal has come to light. Officially sanctioned report after report has revealed the lengths to which the Church has gone to avoid reporting delinquent priests to the civil authorities. Several bishops have colluded in the scandals by moving predatory priests from parish to parish thereby enabling them to carry on abusing children. Rape and buggery of young children have thereby been facilitated by the leaders of the Church. On the few occasions in which the Church has taken disciplinary action against the more flagrant abusers, it has chosen to use canon law. Canon law is a legal code used by the Church to deal with theological and doctrinal errors or misdemeanours. Proceedings are held in secret and those taking part are enjoined, under pain of excommunication, to conceal and keep concealed the details of any hearings. Frequently, such 'trials' are carried out by letter. Punishments usually take the form of enjoinders to mend the ways and pray more fervently. Very occasionally, offenders are laicised and thereby removed from the priesthood. Patently, such anodyne processes are hardly sufficient to deal with matters of repeated rape of young boys and girls, nor the pimping and procuring carried out by senior officers of the Church, for what other terms can be used of bishops who remove offenders and put them in new situations where they can carry on in their merry old ways? The Church has maintained that it has been introducing guidelines to deal with these abuses. Guidelines! For raping children! What are these people smoking? Bishops and cardinals are reported to hold that the priests that serve below them are like their sons. What father can possibly turn over his son to the civil authorities to face trial, imprisonment and disgrace? Let the benign forces of the canon law serve as punishment. Extra Hail Marys and Pater Nosters should suffice.

Such abuses have surfaced just about everywhere the Catholic Church has a presence. Reports have come from the UK, Canada, the USA, Australia, Germany, Belgium, Italy, France – the list goes on and on. In each of these countries, the Church hierarchy has played similar games. It has stonewalled. It has moved offenders from place to place. Sometimes it has enabled the most egregious offenders to serve in another country. When it has been well and truly backed into a corner and a priest has appeared in court, it has refused to cooperate with the local authorities. Where it has been faced with paying compensation, it has been miserly and only eked out cash after legally binding, secret agreements have been signed by the victims not to speak publicly about their cases. The Pope, arch pimp and procurer, has offered bland apologies and spoken about the shame felt by him and the Church. He, however, has not acknowledged the part he has played in the entire global affair. Before he became pope, he held the most senior administrative position in the Church and as such was well aware of what had gone on.

Pope Benedict cannot be said to have actually sanctioned the feeble efforts of his underlings, but he made no effort to bring them to justice. The good name (sic) of the Church and its bank balance were far more important to this ghastly man than seeking justice for so many, who had placed their trust in their priests and, who had been so gravely and seriously betrayed. Everyone else has had to endure homilies on morals and behaviour from this awful man as he trails around Europe at huge expense to his 'hosts.'

Many of the victims report how their lives have been spoiled by their experiences at the hands of clerical rapists. Perhaps they would gain some solace if they could see priests, monsignors, bishops and even cardinals being dragged into the courts to face the rigours of criminal justice. A group of victims has lodged a case at the European Court of Justice seeking to have the Pope charged with crimes against humanity. Sadly, their efforts are unlikely to succeed. The Pope and his Church have far too many friends in high places to allow such an event to take place. For some inexplicable reason, politicians remain in thrall to the diseased institution known as the Roman Catholic Church. Perhaps, the outspokenness and bravery of the Taoiseach marks a change.

The God of Abraham

(First published on 28/11/2008)

In an intriguing essay published on the Butterflies and Wheels website, George Taylor suggests that both Islam and Christianity are derived from the ancient worship of the God of Abraham (TGOA). This god first came to prominence in the eight century BC when two insignificant hill tribes, in the Canaan hills of what is now Palestine or Israel, abandoned polytheism and adopted the worship of a single deity who has variously come to be known as Yahweh, Allah or Jehovah. TGOA was adopted by a political faction among the Israelites and the Judahites, the Canaanite tribesmen. Their political ambitions brought about the conquest of Israel by the Assyrians. The Israelites fled into Judah where they again made the mistake of punching above their weight.

This incautious behaviour led to a second conquest, this time by the Babylonian emperor, Nebuchadnezzar. Most of the Israelites were carted off into slavery. During their period of bondage they rewrote their history to try to justify their sorry position and to exculpate their god. This rewriting became what is now called the Old Testament. It is a fiction and moreover, a political fiction. The template for TGOA was one of a bunch of deities worshipped by the Israelites. He was male. Recast as Yahweh, he created man in his own image. Woman was an afterthought. The legacy of this thinking exists even today: the Christians are reluctant to have women as priests and Muslims look upon them as a sort of cattle.

TGOA had a linear view of existence which remains part of Christian and Islamic teaching. Thus, there is the world as we know it, but of more importance is the afterlife. Good behaviour ensures a seat in heaven. Bad behaviour ensures a one-way trip to hell. Mediating these important matters are priests and mullahs – all male. This philosophy is referred to as dualism. TGOA and his angels and demons exist in the supernatural realm. Humanity lives in the natural world and strives to achieve the translation from one to the other. Those religions that base themselves upon TGOA rely heavily on sacred texts. These texts are held to be divinely inspired. True believers regard every single jot and tittle of these books to be the inerrant word of God and thus not open to revision. On occasions when copies of these books have been burnt or destroyed, riots and mayhem have ensued.

Archeological and historical research carried out during the past 50 years demonstrates that there is little or no corroboration of the events recorded in the scriptures. So the sojourn of the Israelites in Egypt and the subsequent exodus and the establishment of the Kingdom of David are nowhere mentioned in contemporary histories of other empires and kingdoms in the region. Jesus of Nazareth paid special heed to the Old Testament. So, did he also buy into the myth? Islam also pays respect to many personages listed in these scriptures. It has also been taken in. It seems, then, that the Old Testament is largely fictional and certainly not written by Moses and the Prophets.

Taylor goes on to make a very damning claim: *'but does it matter if faith is based on falsehood if the ends are good? In adopting TGOA as their own creator deity, Christianity and Islam have created a fantasy world, the supernatural or transcendent, and set it up to rule this world, and in doing so have created a labyrinth of supernaturally inspired rules, commandments, assumptions and beliefs about this world and its ordering, directed towards a supposed need for divine approval.'* He goes on to outline the damage done to humanity, the environment and general human wellbeing and happiness by the Abrahamic religions. The faithful are led to believe that life on Earth is merely a prelude to the only life that matters. Some go so far as to claim that the end of days is near and that to waste time and effort on environmental concerns is futile because the Saved will be swept up to heaven leaving a severely damaged Earth behind them.

Women generally get very short shrift from the TGOA. In some parts of the world the old German assertion, that women were only good enough for kids, kitchen and kirk, holds true today. Islamic doctrine still maintains that women are so taken up with domestic matters that at least two of them are necessary to bear witness in courts where money matters are to be decided. Much of the Christian world has a hard time imagining women as priests or bishops.

Having power vested in a clique that knows that it is right and that it has divine authority for its views is likely to bring about conflict. *'There is nothing more thrilling than joy of knowing you are right.'* For evidence that this is so, there is no need to go further than the Middle East, a region beset with strife. The protagonists in this endless turmoil are all convinced that their version of TGOA is right and the only view permissible. Views, that vary, are held to be blasphemous and intolerable. So, there are Arabs trying to slaughter Jews; Jews subjugating Palestinians with mainly Christian armies holding the ring. There are, to be sure, political undertones to all of this, but the underlying religious motive is very powerful. Taylor suggests that there are four pillars of Abrahamic religion: a supernatural and omnipotent god, inerrant sacred texts whose truths are a given, hierophants who act as guardians and interpreters of these texts and a worldview dictated by the texts and controlled by the priestly class.

He also compares some nasty, recent ideologies with the Abrahamic model. Communism and Nazism are good examples with their omnipotent leaders (Stalin and Hitler), their sacred texts (Das Kapital and Mein Kampf), their enforcers (SS and KGB) and their worldviews: eugenics, extermination of the Jews, lebensraum for the master race and death to capitalism. The parallels are uncanny. Taylor puts the uncomfortable question: is totalitarianism a godless religion or are Christianity and Islam totalitarian ideologies masquerading as religions? After pondering these and other problems posed by the power and influence of Abrahamic religions, Taylor suggests a few remedies.

Firstly, he holds that Christianity and Islam continue to exert their influence by indoctrinating children very early on in their lives. He considers that religious instruction in schools to be an evil. He maintains that religious indoctrination should be illegal outside the home and that no public money should go towards fostering the ends of religious education. He does, however, consider that religion be taught in schools and universities as a sociological phenomenon that exerts enormous power over the lives of many. In Taylor's view, when religion is dissected as a human construct and looked at through a prism of reason and enquiry, its malign influence will slowly decay,

Furthermore, he suggests that all religious bodies should be regarded as special interest groups with a political agenda and deserving of no special privilege. He would like to see the disestablishment of the Anglican Church in the UK. He considers that the special status held by the Vatican as an independent mini-state to be an anomaly whose use-by date is past. He has no objection to private worship and religious observance and acknowledges that many derive comfort and satisfaction from such activities. It is the political power and influence of religious organisations that he finds intolerable.

Religion has occupied a very privileged position up to now. The priestly class has been afforded automatic respect and deference. The very title of reverend has commanded a degree of respect out of proportion to worth of the individual who held it. It is satisfying to observe more and more thinkers like George Taylor are prepared and able to dissect the claims made by religion and demand that it gives an account of itself. His notion that the various religions based upon TGOA are politically inspired and based upon claims that are entirely fictional is highly engaging. Is it likely that a member of the priestly class will set about refuting these very powerful arguments?

Hilarity

(First published on 15/03/2008)

The Roman Catholic Church has added more to the list of deadly sins. These are the first new ones to merit inclusion for 1500 years! Until yesterday, lust, gluttony, avarice, sloth, anger, envy and pride would get you life in hell unless you were smart enough to have the local priest nip round to hear your confession before you popped your clogs. Now you need to be certain that you have not been involved in polluting the environment, genetic engineering, drug dealing, abortion, paedophilia and causing social injustice. As the list grows longer, you had better make sure the priest arrives sooner or else you might cark it before you plead guilty to all of them. The Church reckons that those who do not die in a state of grace are in for a rough time after death and that the way to ease your pain is through the intercession of an ordained priest.

This new list has come about after a Lenten session of Catholic intellectuals (sic), recently held in Rome who point out that in the face of increasing globalisation, societal sins need to be taken into account rather than only those committed by individuals. Yet you wonder whether these guys understand public relations and if they ran the new list by their spin doctors before publishing it. For example, some of the most egregious instances of institutional paedophilia have been perpetrated by the very priests that have dreamt up this stuff. The Church in the USA has spent a king's ransom paying off the victims of priestly buggeration and other bits of unpleasantness. In all fairness, the Vatican spokesman suggested that the Church was not guiltless but he did rather indicate that priestly, high jinks with altar boys was something of a media beat up and had been blown out of proportion.

The Church has decreed that obscene wealth is wrong. Before making such a claim, it might have been wise for the spokesman to take a stroll through the halls of the Vatican. There he would have discovered a neat definition of obscene wealth. Neither Croesus nor Bill Gates could afford to buy some of the loot on display. And, most of the stuff has been paid for with the pennies and halfpennies of impoverished peasants in benighted places like the backwoods of Africa and South America, who have undoubtedly been persuaded that their pathetic donations would build up useful credit in heaven.

The Church goes on to rail against environmental damage and rightly so. But it inveighs against birth control, genetic engineering and causing social injustice. Church policy along with the policies of other mainstream religions goes a long way to ensuring that the population of this little planet will hit the 9.5 billion mark within the next twenty-five years. Genetic engineering might go some of the way to feeding this lot. Birth control might help ensure that population does not get out of hand. If there is significant pollution right now, imagine how it will be with another 3.5 billion of us milling around.

From the point of view of the theologians sitting pretty in the Vatican, this week's little effort is entirely on message. However, a decent firm of publicity agents might have tempered the announcement and pointed out how unerringly the reverends have shot themselves in the foot. Hilarious! And now for something ominous: the Right Reverend Patrick O'Donoghue, Bishop of Lancaster, has called for a ban on books critical of the Catholic religion from school libraries. A person is always entitled to feel scared when mullahs or other clerics call for bans on reading material. The good bishop maintains that the secular view on extramarital sex, contraception, sexually transmitted disease and abortion might not be transmitted neutrally. Is he implying that the Catholic view on such matters is neutral? Sadly he rehearses the blatant lies of one of the late Pope's henchmen that so-called safe sex is based on the deluded notion that condoms can provide protection against HIV-AIDS. No one has any idea how of many poor wretches in Africa have been condemned to death by that particular Catholic calumny, bruited around a few years ago. This same bishop, who appearing before a Commons committee in London, also claimed that schools should not support charities or groups such as Amnesty

International and Red Nose Day that promote or support 'anti-life policies'

But it gets worse: Islamic states are mounting an effort to curb freedom of expression around the world. Specifically they wish to restrain any 'defamation of religion' on the grounds that it denies believers the right to enjoy respect. Everyone should be entitled to believe in their particular brand of religion or indeed to consider that Jack and the Beanstalk is a story of great cosmic significance. But, are the rest of us obliged to treat such beliefs with respect? Must we refrain from all criticism and comment? May we not poke fun at things we find absurd? Islamic states see human rights in specifically Islamic terms – or in other words they do not really believe that there is any such thing. Islam is all about control and submission. Islamic states seem to be especially sensitive to lampooning of their religious icons. The publication of the notorious Danish cartoons a few years ago really hit home. The cartoons were not that good and sensible people would have ignored them and they would have passed into obscurity. However, the enraged clerics and their puppet followers had their emotions whipped up into a frenzy and consequently the entire affair won greater press coverage than it is was entitled to expect.

The President of Iran – a serious Muslim, if ever there was one – claims that homosexuality does not exist in his country. But when we see serried ranks of male bottoms waving around in the air during prayer, it is hard to keep a straight face in the light of his claim.

The Organisation of Islamic Councils is using its muscle to undermine the 1948 Universal Declaration of Human Rights, which celebrates its 50th anniversary this year. It is trying to promote its 1990 Cairo Declaration of Human Rights in Islam as a complementary set of principles. Various humanist organisations around the World feel that this would seriously undermine the Universal Declaration. A glance at the news from Iran, Saudi Arabia and similar places along with a catalogue of Islamic views on women inclines this author to share those concerns.

Fortunately, there is lighter note on which to end. The same bishop, who announced the new sins, let on that fewer than 40% of Italians attend mass and confession. Perhaps the Italians have seen the light. It does not seem likely that the new catalogue of mortal sins will have them lining up in the aisles soon.

Papa Benny throws in the towel

(First published in February 2013)

Joseph Ratzinger, aka Pope Benedict XVI, surprised the World and the red-hatted gents in the Vatican by announcing his retirement from the job of pope last week. He has well and truly thrown a papal bull among the curial pigeons. He said that he no longer had the mental or physical strength to carry on in the Petrine ministry. It is over 600 years ago since a pope handed in his cards. All the others, since then, have left the post, feet first in a box. Theologists, Vatican watchers and others, who have little else to do, have been analysing the effects this sudden resignation will have on the Catholic Church as well as its possible theological significance.

Firstly, Catholic lore holds that the job of pope is granted through divine influence. After the death of a pope, the College of Cardinals, at least, those members who are less than 80 years old, meet in sacred conclave to elect a successor. Serious Catholics believe that the outcome of these deliberations are divinely inspired, thereby inevitably appointing the one among their number who is most pleasing to God. Once someone is appointed or elected he is greeted by joyful shouts of 'Habemus Papem.' He is then decked out in appropriate robes and presented to the adoring faithful massed in St. Peter's Square. The papal tailors prepare three sets of kit: small, medium and large, so that whomever is elected will have stuff that fits. It is unclear at what point the divine appointment takes place: immediately the votes are counted or when the last qualifying vote is cast and lies uncounted in the ballot box.

For the past 120 years or so, popes have taken upon themselves the notion of papal infallibility. In other words, pronouncements by the Pope, speaking ex cathedra, have the authority of God behind them and to dispute such uttering is tantamount to suggesting that God is talking through his hat. Pope Pius IX claimed this right when, in 1870, he declared that the Virgin Mary had been schlepped off to heaven as is. In polite language, this marvel is now known as the Bodily Assumption of the Virgin Mary. Papa Benny possesses this infallibility right now. But, he has said that he is going to step down at 20.00 hours on February 28, next. Will his infallibility carry on past that time? Can someone granted such a power and privilege just shuck it off because he is disinclined to keep his hand on the tiller? Tricky doctrinal point with no recent precedent to fall back on.

Secondly, as popes are held to be divinely appointed, can they just walk away on a whim? At their swearing in, they undertake to carry out the job until death. The last pope, John Paul II hung on well past his use-by date. He took about ten years to die and he withered away from Parkinson's disease and became more and more infirm as time passed. It was obvious that he was unable to fulfil his duties but was kept on as a sort of icon and trotted out in front of the faithful at the required times of the year. Meanwhile, the friskier cardinals plotted and conspired behind his back to run things as they saw fit. Joseph Ratzinger as Prefect of the Congregation for Doctrine of the Faith, was essentially the number two man in the Vatican and so ran everything to his entire satisfaction. In any case, he held much the same point of view as his ailing boss on the important matters of the day: the status of women, contraception, artificial insemination, assisted suicide, the protection of paedophile priests and the reputation of the Church, above all else. Catholic doctrine holds that sick people have no right to bring their lives to an end. It maintains that each life, however ghastly, is part of God's plan and that human intervention in bringing it to a planned end is tantamount to blasphemy. Persons, therefore, are granted a span of life by God, which can only be shortened at peril of a long stay in Hell. Popes, likewise, are appointed during God's pleasure, for life. Does Meister Benny run the risk of incurring God's displeasure for refusing to bear his cross, however onerous?

Thirdly, what happens to a retired pope? The last one who left office was tossed into the pokey by his successor. Herr Ratzinger has announced his intention to spend his dying days in a monastery. A run down convent within the walls of the Vatican is being refurbished to accommodate him. What will he be called? Ex-Pope Benedict? Cardinal Ratzinger? Were he to be a widowed wife of an English duke or earl, he would be known as the dowager duchess or countess as the case may be. Dowager Pope? Sounds funny. Maybe he will be known as the emeritus Pope Benedict XVI. He will be lurking around in the corridors of the Vatican, a place of intrigue and plotting. Inevitably, he will have his supporters. Might he become a focal point for dissent and unrest?

The Vatican and the Catholic Church are moving into uncharted waters. It is beset with many unresolved problems hanging over not just from the reign of Benedict but also the late John Paul. Its adherents are declining rapidly in number. Much of its priesthood is aged. Postulants are in very short supply. Fewer and fewer people take mass. Congregations are withering. Those, who do show up, are uncomfortable with the party line on matters of doctrine like female priests, priestly celibacy, contraception, abortion, IVF, stem cell research, the sexual abuse scandals and so on.

Countries that once swallowed Catholic doctrine whole no longer do. Ireland, only a short time ago, a Vatican poodle, has recently shut its embassy to the Vatican and its prime minister roundly castigated the Church in the Irish parliament. The only bright spots are in South America, Asia and the Philippines. Press reports surrounding the resignation of Benedict have merrily reported that the Church has more than a billion adherents. It wishes! A large number of these are merely cultural catholics who just about never go near their local church.

Both John Paul II and Benedict XVI seeded the College of Cardinals with like-minded conservatives and the likelihood that the new man on the job will be a progressive is vanishingly small. If an ultra-conservative outlook has brought the Church to its present pass, what chance is there that another of the same ilk will perk things up?

Habemus Papem

(First published on 15/03/2013)

It is not every day that joyous shouts of, 'Habemus Papem,' ring out around the World. Commentators, Church mandarins and members of the public seem to be delighted with the election of Francis, formerly Jorge Mario Bergoglio, as the new Pope and leader of the World's Catholics. He is being greeted so enthusiastically because he is from Argentina, and the first non-European Pope for over one thousand years and the first Jesuit. He is also old, has only one lung and is very conservative in his outlook.

The Roman Church is beset with troubles: shrinking attendance, unresolved sex-abuse scandals, financial irregularities in the Vatican Bank, rumours of a corrupt and gay cabal at the heart of the Curia. Poor Pope Francis has a lot on his plate. Some of the joy surrounding his election stems from the fact that Latin America is the part of the world in which most Catholics live: by some estimates 40%. Francis is characterised as a simple man of the people who eschews pomp and circumstance. It is hoped that his humility will appeal to the masses. Noteworthy and somewhat ominous was his reference to the brotherhood in the first few sentences of his address from the balcony. Presumably the sisterhood was out the back making the tea.

He is also regarded as a conservative and this aspect of his outlook provides comfort and satisfaction to the hierarchy who can rely on business as usual. Whatever changes he might make, he is thought certain to pursue the old policies of priestly celibacy, the inferior status of women, abhorrence of same sex marriage, absolute rejection of abortion under any circumstances, no countenancing of assisted suicide for the terminally ill and no acceptance of artificial birth control. It has not occurred to the hierarchy that it is these very policies that have brought the Church to its sorry pass.

Ireland, until recently, blindly observant of Catholic doctrine, has thrown out the Papal Nuncio and closed its embassy at Vatican City.

Québec in Canada was once staunchly Catholic to the extent that most of the population got down on their knees in front of their wireless sets to pray when the Cardinal Archbishop addressed them on Saturday evenings. Fewer than 2% of Quebeckers attend mass weekly today. Even in South America, the region of the World for which the Church has such high hopes, people are deserting it in droves in favour of Evangelical Protestant Churches. Western Europe is no longer a bastion of the Catholic faith. Birthrates in Italy – home of the Church – are the lowest in the World, because its womenfolk are using contraception in order to limit the size of their families. European women are seeking education and professions and are no longer willing to shorten their lives in the by having huge families. What European women do, others will follow in short order.

And yet, the Church, knowing all of this, does not seem willing or able to change. The old adage, that doing the same thing over again hoping for a different outcome is a sign of madness, applies in spades to this organisation. Few of the doctrines, which are cleaved to so passionately by the Princes of the Church, have much scriptural basis. Priestly celibacy was introduced in the Middle Ages by a Pope, who feared that successive holders of the office would pass church property on to their children. No mention of contraception is to be found in the Bible. Surely, it enjoins people to be fruitful and to multiply, but that applied to a World populated by a few million persons, not several billion as is the case today. Homosexuality was roundly castigated in the story of the fall of Sodom. The little band of brothers that surrounded Jesus of Nazareth had an eerily gay flavour: the disciple whom Jesus loved, for example! The sacredness of marriage and the family, a cornerstone of catholic doctrine, was hardly apparent when Jesus commanded his followers to abandon theirs to take part in his mission. The scriptural basis for the low status afforded women is extremely scanty: two or three scattered verses in the Bible.

Education, modern communications and a general unwillingness of people to obey the dictates of authority figures as unquestioningly as in the past, have created a world in which the Catholic Church finds itself strangely out of touch. Banging on about the old verities is not going to pull it back from the brink. There are other shows in town that look a whole lot more exciting. A seventy-six year old Pope is going to have his work cut out to restore its fortunes. Not only is the new man facing a pile of problems held over from the last administration, he has to deal with the entrenched Curia, the civil service of the Church and the Vatican. One would think that he would be most powerful during the first few days and weeks of his papacy and that now would be the time to fire these plotters and schemers. He could find interesting places for them to go: Tierra del Fuego, Greenland and Mali, come to mind. It has not taken the muckrakers in the media long to dredge up aspects of his behaviour during the reigns of the unpleasant military juntas, who governed Argentina a few years ago. It is said that he was unduly accommodating towards them.

It is little wonder that a newly elected Pope retires briefly to a little room in the

Sistine Chapel, aptly named the Room of Tears, before he emerges in his new gear to accept the plaudits of the Faithful massed in St Peter's Square. Any sentient being would wonder what the hell he had let himself in for.

Schism

(First published on 01/11/2013)

Schism – lovely word – is an affliction that dogs most religions. The Catholic faith is especially susceptible. Schism, which of course, implies division or separation, is derived from the Greek word meaning to split. Many of the matters, that have caused splits in the various faiths, are to the outsider, bafflingly obscure and quintessentially trivial and come into that class of debate characterised by questions like, 'How many angels can dance on the head of the pin?' or, 'Is it wrong to wear pink knickers on any other day than Tuesday?' Such matters are not open to testing and are, therefore, meaningless in the philosophical sense.

The granddaddy of all schisms, known as the Great Schism, occurred in the 11th century, over such profound matters as whether or not it was appropriate to celebrate the Eucharist with leavened bread rather than bread made without yeast and the 'Filioque' problem: was the Holy Ghost derived from God the Father alone or from both God the Father and God the Son? Theologists refer to the latter debate as the 'and or not' problem. There was also dispute about purification after death and what exactly was meant by heaven, hell and purgatory. A more practical problem was the primacy of the Bishop of Rome, but that was merely a turf war and easy for non-theologians to understand. These weighty matters were not resolved and the Church divided into the eastern or Greek Wing and the western or Roman wing. The life of the Catholic Church has been riven by many other schisms over more or less unintelligible matters of doctrine. Dozens are recorded.

The Jewish faith has not been immune from such problems. Nowadays Judaism is split into Reform, Conservative and Orthodox strands. Reform Jews wear their religion lightly and do not fuss much about scrupulous adherence to matters of doctrine. They may well be found turning the lights on or taking public transport during Sabbath. On the other hand, the strict Orthodox Jews do no such thing. They hold that the Sabbath is a day of rest and great efforts are made to ensure that nothing that could possibly count as work is performed. In the most orthodox district in Jerusalem even the traffic lights are turned off on the Sabbath. Lights going on and off are equated to lighting fires and, patently, that is work! Strangers who wander into the Mea She'arim, where the most orthodox live, on a Saturday, may well have stones thrown at them for the Scriptures hold that making journeys during the Sabbath is sinful.

Islam is divided into two main divisions: Sunni (approximately 85%) and Shias (15%) The division stems back to events that took place shortly after the death of Muhammad. The majority felt that Abubakr, one of the Prophet's followers was the right man to succeed as leader of all Muslims. A minority thought that one of Muhammad's male relatives should get the gig. In the interest of peace and quiet, the minority went along with the choice of Abubakr but grew restive and declared that Ali, the Prophet's son-in-law and cousin was really the man for the job. After his assassination, his son Hasan took over and was in turn followed by his son, Husain. Husain was tricked and killed by representatives of the mainstream Sunni camp. It is the death of Husain that the Shias mourn to this day. The feast of Asura features young Shia men lashing themselves with chains while they fall about in paroxysms of grief and to all appearances the grief seems real and profound.

Both Sunnis and Shias regard each other as Muslims but the Sunnis think of the Shias as heretics and are prepared to slaughter them. Shias claim that their imams are direct spiritual descendants of the Prophet and as such are infallible. They cling to a strange idea that there is a hidden imam in a state of occultation who will re-appear at the end of days to sort everything out to the satisfaction of the Shias. Sound familiar?

The Roman Church continued to divide into smaller and smaller sects. A spectacular break occurred in England in the early sixteenth century when Henry VIII decided that he wished to replace his wife, Catherine, with the livelier and bustier model, Anne Boleyn. Divorce was then out of the question and discrete enquiries made to Rome by Cardinal Wolsey were rebuffed. Henry, never a man to be thwarted, declared himself to be the Head of the Church and so the Church of England was born. Now it can be argued that Henry did not behave very gallantly towards poor Catherine, but if a schism is being engineered, a change of wife as a reason seems more earthy than a dispute over the Holy Ghost!

The three monotheisms are beset with curious, obscure and entirely unfounded beliefs about their version of God and his servants. Not only do followers of these faiths regard members of the other faiths as heretics, they have profound differences among themselves, which are often so strongly held, that violence and division can occur. This continues to be true among Muslims. The majority of all contemporary terrorist activities are inflicted by one branch of Islam on the other. Christians have matured and no longer burn one another at the stake or inflict ghastly torture upon each other over obscure doctrinal points. The Haredim the ultra-orthodox Jews, content themselves with throwing stones at those who do not observe the Sabbath.

Doctrinal differences among churchmen, that have provoked so much commentary, largely pass over the heads of the faithful. They want a god to whom they can pray and whom they believe has their interests at heart. Getting bent out of shape over the mysteries of the Trinity or the resurrection is of little moment to those in the pews. It is the religious scholars who agonise over such obscure matters. Consider the priest, who announced to his flock, comprised of average punters that he proposed to preach on the Filioque question. He would be met by looks of total bafflement. Imagine such a sermon being delivered to faithful Catholics in the Third World. Such folk have more pressing needs that would not be met by a discourse of that nature.

It can be argued that use of the word scholar is inappropriate to describe one who expends much effort dealing with matters of this sort. Whether or not the Holy Spirit proceeds from the Father and not the Son or whether it is right to use yeast in the bread for the Eucharist are matters of faith and cannot be subjected to scholarly analysis. However, the state of mind that grips those who argue about such matters can most certainly be studied. Thus, the phenomenon of faith is a legitimate subject for scholarship but faith itself is not. Notwithstanding, there are extensive libraries full of closely argued tomes written in the most impenetrable and polysyllabic language on matters of faith and points of doctrine. How such collections contribute to general human well being is open to argument.

Evidently, religion is a matter that provokes dispute and division. The majority of people in the West are no longer much concerned with it and look upon it and its effects as irritating nuisances. Most liberal minded individuals are happy that others find help and consolation in their faith but do not want it to spill over into the everyday conduct of affairs. Feeble efforts, under the rubric of ecumenism, are made to try and reconcile the principal faiths but they do not convince. Popes continue to suggest that prayers for the forgiveness of the Jews for the crime of deicide are in order! Pope Benedict, in a speech at Regensburg University, compared Muslims unfavourably with Christians, suggesting that the latter were all about faith and the former, violence. The Koran demands that non-believers be forced to convert, or to be killed. Such views do little to lower the emotional temperature surrounding faith.

Religious strife and division are not going to disappear soon. Whereas in much of the formerly Christian world, religion is seen as increasingly irrelevant, Muslims have not yet arrived at this point of view they and continue to take religion dauntingly seriously. Perhaps they will come to realise that most of the claims made by their faith are unfounded and indefensible and slowly but surely become less intoxicated by it.

Sex!

(First published on 21/06/2008)

The Anglican Communion is tearing itself apart. It has got its knickers in a very tight twist over homosexuality. On the one hand there are the literalists who cite a verse from Leviticus, which holds that for a man to lie with man, as with a woman, is an abomination. The other side holds a more relaxed view of matters. A year or two ago, an openly gay priest was consecrated as a bishop in New Hampshire and that really set off the conservatives. Their ire has been even further aroused by the notion of gay marriage sanctified by church ceremonies. These have taken place around the world and have caused great controversy. Famously, the vicar of an ancient church in the City of London married a pair of male clergymen a few days ago. This caused great uproar and was declared to be un-biblical. There were newsreels pictures of the ceremony in the church with all concerned dressed up in ecclesiastical robes, complete with smoking handbags. With unconscious humour we were next taken to a beautiful Oxford garden where a distinguished female academic theologian railed against the sinfulness of the proceedings and demanded that all concerned be defrocked! This writer felt that the thing that the participants would have most welcomed was a ripping of frocks from their persons.

The struggle goes on and is the issue most likely to tear the Anglican Church apart. Already several conservative parishes are breaking away from their liberal bishops and seeking rule by other more traditional leaders. The decennial gathering of the Anglican clans is due to take place in London under the chairmanship of the beleaguered Archbishop of Canterbury. Several prelates from the around the World have announced their intention not to attend. Instead they are going to another gathering in Jerusalem to sulk and to snipe from the sidelines.

One never ceases to wonder at the prurient interest holy men take in the sexual behaviour of others. A person could be the greatest benefactor ever known to mankind but should his sexual practices not pass muster, his other activities would be set at naught. While all of these shenanigans were going on, a beauty contest was taking place in Saudi Arabia! Many Saudi princes, done up in traditional garb, attended and waxed eloquent over what they had seen. Beauty contest in Saudi Arabia? How can it be possible to judge the contestants if they are swathed from head to toe in burkas? Gotcha! It was not a beauty contest featuring women but goats! Poor sods!

The role of God in natural disasters

(First published on 25/04/2008)

It is possible to be rather bemused by the contortions of religious folk where natural disasters are concerned. In recent weeks two very grave events have occurred. First came the cyclone that ravaged much of the Irrawaddy Delta region of Burma and second the huge earthquake in Central China. Political shenanigans have concealed the true extent of the damage cause by the event in Burma. The Chinese have been more open about their earthquake. It seems that over 100,000 people perished in Burma with up to two and a half millions displaced and now threatened by all kinds of water borne diseases. In China the death toll is probably less than 100,000 but many more have lost their homes.

Religious people entertain the notion – some would say the delusion – that the universe was created by a supernatural being variously called God, Allah, Yahweh among many other names. This being is held to be omniscient, omnipotent, benevolent and merciful. It is also held to have endowed humanity with freewill. Every few hundred years or so, it sends a messenger into the world to inform us all what sort of behaviour is expected. These messengers include Moses, Jesus Christ and Allah. Many people in the USA would want the Angel Moroni included in their number. In spite of endowing us, mere mortals, with freewill, the deity pokes its nose into the most trifling aspects of personal behaviour. So there are rules about what is fit to eat, how fabric for clothing is to be made, how women are to dress and manage their menstrual lives. The deity seems to be especially concerned with sexual behaviour: who may have intercourse with whom and whether steps may be taken to prevent conception.

It is hard for the observer to reconcile the pettifogging nature of these rules with the notion of any substantial measure of freewill. Some even believe that ones' every waking thought and deed are noted and will have to be accounted for on some distant day. Freewill? What's free about that? More modern religious practitioners are ready to cherry pick bits and pieces out of the holy books and discard some of the more arcane proscriptions. However, we are dealing with the word of the deity in these books and it could be seen as presumptuous to ignore some bits and follow the rest.

If the Bible and the Koran are the word of God, then it is not open to a believer to parse the good bits and ignore the bad. A deity that so deeply interests itself in the quotidian affairs of its creation paradoxically seems quite ready to allow the most shocking and appalling events to occur and to have devised gruesome ways of afflicting human kind. What possible purpose can there be to allow natural disasters of the kind mentioned above to take place? In the space of a few minutes, thousands of people died and many more died in the subsequent muddle during the rescue phase. It is hard to find any sensible explanation to excuse an all-powerful deity for allowing such mayhem to occur.

Theologians, faced with such questions, opine that God is unable to interfere, or having

79

set things in motion and provided humanity with freewill, chooses not to interfere. Perhaps, most chillingly, He does not wish to interfere. And yet, this is a god who decrees that meat not be eaten with dairy produce and that knickers not be made from fabric consisting of two or more different fibres! Our deity sweats the small stuff but stands back from what really matters. Imagine the clamour that would happen were a political leader to drop an atomic bomb on a densely populated area of the world. The damage caused would be equivalent to that that occurred in Burma a few weeks ago. No impotent outrage has been expressed – just a feeling of bewilderment. Indeed, many of those who escaped death, give thanks for their deliverance. To whom? Presumably the agent that brought about the disaster.

Perhaps the religious and the sceptical fundamentally hold the same views about these issues. The religious need to ascribe happenings to something and 'god' does very well as the scapegoat. The sceptic has come to terms with the fact that we are all on the same pointless journey from nowhere to oblivion and does not need to point the finger or find anyone or anything to blame. Such persons can find solace in knowing that we are tiny insignificant scraps of sentient protoplasm and that we may as well find amusement and happiness where we may during the tiny interval that life affords us.

Chapter Two – Prophets

Suicide Bombers

(First published on 06/04/2008)

Suicide bombers have been much in the news during the past few years. The vast majority of these murderous thugs are Muslims and come from the Middle East or from among the ranks of Muslims who have settled in the West. Several young men fitting this description are on trial in London for plotting to blow up transatlantic passenger jets. Others were responsible for the Madrid and London outrages as well as the attacks on the Pentagon and the World Trade Centre.

Islamists or Jihadis did not invent the idea of killing oneself to make a political point. Jan

Pallach set himself on fire in Prague after the Soviet Army moved in to crush the so-called Prague Spring. Bobby Sands starved himself to death in a British jail in Northern Ireland during the 'troubles'. The Tamil Tigers in Sri Lanka have used the technique of suicide bombing for political ends during their protracted battle for self-determination. Japanese fighter pilots, or the Kamikaze, made their mark in World War Two. However, it is the Islamic community in Iraq, Afghanistan and Palestine that have been the most prolific protagonists of the idea of strapping a large quantity of high explosives to your person and wandering off to a crowded school or market and blowing yourself to smithereens along with as many other bystanders as possible.

Al Qaeda, Osama Bin Laden's group has recently published a video clip showing a young terrorist setting off on his last journey. He is shown in a passionate and prolonged embrace with another man, presumably his handler. He is then seen climbing into a small truck laden with explosives and driving off towards a US military outpost. The clip then shows the explosion from a number of angles and finishes with the celebration of the bombers martyrdom.

It might be interesting to reflect on the thought processes of those who either act as human bombs or persuade others to do so. There does seem to be disagreement about the motives behind these acts. Some claim that they would cease if Western soldiers were to leave Islamic territories, especially Iraq and Afghanistan. Others claim that these acts are done purely in the name of Islam as a way of punishing the sinful, immoral West and leading it towards the embrace of Allah. Militant Islam finds the West, in general, and the United States in particular, to be repugnant. That being so, anything that can be done to harm their interests can be justified by a careful parsing of the Koran. Books like the Koran and the Bible can be used to justify more or less anything the reader cares to choose.

So, a successful suicide bomb attack that kills lots of people is entirely acceptable to the religious hooligans that carry them out. Most of the bombers who carry out their gruesome acts in the Middle East are unlettered peasants whose only education has been study of the Koran and related materials. The Western media suggests that they are persuaded that the successful commission of their missions will lead to an immediate passage to paradise and priapic rewards beyond their most fevered dreams. Of course, death is instantaneous and they never realise that they have been duped – poor bastards. Large numbers of virgins they do not get – just oblivion! Do their handlers believe the same line? Do they think that they are doing God's work? Do they consider that the use of suicide bombing as a tool will weaken the resolve of Western nations and cause them to withdraw their forces from the Middle East or to mend their ways and start behaving in a way that would cause Allah to smile upon their societies? It is likely that some of the handlers believe the same toxic mumbo jumbo as the poor deluded bombers. Much more likely, surely, is that they are sinister manipulators who will stop at nothing to prosecute their war aims.

Those naughty Swiss

(First published on 11/12/2009)

On November 29 last, the Swiss voted to ban the construction of any more minarets in their country. A referendum was held and passed by a margin of 57% in favour to 43% against. Consequently the Swiss constitution will be changed and further mosque building will be prohibited. The population of Switzerland is just over 7.5 million including 400,000 Muslims, most of whom come from the Balkans. There has been a good deal of multicultural hand wringing about this decision and accusations of xenophobia have been levelled at the Swiss. The Muslim population of the country has expressed fears that they will be singled out for discriminatory treatment and that their lives will be made miserable.

External commentators have suggested that Switzerland will be in breach of its obligations under various United Nations Charters that guarantee freedom of religion and that she will face challenges at the World body. Some, or all of this, may be true but the issue is not a simple one. The Swiss, in particular, and Europeans, in general, are not the only people on Earth who are suspicious of newcomers. Xenophobia is not a pleasant trait but it is just about universal. Fear of the other is widespread and not confined to the developed World. Many national groups have a visceral dislike of their neighbours and of foreigners in general. Many African tribes have been at war with their neighbours forever and often the original reasons for these conflicts have been long forgotten. The Hutus of Rwanda hate the Tutsis. The Hausa speaking people of Northern Nigeria hate and despise the Ibos from the South. Koreans look upon Caucasian visitors with a good deal of suspicion and dislike it when white men marry Korean women. The Japanese have a similar outlook. Arabs find little good to say about Jews. There is a movement in India to break up large states into smaller units in order to preserve language and customs and to separate peoples. The huge state of Andhra Pradesh in India is about to split into two to allow a Telangana speaking state to be created.

Many languages contain words used to designate "the other.' 'Goyim' in Hebrew refers to all those who are not Jewish. Muslims use the word, 'kafir' to refer to non-believers or apostates. It is not a complimentary term. There are many other similar examples but the point has been made. Europe has experienced a very large influx of immigrants since the end of the Second World War. Most of the newcomers have come from former colonial empires and many of them have been Muslims. The make up of many European countries is now very different from what it was before the Second World War. A glance at a UK telephone directory shows scores and scores of 'foreign' sounding names. Forty years ago, the names were almost all English: Smith, Robinson, Brown and so on. A 'foreign' name was an exception.

Immigration into Europe has been largely unplanned and unregulated and there are now many enclaves in European countries in which the language on the street is Arabic, Hindi or Urdu. French, German or English, for example, are not much heard in such districts. Enoch Powell, a former Conservative politician attracted enormous opprobrium when he asked whether the consequences of these immigrant waves had been fully appreciated. He did not suggest that immigration should be stopped. He suggested that unbridled inflows of newcomers were likely to be troublesome and that some thought should be given to their management.

It is hardly surprising that newcomers tend to flock to areas where they can find their own people. Such was the habit in the United States during the time it accepted hoards of people from Europe between the wars. In New York City, for example, there were wholly Jewish, Polish or German districts. In London, the traditional place for new immigrants was the East End. People settled there and slowly moved to other parts of the city as they became more prosperous and established. Characteristically, these immigrants learned to speak English and to adopt the ways of their new country. The second generations tried even harder to do so and fit in as best they could in order not to draw critical attention to themselves.

There is a good deal of unease about the large numbers of Muslims that are flowing into Europe. These folk come with ideas that are very different from those possessed by their generally, reluctant hosts. Men frequently show up with multiple wives. Women are often shrouded from head to toe in burkas. The newcomers insist on having much of their daily round mediated by Sharia law, which system is quite foreign to the British common law or the Napoleonic code of France, for example. They demand the right to institute halal codes for food preparation. This involves the slaughter of beasts without prior stunning and is regarded by host peoples as unnecessarily cruel.

More disquieting still are the very high birthrates in these new populations, giving rise to fears that within a few decades European societies will have changed beyond recognition. The frequent refusal to integrate into the receiving society but to remain separate is the source of much unease. Germany has been the host of large numbers of poor people from rural Turkey, many of whom have made no attempt to learn German. Consequently they remain trapped in their little enclaves. Several radical preachers insist on using Arabic for their sermons. It often turns out that the content of these sermons is violently anti-Western. Many mosques are responsible for promoting unrest and sedition. Such activities are all the more disturbing against the background of widespread Islamic, fundamentalist terrorism taking place throughout so much of the World today.

Many Muslims are understandably irritated by what they see as unwarranted interference in Middle Eastern affairs by Western powers. The almost unanimous support given to Israel by the West at the expense of the Palestinians likewise promotes a sense of unfairness. Young Muslim men, especially those who are out of work and poorly educated in places like the UK or France, fall easy prey to radical imams in the many mosques that are now scattered throughout both countries. They are easily persuaded that the West is the seat of iniquity and out to scupper Islam. There have been a number of spectacular terrorist outrages that have been carried out by young Muslims born and bred in Europe. A plot to bring down six or more jets over the Atlantic was recently scotched. The plotters were almost all homegrown, young Muslims. Loyalty to other Muslims, right or wrong, appears to be more crucial in the thinking of young radicals than loyalty to their newly adopted countries. Europeans have only to open their newspapers or turn on the TV news to learn of daily abominations that take place throughout the Muslim world. It is not uncommon to learn that more than a hundred men, women and children have been casually slaughtered by various fundamentalist religious splinter groups in the name of who knows what.

Europeans have become accustomed to thinking that if terrorism is taking place anywhere, it is carried out by Muslims. By and large that is true. Thus it is not altogether surprising that the people of Switzerland, when given the chance, decided to react viscerally and vote to prohibit the construction of any more mosques, which they see as nests of subversion and reaction. Muslims say that as there are thousands of church steeples in Switzerland, why can't there be minarets? Churches summon their flocks to prayer ringing bells. Mosques call the faithful to prayer by chanting passages of the Koran. One quantitative difference is that church bells ring for thirty minutes on a Sunday whereas mosques blast out their summonses five times a day, every day! Another is that church steeples have been part of the landscape for hundreds of years whereas minarets have not.

Surely countries do have the right to decide who should move in and settle. Can they not expect newcomers to integrate and accept the status quo and not insist on radical changes ten minutes after arriving? An incoming population that insists on being ruled by the mores of fifth century, nomadic, Arabic tribesmen will find itself unwelcome in post enlightenment Europe unless it is willing to make considerable efforts to acculturate. After all, it is the visitors who come and the hosts who set the ground rules. It is up to the incomers to make the greater effort to fit in. Muslims, who find this hard to accept could ask themselves how welcome would the widespread construction of churches, public houses and dance halls be back home. Would they permit Western women to wander the streets wearing summer frocks? Openly gay and lesbian parades in Jedda, Damascus or Kabul would not prosper. Immigration to the West from the poorer parts of the world is not going to stop. Strenuous efforts will be needed from hosts and visitors alike. Success will not be achieved if intellectuals and liberals automatically cast the hosts as being at fault. Germans, Frenchmen, Swiss and Britons have rights too.

On Saudi Arabia

(First published on 15/03/2014)

Karen Elliott House, Pulitzer prize winning journalist, has written an interesting book on Saudi Arabia. (On Saudi Arabia – Its People, Past and Religion, published by Alfred A Knopf, 2012) This book was based on thirty-five years travelling backwards and forwards to that country and upon thousands of interviews that she carried out during her many visits. As a western woman, she had unparalleled access to all strata of Saudi society. As long as she dressed modestly and covered her hair, she was able to speak to men and women alike. No Saudi Arabian writer of either sex would have been allowed such privileges. The story she tells is of a dysfunctional country, entirely controlled by the dictates of Islam, burdened a large royal family numbering some seven thousand princes, riven by corruption, mired in ignorance, and living off the proceeds from the sale of a dwindling supply of oil. In short, a depressing hole in which *everything that is not absolutely compulsory is absolutely forbidden.'*

The late Christopher Hitchens made that observation about North Korea but it applies in spades to Saudi Arabia.

Three hundred years ago, what is now known as Saudi Arabia was a barren, harsh desert over which roamed several tribes of endlessly warring Arabs. A tribal chief, Muhammad al Saud, along with a fanatical preacher, Muhammad ibn Abd al-Wahhab, conquered them all and founded the first Saudi kingdom in 1745. Al Wahhab's dream was to return to the austere and simple life, that Muslims believe, was led by the Prophet. The system that was set up by this pair lasted for about 80 years. After its demise, there was another extended period of lawlessness which was replaced by another Al Saud dominated kingdom, which in turn lasted a further 80 years. The most recent iteration was founded in 1932, led by Abdul Aziz bin al Saud, father of the present king. Abdul fathered 40+ sons and uncounted daughters. The present king, Abdullah bin Abdulaziz al Saud, is the son of the founder. He is in his 80s and in failing health. During his reign, he has outlived two or three crown princes. Succession passes from one brother to the next and all of the founder's living sons are old men. Sometime during the next few years, the throne must pass to the next generation. It is likely that there will be a struggle over competing claims at that time. Each of the founder's sons had many wives and produced dozens of sons, who in their turn, were equally fecund. His progeny now amounts to some 7000 souls, all of whom are entitled to the title of prince. Hardly anyone in a cushy post in the country is not a prince.

Statistics are dull but there are a few, given by Ms House, that paint an illuminating picture of today's Saudi Arabia:

-70% of Saudis are under thirty,

-60% are under twenty,

-40% of the entire population lives in abject poverty, unable to afford a house,

-40% of those aged between twenty and twenty-four are unemployed,

-90% of persons working for private enterprise are imported foreign workers, most of whom are savagely exploited with few if any rights.

-Twelve international patents have been granted to Saudi citizens since 1971.
-The governor of each of the thirteen provinces is a prince.

Young Saudi men seek government jobs for they seem to consider working in service industries beneath them. Such jobs are at the gift of a prince to whom a bribe must be paid. The majority of the population lives in Third World conditions in a country with $400billion in cash reserves and an annual income from the sale of oil of $100billion. The monarchy claims to personify, propagate and protect the one true religion and it has granted itself the title of Custodian of the Holy Mosques: Mecca and Medina. The Haditha, of which there are thousands, are the reported words and deeds of the Prophet and are used, along with the Koran, as a guide for the devout. Ms House recounts in detail the effect that religion has on the daily lives of Saudis and how modern pressures from abroad are slowly forcing unwelcome change on society. The religious police, the Mutaween, are charged with ensuring that the precepts of Wahhabi Islam are followed to the letter but are finding their task ever more difficult in the face of intrusions from outside, via the Internet and social media.

Devout Muslims believe that men must obey Allah and that women must obey men. Ms House observes that, *'Fortunately for men, Allah is distant, whereas for women, men are omnipresent.'* One especially religious woman, with whom the author lived for a spell, is quoted as saying, *'Righteous women, in their husband's absence, must fiercely guard what Allah would have them guard!'* May one assume that Allah is pruriently pre-occupied with the more intimate parts of women's anatomy in that he fears that all men are no more than ravening sex maniacs? Shopping malls, airports, hospitals and all government offices are spread with prayer mats, conveniently pointing towards Mecca so that anyone, anywhere can drop to his or her knees and follow the five time daily prayer ritual. Hotels rooms have little signs pointing towards Mecca and many cars are sold with complementary prayer mats to enable their owners to stop by the roadside and carry out their devotions. It seems that the devout regard change as the pathway to hell. They are more concerned with the hereafter than life on earth. All public displays of affection are forbidden except men walking along hand in hand. Women outside the home are supposed to cover themselves completely. Waving to an acquaintance is frowned upon as being a western habit. Abdul bin Abdullah bin Bay was the Grand Mufti until 1999 and he proclaimed that the world was flat! During his period in office he was the unchallenged voice of Wahhabi Islam.

Ms House devotes a good deal of her book to the subject of education. In general, education in Saudi Arabia is a matter of rote learning with great emphasis placed on being able to churn out the Koran. More hours per week are spent in school on religious studies than all other subjects combined. Wahhabis see education as an extension of religion and that the sciences and foreign languages as a distraction luring the youth towards worldly wickedness. Religion is not a matter of debate, just acceptance. The teaching of philosophy is banned for it entails the art of questioning. Chemistry is regarded as magic and physics as atheism. Some anxious professors approached the minister of education with their concerns that students who hoped to attend the University of Cairo needed these subjects for entry and that the religious authorities would not countenance the teaching of them. The minister, with uncharacteristic wit, told them not to teach chemistry Instead he suggested the nature of matter as an alternative title for the topic. Physics was similarly disguised as the nature of things. Teaching is very poorly paid and attracts the bottom 15% of university graduates. Women are not allowed to teach, firstly, because they would come into contact with men, to whom they were not related, and secondly, because Islam holds that women may not provide instruction for males.

By some means or other, the House of Saud has managed to exert its hold over the Saudi population with the help and active cooperation of religious authorities. Helping them to hang on to power has been their exclusive access to the proceeds from the oil wealth. Unfortunately, there is a growing pool of young people who are poorly educated with no prospects of useful and profitable careers. Allied to this is the cultural distaste that the young men have for doing jobs that are seen as being beneath them. Younger women are likewise becoming more and more restive and bucking against rules that forbid them to go about, drive cars and have careers other than that of breeding stock. When prominent clerics proclaim that driving motor vehicles is bad for their ovaries and likely to result in the production of damaged children, female anger and derision results. (Sheik Saleh al Lohaiden)

Karen Elliott House generally writes sympathetically about Saudi Arabia and its people. She is reminded in some way of the dreary hole she grew up in deepest Texas where religion trumped everything. She does, however, have grave misgivings about its future. The oil stocks, upon which its wealth relies, are dwindling. The West is less and less dependent for its supply of fossil fuel from Saudi Arabia. The deadening grip of religion is weakening in the face of the onslaught from outside through the Internet and other social media. Saudi Arabia lies in a very dangerous neighbourhood. It is the main champion of Sunni Islam, but its neighbours: Iran, Iraq, Syria and Bahrain are Shi'ite countries with no love for the Saudis, who proclaim loudly that Shi'ites are heretics. The pool of restless young men, unemployed and ill-educated, represents a danger to the establishment. The succession from the generation of the founder's sons to that of his grandsons is likely to be turbulent. Saudi's principal western ally is the United States. This does not come about because of any deep-seated affection for the regime. It is entirely pragmatic, for in recent decades, that's where the oil was. The other great American ally in the Middle East is Israel and were the Americans forced to choose, things might not go in favour of Saudi Arabia, especially as North America becomes less and less dependent upon oil from the Gulf. Elderly conservative Saudis shrug off the depressing prospects for the future. They happily point out that their ancestors lived off dates and camel's milk and that they, too, could return to that practice.

The next ten to fifteen years will be interesting. The stifling grip of Islam over all aspects of life, commerce, education, and the treatment of the young and of women will surely weaken. 'On Saudi Arabia' hints at this. For an easy to read and competently written account of this strange place, $15 spent with amazon.com for the Kindle edition is money well spent.

Jihad

(First published on 29/06/2013)

One hears much about 'jihad' in the Western media nowadays since the arrival of so many Muslim immigrants in Europe, North America and Australia. Once they began to draw attention to themselves in the unwelcome fashion of espousing violent terrorism, the natives, who had lived more or less contentedly in these countries, were obliged to sit up and take notice of these exotic people who dressed strangely and appeared to have very curious ideas about life, culture and, above all, the centrality of religion in day to day affairs. Some of the more fiery Muslim clerics banged on about Allah, Muhammad, jihad and fatwah – terms that had, heretofore, not cut much ice in London, New York and Sydney. Allah and Muhammad need little explanation for there are similar entities in the Christian worldview. Jihad, however, is a bird with very different feathers.

In classical Arabic, the word means struggle. There are two kinds of jihad: the lesser and the greater. Lesser jihad is the struggle against those who do not believe in the Muslim divinity. Greater jihad is the inner struggle to fulfil ones' religious duties. For purposes of this piece, greater jihad is not a concern, for the experience of an individual who is quietly going about his private convictions concerning his obligation to his god is unlikely to butt up against the life and habits of fellow citizens. After all, belief in god and taking on a pile of obligations as a result, is a personal burden and is undertaken voluntarily. Those who wish to don the hair shirt of strict religious observance can do their own scratching.

Lesser jihad, on the other hand, is a much greater worry for it entails interference in the lives of those who do not care overmuch about Allah and his Prophet and most certainly do not wish to be blown up by the actions of some crazed jihadist wearing a suicide vest who objects to actual or perceived slights against the whole box of dice. In passing, it should be noted that a jihadist is more accurately called a mujahid and his mates, mujahideen.

Islamic terrorism is a comparatively new phenomenon and many Western writers and thinkers have sought to find reasons to explain it. The question of Israel and the Holy Lands, postcolonial anger and resentment at the presence of Western military forces on Muslim lands are the usual suspects. That there might be religious reasons for jihadist behaviour sits less comfortably with Western commentators. It is one thing to blame the actions of the Israelis as they seek to defend themselves against attacks and threats from the Muslim world or to sympathise with the feelings of those who have so recently thrown off the colonial yoke but quite another to blame a major religion for terrorist attacks. But it does seem that Islam comes with inbuilt imperatives to attack those who do not care to follow its dictates. Passages from its scriptures actually enjoin its followers to do all they can to restore the long lost caliphate and to spread its beliefs across the world.

Some strands of Muslim thought maintain that the World is innately Islamic and that it was so before the Jews set up their version of monotheism and carefully edited out all references to Allah's laws from the scriptures. According to this view, Muhammad was sent to reassert the primacy of Islam and so, is believed to be God's last messenger whose purpose is to restore the world to its rightful, pristine state. Hard line Muslim fundamentalists believe that the world is divided into two realms: good or haram and evil or halal. Islam holds that all should submit to the will of God. Not to do so is impious and forbidden. No debate on this point is conceivable. In the 13th century, ibn Tammiyah encouraged Muslims to rebel against leaders who were not truly pious. He sought to purify the religion from distortions. His writings influenced later prominent preachers. In the eighteenth century, Muhammad ibn Abd al-Wahhab popped up in Arabia. He preached much the same line of thought, suggesting that Islam had gone into decline and had regressed to pre-Mohammadan ways and this had allowed European modernity to commence its long climb to world ascendancy. He demanded that the faithful return to the ways of the Koran. Incidentally, he is the founder of the Wahhabi strain of Sunni Islam and is the spiritual godfather of al Quada and religious practices in modern Saudi Arabia – beheadings, amputations, stonings and the subjugation of women along with the rest of the poisonous doctrines to be found there.

After the fall of the Ottoman Empire, the nearest thing in modern times to the Caliphate or universal rule of Islam over the entire world, the Muslim Brotherhood was founded. They rejected modern political ideas on matters such as democracy, holding instead, that God's law or Sharia was all that was necessary to govern the affairs of man. Allowing mere humans to vote and to pass laws, as happens in democratic systems, was thought to be blasphemous and Un-Islamic. An important influence upon the early days of the Brotherhood was Syed Qutb, an Egyptian who spent some time in the United States and was deeply offended by what he encountered there. He was particularly exercised by the behaviour of American women. His most famous quotation was provoked by a visit to a church social in Greely, Colorado. *"Humanity is living in a large brothel! One only has to glance at its press, films, fashion shows, beauty contests, ballrooms, wine bars and broadcasting stations! Or observe its mad lust for naked flesh, print, provocative pictures and sick, suggestive statements in literature, the arts and mass media! The American girl is well acquainted with her body's seductive capacity. She knows it lies in the face, and in expressive eyes, and thirsty lips. She knows that seductiveness lies in the round breasts, the full buttocks, and in the shapely thighs, sleek legs – and she shows all this and does not hide it."* Apparently his over excited reaction was provoked by the playing of "Baby, it's cold outside!", the dim lighting and dancing, *'chest to chest!'* This obvious terror of the human female body would be laughable if it were not so sad and it hardly squares with the rewards for martyrs who die in the cause of jihad: seventy-two virgins! En passant, it is fair to ask what a psychiatrist would have made of these fulminations.

In short, those who firmly believe that the lesser jihad must be pursued regardless of the opinions and feelings of others, lap up the teachings of Tammiyah, Wahhab, Qutb and others. They are trapped in a *'hermetically sealed thought system'* (Melanie Phillips) that allows of no view of the world other than the one that demands total submission to the will of Allah and the teachings of his Prophet and the Sharia. The alternatives are bleak: submit and convert, be killed or live as second class citizens under Muslim hegemony and pay jizyah, a special tax extorted from those who live under Muslim rule but refuse to follow its precepts.

Unfortunately for the West, there is a substantial number of people living there who believe strongly in this stuff and who are determined to impose it upon their new hosts whether they like it or not. By no means do all recently arrived immigrants from Muslim countries hold these views but most of them find it hard to challenge the ideologues for fear of being termed apostates or blasphemers. More sinister still is that several of the most radical Western mujahideen are second generation immigrants. They have grown up in the West, gone to school there, seemed to have settled but then have become radicalised and have taken to violence. Those, who carried out the attacks on London Transport in 2007, are prime examples of this phenomenon. It is unclear what has caused such distaste for their fellow citizens to emerge after several years' residence in the West. Several theories have been put forward and the most likely explanation seems to be that that those Muslims who have arrived from the Indian sub-continent have cultural imperatives on top of their religious feelings that impede their full integration into their new host countries, which in turn leads to lack of economic success and then breeds resentment.

The West, especially, the United Kingdom, is not short of fiery, hate spewing clerics who prey on deracinated young men and set them on the path of violent jihad. This, coupled with the squeamishness of progressive thinkers in the West to vigorously question religious beliefs and practices, feeling somehow, that such matters are off limits, is bringing about a dangerous state of affairs. Multiculturalism is all very well but can it be allowed to distort and destroy the native or original culture? Are culturally Christian nations obliged to refrain from pointedly questioning the practices of incomers on the grounds that it can be termed racist and disrespectful to do so?

The steady advance of jihadism in the West is something to be taken note of. Passive, supine tolerance and fear that intrusive questions and debate may not be conducive to the public good – the excuse so often trotted out by the 'bien pensants' in the West – may well permit, unconsidered, irreversible change to Western societies.

Dangerous waters

(First published on 01/11/2013)

The Holy Bible, that venerable collection of myths, legends, horror stories, history and poetry, leads its readers to accept that Abraham fathered children with two women: Sarah, his wife and Hagar, his concubine. Sarah's son, Isaac, is held to be the ancestor of the Jews and Hagar's son, Ishmael, the ancestor of the Arabs. In order not to offend the amour propre of the Arabs by considering them to be descended from Abraham's 'bit on the side', Hagar has been tarted up and deemed to be an errant Egyptian princess who somehow found herself in Abraham's bed. If there is anything at all to these stories, then the Jews and the Arabs are closely connected. More sophisticated anthropological and linguistic studies show that to be the case. The diverging pathways taken by these two closely related peoples is the burden of this essay.

In the ancient world, scholarship was the preserve of the ancient Greeks. Plato, Aristotle and Socrates are figures that stand out among a host and whose works still have resonance today. Various schools of philosophy came and went in Ancient Greece and the last of them was closed by the Roman Emperor, Justinian, in 529. Greek scholars drifted away and many settled in the Persian Empire. Forty years later, Muhammad was born and during the next couple of centuries the religion of Islam was established. It began its spread across what is now known as the Middle East and North Africa. Its main rivals were the neighbouring Persian Empire and the residual, Byzantian Roman Empire based in Constantinople.

An inevitable cross fertilisation occurred and much of the ancient Greek learning was adopted by Arabs and this led to the astonishing flowering of their scholarship in the four to five hundred years up to the middle of the 13th century when Mongol invasion destroyed the remainder of the Abbasid Empire with their conquest of Baghdad, the principal home of most Arabic scholarship of the period. During this so-called 'Golden Age', Arab thinkers developed algebra, devised an easier numbering system to replace the cumbersome Roman method. They also wrote extensively on astronomy, medicine, physics and optics. Al-Burini, a prominent enquirer, using a trigonometric method of his own devising, calculated the circumference of the Earth to within 200 miles of the figure accepted today. Perhaps the greatest contribution made by this era of enquiry was the movement that resulted in the translation of many of the works of the Greek ancients into Arabic. It is via these Arabic sources, that so much has come down to modern times, which might otherwise have been lost.

After the Mongol invasion and consequent fall of Baghdad in 1258, Arab scholarship declined rapidly. Arabs were split into small tribal groups. The blinkers were put on, the earplugs inserted and a headlong rush into the cul-de-sac of religion took place. The infantilising effect brought about these changes led to little more than an endless parsing of the Koran, Sharia and the Haditha. Today, Islamic scholarship in general and Arabic scholarship in particular is in a sorry state. There are 1.6

billion Muslims worldwide. Only two persons living and working in Muslim countries have won Nobel Prizes. Residents of these countries publish a tiny fraction of all scientific literature. Spain translates more books into other languages annually than the Arab world has done during the past one thousand years. The USA produces about ten thousand peer reviewed, scientific papers each year and the Arab world, only four. Arabs comprise 5% of the world's population but publish only 1% of all books.

On the other hand, Arabs and Muslims who live in the West are as productive and inventive as any other group of people and so can it be concluded that there is something stifling about Islam as practised in the Muslim heartlands? Islam does not encourage scientific enquiry for that would undermine the dicta of the religion. If the Koran and the Haditha are held to be the founts of all necessary knowledge, then seeking answers elsewhere is heretical. Islam further hobbles scientific enquiry by suppressing the female half of its adherents. Even today, in many parts of the

Islamic world, female literacy is actively discouraged. It is hard to imagine a university department of physics in Saudi Arabia being headed by a woman.

Shortly after the end of the Arab Golden Age, European scholarship began to flourish. Roger Bacon (1214-1294), René Descartes, (1596-1650), Galileo (1564-1642) and Isaac Newton (1642-1727) are links in a chain of early scientists, some of whom ran into serious trouble with the Church over their work and publications. The Christian Church felt as threatened as Islamic authorities by independent speculation. The efforts of such men led to the burgeoning of enquiry that fostered the age of reason and enlightenment and which laid the foundation for today's scientific advances. Speculation, unhampered by dogma, allowed knowledge to progress and accumulate. By the time the 18th and 19th centuries arrived, scientific enquiry was in full flood and has continued to be so until the present day.

Jews were widespread throughout the Fertile Crescent and what is now known as the Middle East, during the period of the Arab Golden Age. They made substantial contributions to the scholarship of the day. During the Middle Ages they settled across much of Europe and established thriving communities. They were mainly engaged in various aspects of trading and banking but were not immune to intellectual developments taking place in their new homes. Religious reform among Jews began in earnest during the eighteenth century, since which time, Jewish scientists and thinkers have made remarkable contributions to modern thought across many fields. People such as Karl Marx, who revolutionised political theory, Sigmund Freud, who made profound contributions to ideas about mind and behaviour, Albert Einstein, the founder of modern physics and cosmology, Noam Chomsky, linguist, philosopher, mathematician, computer scientist, thinker about artificial intelligence and one of the most cited scholars of all time, are all Jewish. Just over eight hundred and fifty Nobel prizes have been awarded since their foundation. Jews have won approximately 20% of these, although they make up just 0.2% of the population of the World. It can be said with confidence, that in matters intellectual, modern Jews have punched well above their weight.

Why then have the two races: the Arabs and the Jews experienced such different courses? Notions that one racial group is smarter than another have long ago been discredited and shown to be unfounded. Intelligence tests are encumbered with great cultural bias and unhelpful when comparing the performances of different populations. After their Golden Age, Arabs appear to have become pre-occupied with religious matters, to the exclusion of almost everything else. A religion that insists that it provides answers to every question pertaining to the human experience must inevitably stunt intellectual growth. It is curious that Arabs lived in such a lively intellectual milieu during the time when their religion was relatively new and fresh. Among Jews today there are the ultra-orthodox Haredim whose ideas about the primacy of religion in day-to-day life closely mimic those of devout Muslims. Jews, that have made their enormous contribution to science, medicine and philosophy, have discarded the blinkers imposed by faith. Few Haredim are known for their contributions to scientific advancement! Their time is spent studying the holy books.

This essay has taken on quite a task: tracing 1500 years of history and the fate and fortune of two ethnic groups during that time. Many authentic scholars have spent their lives treating just one facet of these stories. However, the meagre contribution made to the sum total of modern knowledge made by one of the groups compared to the astonishing successes of the other stimulates enquiry. If this piece provokes only one of its readers to wonder about the contrast, it will have served its purpose.

Holy War

(First published in 2014)

Perhaps it is time for the West to wake up and acknowledge that a substantial number of Muslims are engaged in Holy War and that they are actively seeking to bring an end to the Western way of life. Commentators have not been comfortable with the idea that much of the strife raging in the Middle East has its origin in religion and not politics. After all, in these inclusive days, it is one thing to object to another's politics but to question his religion? That is a step too far. Most will have taken notice of the recent fighting in Iraq. A group of Sunni militants have made a sudden move and blindsided the central government, led by Nuri al Malaki, a Shia. These Sunnis belong to an organisation known as ISIS (Islamic State of Iraq and Syria) whose stated aim is to establish a caliphate extending throughout the Middle East. They are Salafis or Wahhabis – these terms are more or less interchangeable – who practise an austere form of Islam that seeks to resemble that religion's very earliest days. That was the time when good Muslims believed that the word of God was given to Muhammad by an angel in a cave; when all should submit fully to God; when it was OK to seek out and murder unbelievers, especially Jews; when the inferiority of women was fully established by God; when heretics, apostates and idol worshippers should be publicly stoned to death; when adulterers should suffer the same fate; when education should be limited to a study of the Koran; when the study of the natural sciences should be banned as magic and sorcery; when the righteous went off to paradise and enjoyed seventy-two virgins who were miraculously 're-virginised' after every sexual encounter; where these same virgins had 'appetising vaginas' and where the righteous had eternal hard-ons; where the women who went to paradise had to make do with their earthly husbands; where rivers of wine flowed freely. The list goes on and on.

ISIS adherents believe that they have a divine obligation to slaughter all Shias, the majority people of Iraq, for in their view, they are heretics, equivalent to unbelievers. Having overthrown them, they will be on the way to setting up a Sunni caliphate that could take in Jordan, Syria, Palestine, Israel and who knows where else. Why should any of this be of interest to the self-absorbed hedonists that make up most of the West? Would not the ambitions of these fanatical Sunnis be satisfied with their fine new caliphate in which they can order everything according to their holy book and ensure that their people remain mired in ignorance and backwardness? Perhaps they wouldn't. In any case, they would have established a nice little territory from which they could plan and execute plots and attacks on Europe and further afield. Western powers have spent huge sums of money, sacrificed the lives of thousands of young men during the past decade to prevent that very thing happening. The invasions of Iraq and Afghanistan attest to Western concerns. But it looks as if all of this expenditure may come to naught.

It is important to remember that good Sunnis have an obligation to spread their religion as far as they can. The doctrine of Jihad

– struggle – has been interpreted to mean the conquest of unbelievers or non-Muslims. Like most Koranic expressions, it has as many shades of meaning as there are so-called Koranic scholars to pronounce upon them. In that regard, there is no difference between theologians of all faiths: keep it complex and baffle the punters! Islam was initially spread throughout Arabia and adjoining lands by means of the sword. It attempted to take over Europe but was stopped at the gates of Vienna in 1683 when an alliance of Christian forces defeated the Ottoman army. A few pockets of the Muslim faith hung on in the Balkans into modern times: Albania, Kosovo and Bosnia-Herzogovena. Several Arabic words live on in the Spanish language.

European empires collapsed during the middle of the twentieth century and peoples in Africa, the Middle East and the Indian Sub-continent acquired self-rule. In practice, freedom from the colonialists was followed by life under home brewed dictators. However, increasing numbers of Muslims arrived on European shores during the last thirty years and now make up significant proportions of national populations: Austria 4%; Denmark 5%; France 7.5%; Germany 5%; Netherlands 6%; UK 4.6% are a few examples. Also worth noting is that Caucasian women in Europe bear an average of just over two children, while their Islamic sisters have five. If current trends continue, Muslims will find themselves in the majority in several European countries by the end of the century. It is, of course, mistaken to conflate a religion with a nationality. It is even deemed racist to discuss the matter in these terms. The dictates of political correctness muzzle discussion of many important topics. But it is worth remembering that Muslims act pretty coherently when something is considered to be insulting to their religion. The Salman Rushdie affair, the fuss over the Danish cartoons and the Dutch movie, Fitna, by Theo van Gogh illustrate that tendency.

Jihadist struggles in the Middle East have begun to attract disaffected young men from Europe, who see themselves going off to fight the infidels and perhaps drawing their tickets to Paradise. Those that escape a bullet and return to their homes have the potential to act as recruiting sergeants for others, similarly disposed. Sharia law is making its presence felt in Europe by degrees. There has been a recent endorsement by the Law Society of England, which advised its members on how to draw up Sharia compliant wills. Many domestic disputes are now settled by local Sharia councils instead of by the officially sanctioned authorities. There have been reports of young radicals declaring parts of London –Tower Hamlets, for example – to be Sharia areas and not open to non-Muslims and certainly not those wearing scanty clothing or drinking beer out of cans as they mooch about. Londoners unwise enough to amble into these areas have been hassled. Several instances of Muslim groups in British universities demanding that public lectures be delivered to audiences segregated by sex have been reported. In some instances, the university authorities have backed their demands. Radical clerics are known to preach inflammatory sermons encouraging civil disobedience from certain mosques in both UK and France. Local authorities seem reluctant to interfere with such activities for fear that they could be accused of racism or discrimination. So, like it or not, there are worrying signs that some immigrant groups are hell bent on stirring up trouble.

It is entirely true that many Muslims, living in Europe, wish to get on with their lives, bring up their children and earn their livings. By no means all Muslims newcomers are troublemakers. It is also true that many are not so keen on integrating and are ready to cause trouble. Most regrettably, those who seek the quiet life are most reluctant to castigate the troublemakers and to tell them to mind their manners. Accounts of outrages taking place in Europe or in Muslim heartlands are not met with choruses of disapproval and protest. Is it reasonable to assume this silence implies assent?

Aspects of terrorism

(First published on 05/10/2008)

James Cook University academic, Dr Mervyn Bendle, has drawn attention to the large amounts of Saudi Arabian money flowing into Australian universities. He maintains that some of this money is going towards funding a new academic discipline known as Critical Terrorism Studies. In his view this discipline is sparked by Neo-Marxist post-modernism and treats terrorism as a construct of Western imagination.

A leading proponent of this new discipline is Professor Anthony Burke, who teaches at the Australian Defence Force Academy in Canberra. Critical Terrorism Studies seek to deconstruct the causes of terrorism. It concludes that most, if not all, Islamic terror strikes are the result of Western actions around the World. Furthermore, they are provoked by Western Imperialism, both past and present and are a kind of pay back for Western imperialist policies of the past. Professor Burke is especially critical of the Israeli-Palestinian conflict and claims that many arrested Islamic terrorists cite that conflict as the main reason that they involved themselves in terrorist activities. He seems to claim that were the West to stop supporting Israel so ardently and to assist the Palestinians in regaining their homelands, most of the terrorist activities, that we see today, would stop. He pays little heed to the holy injunction placed upon all Muslims to spread Islam by means of the sword if all other means fail. He downplays the role of Islam in fomenting anti-Western attitudes. In short, this new discipline says that the West has only itself to blame for the unrest and hostility that runs throughout the Islamic World and that is being exported to Europe, Australia and North America.

Channel Four TV in Britain has recently broadcast some programmes on the findings of some of its journalists, who went 'underground', and were able to report the goings on inside the Regent's Park Mosque in London. Most spectacularly they were able to insert a female journalist into the women's section of the mosque. She went along suitably swathed in head to toe garments and was able to listen to some vitriolic statements by senior female instructors from Saudi Arabia. They were preaching the necessity for all Muslims living in Britain to hold themselves entirely separate from the native population and to avoid all contact if at all possible. These women emphasised the Islamic view that adultery, homosexual activity and apostasy were all capital offences for which the punishment was death. These instructors claimed that Westerners were immoral, tainted and evil. The Regent's Park Mosque had been thought to be a bastion of Islamic moderation and several interfaith meetings have been held there. Its supervisor is a Saudi Arabian diplomat from the embassy in London. Channel Four managed to film some inter-faith meetings that had taken place. It appears that all is sweetness and light during the meetings but that as soon as the other delegations leave, all kinds of vitriolic and abusive statements are made. This sort of hypocrisy is justified by the doctrine al-taqqiya, which states that it is not necessary for Muslims to be truthful towards unbelievers!

Many very hostile DVDs and books are on sale at this mosque. When this fact is pointed out, the managers undertake to withdraw them. Repeated checks have shown that this odious material is still available.

Lastly, Random House Inc., a prominent publisher, cancelled a deal to publish 'The Jewel of Medina' by Sherry Jones on the grounds that it might offend some Muslims. The book is a fictional life of A'isha, one of the Prophet's wives. They were afraid of legal action or worse and did not want a reprise of the Salman Rushdie Satanic Verses affair. Gibson Square Books have taken on the job of publishing this book in England. They have already been rewarded for their pains by a firebombing of their London offices. Three men are in custody awaiting trial on a number of serious charges. Beaufort Books, which holds the rights in the USA have announced that it is bringing forward its release date. The London publisher describes the book as a moving love story whereas the Ramadan Foundation, a Manchester based youth group, calls it an attempt to belittle one of the most prominent women in Islam. Unless the book sees the light of day, who will know which view is the right one?

Surveillance

(First published on 13/06/2013)

The media are, recently, full of expressions like, 'Orwellian' 'Big Brother is watching you,' and 'NewSpeak,' as the activities of whistleblowers, like Robert Snowden and the pathetic, little, private soldier, Bradley Manning occupy the front pages. The events of nine-eleven were an enormous shock to the American body politic and to the people. Remnants of this shock remain today and are a compound of anger, fear, and astonishment and wonder that there are people out there who would do such a thing to the nice people who inhabit the USA. Shortly after the destruction of the Twin Towers, the then president, George W. Bush, initiated a war on terror that involved invading Iraq to depose the egregious Saddam Hussein which, in turn was followed by the Afghanistan adventure. The war in Iraq lasted for about ten years. One of the pretexts for the invasion was to seek and destroy weapons of mass destruction. It was assumed that Iraq was ankle deep in such weapons and that these might well be used to mount further attacks on the American homeland. No such weapons were found. Saddam was deposed and eventually hanged. Iraq was turned into a quagmire and remains so to this day. It is on the brink of a bloody civil war between the Sunni minority and the Shi'ite majority with the Kurds sitting on the sidelines egging on those who appear to be gaining the upper hand. The war in Afghanistan was mounted to stop its very difficult territory being used as a base by al Qaeda-like groups. By no stretch can the forces of the Coalition of the Willing (USA, UK, Australia with smaller posses from sundry European countries) be said to have won that conflict, either. All foreign troops will have left within a matter of months, leaving the field open once more, for the Taliban to resume control and turn the place back to the Middle Ages run by a crazed theocracy.

During the last decade, there has been a string of Islamist attacks on sundry targets in the West. A detailed recital of these would be tedious but the most significant were in New

York, the London Transport System, the nightclub in Bali and the Mumbai assault. The Website, Islam the Religion of Peace, documents more than 21,000 'minor' bomb attacks since 2001. The Arab Spring has rocked the Middle East and overthrown a handful of dictators leaving the countries involved in an anarchic mess. There is a ghastly struggle going on in Syria on increasingly sectarian lines. Northern Nigeria has burst into flames. Mali nearly fell to an insurgency. In a more minor key, Islamists have slaughtered people taking part in a celebrated foot race in Boston and a poor unfortunate, off duty soldier had his head hacked off in broad daylight on the streets of London. In total, about 20,000 people have been killed and twice that number injured. Without doubt, today's menace comes from some perverted Muslims espousing a doctrine of Jihad and wanting to cause as much disruption to civil society as possible.

Western authorities have naturally sought to put a stop to this and have geared up their security services to spy on those they feel might be in the process of plotting further bombings and rampages. If the benefit of the doubt is given to Jihadist groups and it is decided that they are motivated by the desire to right the wrongs, as they see them, of the recent colonial past, to do something to help the wretched Palestinians suffering under the Israeli jackboot, to bring Western societies and culture to heel for what they feel is rampant immorality and, finally, to establish an Islamic caliphate and impose Sharia, then it is likely that these sentiments are slowly morphing into a dangerous and threatening movement that will ultimately change the way society in the West conducts itself. Evidently, this is a real threat not to be taken lightly. An Islamic caliphate would turn out to be totalitarian and intolerant of dissent. Notions of democracy would be tossed out and citizens' actions and thoughts would be judged through the prism of Sharia – a far cry from present day Western democracy with all its faults. Hardly surprising then, that the West seeks to prevent this and to pre-empt further terrorist attacks. Ironically, the means it is employing to achieve this laudable aim are becoming increasingly onerous and turning society into the sort of totalitarian affair that the Taliban would engineer were they able to realise their ambitions.

No one who has travelled internationally by air during the last 10 years can have failed to notice the tedious security measures that all must face before boarding an aircraft anywhere in the World. It is understandable that precautions taken in Los Angeles or London would be thorough, but it does not stop there. Little old ladies catching planes in Coffs Harbour, NSW or Grande Prairie, Alberta have their belongings routinely screened for explosives! Little or no discretion is used with airport searches. The guiding doctrine seems to be if it moves and breathes then it is a potential suicide bomber. The aged, the infirm, those requiring oxygen cylinders, mothers carrying tiny babies, all are subjected to extensive body searches and an examination of their personal effects. Such policies are plainly fatuous. To date, not one eighty year old, white, Chinese or Afro-American woman has been discovered to be carrying a bomb. On the other hand, several, swarthy, young men from Pakistani,

Bangladeshi or Middle Eastern backgrounds have been. To search everyone, regardless, is to waste limited resources. A more nuanced approach would save money and permit better training of airport security officers and would almost certainly achieve an acceptable level of security. Thus, authorities would have to lay down criteria laying out who was to be thoroughly searched and those who could be subjected to minimal scrutiny. Such a policy would provoke the human rights lobby, who would cry, 'Profiling!' They would, of course be right but the aim would be to prevent would-be bombers boarding aircraft, not to protect everybody's feelings.

It is not universal bodily searches at airports that has got the media crying after the late George Orwell but recent revelations about widespread, clandestine probes into phone, email and social network accounts. Edward Snowden, a former American security officer, has let the cat of the bag by revealing that the government of the USA has been nosing its way into huge amounts of private data. It has managed this trick legally by passing secret laws that give it the right to snoop on its own citizens as well as many foreigners. Mr Snowden has brought the wrath of the USA down upon his head and has fled to Hong Kong in order to escape the US authorities, who dearly wish to capture him and lock him up for several decades. He has given details of a process, code named Prism, that allows the security agencies to pry into personal affairs without first obtaining a properly executed warrant from a judge. He has also revealed that the security agencies have obliged Google, Verizon, Facebook and Microsoft to provide backdoor access to their servers. Patently billions of transactions go on through these vast companies every day and there are just not enough snoops to listen to and to read all of the material obtained. However, metadata is gathered and scrutinised to permit the detection of unusual patterns of communication. Anything that draws attention to itself can then be further examined and actual phone calls or emails listened to or read. Similar antics have been going on covertly in Australia, the UK and Canada! It appears that several members of Congress were unaware of these clandestine activities and have reacted angrily. They point out that the fourth amendment to the US constitution was drafted to hold off government snoops. But, the Secretary of State, John Kerry has said, 'There is a very delicate but vital balance between privacy and the protection of people in our country.'

Undoubtedly, the threat of Islamic terrorist attacks upon the citizens of Western countries is a very real one and governments have a difficult task to protect their citizens but the question is how far is too far? It is impossible to provide complete security: to ensure that no bombers board planes; no significant messages are passed from one potential terrorist to another; that all plots are unmasked in a timely fashion. To provide absolute security is bound to fail as well as being unacceptably intrusive and onerous to law abiding people. The East German security agency, the STASI, employed one person in six at the height of its powers. Family members spied on each other, colleagues at work reported each other to the secret police, and children reported their parents. Even so, resourceful plotters managed to evade detection. Does the West wish to go down this sort of path? In the interests of unobtainable, absolute security, is it prepared to allow the perfect to become the enemy of the merely good? Is a way of life worth having if measures to ensure its continuance become so onerous, that those who would seek to destroy it, have virtually succeeded by co-opting security services as their unwitting assistants? Just as there must be discretion employed in airport security with enormous efforts directed towards likely miscreants, so must similar discretion be used in surveillance.

Hate preaching clerics need to be watched extremely closely: phone calls, emails, social media posts. Mosques that employ them should have large numbers of closed circuit television cameras installed. All sermons at such mosques should be recorded and translated into the vernacular for examination by the security services. Islamic societies in schools and universities need careful oversight. People travelling from or to Islamic countries must be carefully monitored. All such measures will outrage those in the West who regard multi-culturism as the prime goal. But unless the enemy realises that its activities are being closely watched and that Western societies prefer things as they are and not how the Jihadists would like them to be, then threats and outrages will continue. These onerous measures would be modified as soon as the elders of Islamic immigrant communities, in countries like Britain and France, managed to persuade their young men that their religiously motivated, destructive, activities were bringing hardship upon their own families and were actually counter productive

Blasphemy

(First published on 03/02/2008)

Moves are afoot in the United Kingdom to revise or abolish the laws pertaining to blasphemy. Blasphemy is an archaic crime, which forbids the defamation of religion or the sacred in speech or writing. Today, such prohibitions run counter to other laws about free speech. The Archbishop of Canterbury has recently delivered the James Callaghan Memorial lecture and he devoted his talk to the tension between blasphemy and free speech. To summarise a very long lecture in a sentence, he proposed that unbridled free speech might not be an altogether good thing. He suggested that there are those whose sense of identity is bound up with their religion and these people would see an attack on their religion as an attack on themselves. He did not come out and say that Muslims were the group he was talking about but it was pretty obvious whom he meant.

If one goes to the Middle East, Saudi Arabia for example, and says that Mohammed most certainly did not write down the Koran from divine dictation and that the book is not the word of God and that God does not exist, the local authorities will regard your remarks as blasphemous. The punishment for blasphemy is death. In Afghanistan, a journalist is on death row because he has downloaded and distributed some material critical of the Islamic attitude to women. Muslim countries take this stuff pretty seriously. In Western Europe, most people do not care much what you say about the religious or the sacred. One can openly espouse an atheist point of view and run no danger. Desecrating churches or other places of worship is frowned upon more as a breach of good manners and taste rather than as blasphemy. However, immigrant Muslim communities will rail against unfavourable comments. Remember the furore about the Danish cartoons that were deemed to be uncomplimentary to the Prophet. These communities are liable to make such a fuss and to make such outrageous threats that the rest of the population is likely to tread very warily for fear of a violent backlash.

Some religious people are often offended by non-believers who express their scepticism. Such people hold that religious beliefs are somehow privileged. Imagine, therefore, how irritating it is for an atheist to be told by no lesser authority than the Pope, himself, that most mental illness comes about as the result of possession by devils! Or that abortion under all circumstances is an offence. Consider how provoking are Islamic attitudes to women and its notions about dress and demeanour. The most egregious offence, carried out by religious folk, is to talk of Catholic children or Muslim children, instead of children whose parents happen to Catholic or Muslim and who indoctrinate these children with the bizarre beliefs that these religions adhere to, before they are old enough to know better. Surely, a clear case of child abuse!

The Archbishop spoke of militant atheists who are stirring up trouble. I am not quite sure what he means. If a Christian publicly proclaims that Jesus of Nazareth was born of a virgin and that he was executed by the Romans and then rose from the dead three days later and went directly to heaven, I am likely to say, 'Nonsense!' I would use the word in the sense that such wild propositions are not rational – that they make no sense. I do not feel that my position is militant. I am merely saying that there is not a shred of evidence for such claims and very probably Jesus of Nazareth never existed in the first place. There is very scant historical evidence of his existence. When I use the word nonsense in this context I am not using it as synonym for rubbish, which is the colloquial usage.

When I am told that Mohammed received the word of God from angels and that he wrote them down in what became the Koran, I am also justified in saying, 'Nonsense. Show me the evidence!' I can equally well make the same observation when the Mormons tell me about Joseph Smith and his stainless steel tablets or when the Jews talk about Moses and his tablets of stone. My position is reasonable for I am asking for evidence. I am prepared to change my outlook if any can be produced but I do not think that I am in much danger of being obliged to make the change.

In a civilised, advanced country like the United Kingdom my publicly proclaimed scepticism does not need to be restrained by law. The law only needs to be invoked if I become insulting or if I start to spray paint graffiti on the walls of a mosque, synagogue or church. Merely affirming that practitioners of this or that religion are talking through their hats should not be regarded as unduly provocative, insulting or even offensive. One side adopts one intellectual position and the other a contrary one. You believe in magic books and miracles and I do not. Convince me and make me change my mind. Show me the evidence. Should I be so silly as to shoot my mouth off in a primitive country such as Saudi Arabia or Afghanistan where the dictates of religion are accepted unquestioningly; where the most outrageous propositions are swallowed willy nilly, by the faithful, then I shall need to watch my back for I am dealing with irrational people who are mired in the dark ages.

So back to the Archbishop. I can well see that he feels that some legislation is required to curb the most extreme forms of free speech. He almost certainly has a vested interest in protecting the dafter claims of Christianity. My position is that any contrary comments made about any religion in a free society should only be tempered by good manners and good taste. A well reasoned argument aimed at undermining the religious point of view should not be restrained by any kind of law. Members of religious groups who feel that their particular brand of mumbo jumbo needs the protection of the state should learn to argue coherently and persuade us all of the rightness of their views by the logic and cogency of the arguments. I believe in whatever, just does not cut it.

Mischief in Mali

(First published on 14/01/2013)

Robert Fowler, a senior Canadian diplomat and former Canadian ambassador to the United Nations, was seized by al-Qaeda in December 2008, while working as the United Nations representative in the Maghreb, and held captive in the Sahara until April 2009. During his captivity he learnt that al-Qaeda and its affiliates intended to organise an jihadist takeover of the strip of Northern Africa that runs from Mogadishu on the Indian Ocean to Nouakchott on the Atlantic, a distance of 10,000 kms, and turn it into an ungovernable region in which their jihad would flourish and from which Islamist terrorists could mount attacks on Europe and the rest of Africa. Potentially, they would link up with Boko Haram in Nigeria and al Shabaab in Somalia, both of which are especially blood thirsty, fundamentalist organisations pledged to the destruction of the West. Fowler considers that even a partial achievement of their aims would result in an appalling humanitarian and economic disaster which would make that which occurred in Darfur seem benign in comparison.

In March 2012, the army in Mali staged a coup and overthrew the sitting president. The Tuareg in Northern Mali seized their chance and declared the north of the country independent and they set up their own state with the help of al-Qaeda linked, dissident groups. Mali is an odd shaped country situated in the heart of West Africa. Essentially, it consists of two unequally sized triangles. The southern triangle abuts on to the Rivers Niger and Senegal and is relatively fertile. The capital, Bamako, is situated here. The northern triangle is a chunk of territory as large as France, right in the centre of the Sahara Desert, and is very sparsely populated. Its people, the Tuaregs, are nomadic. They are Muslims and consider themselves to be oppressed by the people in the South. Once they had thrown off the southern yoke and were all set to declare a Tuareg homeland, their erstwhile allies, the al-Qaeda related groups, did an end run around them and took over. Recently, the latter have been consolidating their hold, recruiting foreign jihadis and preparing to move south to take over the whole country. They have also instituted a harsh version of Sharia – hand lopping, beheading, flogging and stoning. They have also set about destroying priceless Islamic artefacts, banning all forms of entertainment and razing Timbuktu, an ancient centre of Muslim learning.

Mali's neighbours have become alarmed by these developments and have responded to pleas from its government to come to its aid. The Economic Community of West African States (ECOWAS) and the African Union have pledged a few thousand troops to assist the Malian army to drive out the jihadis. But, and it is big but, they cannot get their act together before September 2013. This is a little like phoning the local fire brigade for help to save a burning house only to be told that they will turn up next Tuesday fortnight. It appears that those who run ECOWAS and the African Union would have trouble organising the proverbial piss-up in a brewery or sexual congress in a brothel, at least in short order.

Events are moving fast. The Jihadis are moving south very quickly and have threatened Konna, a city only 600 kms from the capital. France the former colonial power has sent in special forces to halt their advance. They have also employed air strikes. The United Nations have asked for additional western help but the UK, Canada, the US and other NATO powers are distinctly war weary having spent much of the last decade and a half fighting nightshirt clad gentlemen, careless of their own safety and armed with AK 47s, rocket propelled grenades and improvised explosive devices – all the while crying out, 'Allahu Akbar', until their opponents were ready to scream – in far off dusty places like Iraq and Afghanistan. The Western forces have not had a very successful time of it and are trying to get their troops home just as fast as they can. A call to retake up arms and go traipsing off to another desert to face up to another bunch of fanatics is distinctly unappealing. Canada has said it will offer a few trainers and the UK has sent a couple of large transport planes to move other people's troops. The US has remained mum. Robert

Fowler, in an article in the Toronto Globe and Mail, 8/1/13 argues that the West has little option but to go in and sort out yet another mess. He is fearful that al-Qaeda and its allies could very well take over Mali and its neighbours and turn the entire, huge region into a terrorist stronghold right on Europe's doorstep. Such an outcome would have imponderable consequences.

During the past half century, the West has set off on any number of military adventures in the Third World. Its win loss ratio is not impressive. The US was more or less defeated in Vietnam. In the second Gulf War, the US and a Western coalition smashed Saddam Hussein's military very quickly in Iraq, but then got thoroughly bogged down in the ensuing mayhem and, ultimately, fled the scene leaving a right royal mess behind them. Their earlier foray into Kuwait, known as the first Gulf War, provoked by Saddam's illegal invasion of that country, managed to drive out the Iraqis but their subsequent early withdrawal from the area allowed Saddam to slaughter the Marsh Arabs, who rose up against him, thinking that the West would hang around and support them. The US and its allies have also been tied down in Afghanistan for nearly twelve years with the aim of ridding the country, once and for all, of the Taliban, but that has proven to be a task too hard. All Western forces will be gone from that unhappy country by next year and the Taliban look well set to come back. Would another military adventure, this time in the Sahara, have a happier outcome?

Western armies are potentially very powerful and have enormous firepower at their disposal but for the most part they do not use it. They spend far too long pondering the rules of war and various Geneva conventions. This time round, perhaps all of their strength should be deployed. No trying to win over hearts and minds; no consideration for civilian casualties; no fostering education for women and girls; no setting up of clinics for the sick and elderly, no thought for hostages or human shields, no concern about collateral damage. On the contrary, just pitiless slaughter and destruction, employing all the means at their disposal: aerial surveillance, drone attacks, and, perhaps, even the use of tactical nuclear weapons, if that looked profitable. In short, total war with the aim of eradicating all of the Jihaids and supporters of al-Quada wherever they may be in Northern Mali and neighbouring countries.

Such tactics will cause outrage around the World and at home. Many European countries and others like Canada, will claim that to be so remorseless would be quite of character. But, it is worth noting that Islamic terrorists have no hesitation in bombing buildings where women and children are known to be. They do not resile from setting off bombs in crowded markets or outside schools. Just this week, Islamists have exploded an enormous bomb outside a sports club in Pakistan killing over one hundred people and maiming and injuring scores more. One of the principles of warfare calls for maintenance of the aim. Jihadis follow this to the letter and to hell with the consequences. Should the West follow suit? If events taking place in Mali are considered to pose an existential threat to Europe and the West, then a very vigorous response is called for which does not take into account the niceties of international behaviour but focusses solely upon putting an end to the threat as thoroughly and as quickly as possible.

Three cases of temporal lobe epilepsy

(First published on 21/01/2015)

Saul of Tarsus, Muhammad of Mecca and Joseph Smith of Upper New York State all had something in common: they claimed to have had visions. Their claims have had wide ranging consequences for the rest of us.

Saul, a Jew, was born a Roman citizen in Tarsus, a city on the Mediterranean Coast, just about where modern Lebanon and Syria meet. He became a Pharisee and spent a good deal of his early adult life persecuting the followers of Jesus of Nazareth. The latter was a Jewish preacher who came from Galilee and who spent three years as an itinerant, before getting up the noses of the Jewish authorities in Jerusalem, who in turn, persuaded their Roman overlords to put him to death. He had attracted a handful of followers who were overwhelmed by his death and who returned home to take up their former lives. There, the story may well have come to an end but for the efforts of Saul.

Saul was on the way to Damascus when he was struck down by some kind of fit during which he claimed to have had a vision. He recovered and thenceforward turned into a staunch advocate of the teachings of Jesus and spent the rest of his days travelling around the Roman Empire encouraging all and sundry to join the new religion, Christianity. After his vision, he called himself Paul and is today better known as Saint Paul. History does not relate that he ever actually met Jesus. The historical record about Jesus and Paul is scanty. Many modern Christian scholars consider that St Paul, rather than Jesus, was the founder of what we now call Christianity.

Muhammad was born in Mecca in 570, was orphaned, taken in by an uncle and employed in his uncle's business. He is also said to have been a shepherd. Aged 40, he took to going off to a cave where he claims that he encountered the Angel Gabriel who dictated the Koran to him. Apparently, this process took more than twenty years. As far as we know, Muhammad was illiterate and that could not have been too helpful during the enterprise.

Twenty years does seem a long time, for the Koran has fewer words than the complete works of Shakespeare. Anyway, the Koran is now considered to be the actual word of God and also God's last message to humanity. It forms the basis of the religion of Islam and the very book is revered and considered sacred by adherents of that religion. There is no record of any corroboration of the story concerning the frequent visits to the cave or any speculation as to why Muhammad spent so much time there. The faithful take the story on trust, warts and all.

Joseph Smith, born in 1805 in Vermont, moved to Upper New York State. He claimed to have had visions in which he saw Jesus Christ and God and another figure. He then met the Angel Moroni, who directed him to a cave in which were buried some golden plates on which were inscribed a history on an ancient Judaeo-Christian civilisation based in what is now known as the United States. He published these writings in 1830 and so founded the Church of the Latter Day Saints. He died in 1844. No trace of the golden plates exists.

These three historical figures have had an enormous effect upon humanity. The religions that were founded as a result of their efforts claim over 2.7 billion adherents today, or 36% of the population of the World! (Mormons only make up 15 million of this vast number.) That they all seemed to have experienced visions prompts some questions. On encountering a person who claims to have undergone some kind of paranormal experience, one is entitled to consider a number of possibilities: he may be telling the truth; he may be a liar or he may be suffering from a neurological or psychological disease. Most skeptics will throw out the first possibility. Encounters with angels seem to be highly unlikely and quite outside the normal run of things. To conclude that the trio were liars seems a little harsh, although Mr Smith was a dodgy fellow by some accounts. The third possibility is worth exploring in a little more depth.

Those who suffer from epilepsy are known to experience a disordered and uncoordinated firing of nerve cells in the outer lining of their brains, known as the cerebral cortex. If this disturbance is confined to that part of the cortex that controls motor function, then they have classical fits: convulsions, unconsciousness and bewilderment on recovery. However, there are several types of epilepsy whose external manifestations vary according to where in the cortex the disturbance is situated. Fits arising from the temporal cortex are known to be associated with feelings of bliss, visions, and the sensation of being in touch with God. Indeed, some sufferers have said that they felt as if there was a wire coming directly from God buried inside their brains. It is possible that this type of epilepsy could account for the visions experienced by our three heroes. Such an idea is pure speculation for no very comprehensive accounts of their experiences are available to us today. Equally possible is that all three were in the grip of some psychosis or other and that they hallucinated from time to time. Smith, who tells us that he was directed by the Angel Moroni and Muhammad, who claims to have been told to write down the text of the Koran, could both have been obeying the voices commonly experienced by schizophrenics.

It cannot be proven either way, but that these three men were able to influence so many on the basis of their mysterious experiences demonstrates the in-built need of humans to have some kind of religious belief to cling to, notwithstanding that religion is, 'a kind of mediaeval unreason' (Salman Rushdie) and does not stand up to analysis and can only be accepted on the basis of blind faith. Consider the consequences that have followed the establishment of the three religions: libraries of writing, art works galore, slaughter on an industrial scale in the name of God, vast building enterprises, immense amounts of time spent in prayer, pilgrimage and parsing the minutiae of scripture. Paul, Muhammad and Joseph Smith have much to answer for. Einstein maintained that, 'God does not play dice.' But, perhaps he plays jokes. Just imagine that it could be shown that Christianity, Islam and Mormonism came about because their founders were suffering from mental or psychiatric disease. In that case, that so many cling very fiercely to these faiths would be a joke of cosmic proportions.

Certainly worth a thought.

Chapter Three – Politics

The feminisation of the medical

profession

(First published on 21/06/2013)

Sixty years ago only 5% of the average annual intake to British medical schools were female. Things have changed drastically recently and now women constitute about 70% of each new cohort. Furthermore, they are doing very well and winning all the prizes. Women occupy more and more senior posts, such as Presidencies of Royal Colleges and National Medical Associations. Before the tide turned, there was a little reluctance on the part of women to enter certain fields such as orthopaedics, but such squeamishness is a thing of the past. A trip to a graduation ceremony at certain prominent Australian universities reveals that Caucasian males are rare birds indeed. Those men who obtain medical degrees are overwhelmingly from 'ethnic' backgrounds. Whether all of these dramatic changes can be considered a good or bad thing is beside the point: the situation is what it is.

A hapless junior minister of health in the UK fell foul of the feminist lobby recently because she pointed out that having so many women in the profession had certain unwelcome consequences. She suggested that many would want to have families and to take up to five years off work while they reared their infants. Furthermore, she added this practice had negative consequences for the service and perhaps contributed to an overall shortage of general practitioners. The shit hit the fan big time and various prominent female doctors were infuriated that the minister appeared to blame women for the problems of the National Health Service. Dr Clare Gerada,

Head of the UK College of General Practitioners was especially miffed at what she took to be implied criticism of women practitioners. Dr Hannah Mitchell, in a letter to a newspaper, suggested that minister had used sexist language. Of course, all had missed the point, for the minister had merely observed, that where many staff work part time, it is necessary to employ extra people to make up the shortfall. By no stretch of the imagination did she suggest that women were letting the side down by starting families.

It is perhaps a general observation that 'Ismismists' (sic) are especially thin skinned when anyone who does not belong to their particular 'ism' pipes up and says anything at all about it. Islamists hate any mention of their activities or reasoning by non-Muslims. Feminists are very sensitive to observations made by non-feminists — especially men. Communists were very prickly about their particular ideology during the days when it mattered. Catholics are very easily hurt when critics make unfavourable observations about the Church. But all of that is a matter for another essay.

Some 'back of an envelope calculations' clearly point out the problems that arise when large numbers of the work force take prolonged periods of family leave. Medical practitioners are ready to enter full time, independent practice by age thirty. If they work until they are sixty-five, they clock up 1820 weeks. To expand this to a cohort of 1000 doctors of whom 70% are women and who will take five years off for family reasons, then for the whole group there is a shortfall of 172,000 weeks which requires an additional 95 practitioners to make up for the lost hours. If it costs £250,000 to train a doctor in the UK, then it costs an extra £24 million to train these extras. Figures for Australia and Canada would be comparable.

It is forecast that 70% of all medical practitioners will be female in twenty years or so and these extra training and recruiting costs will have to be factored in when planning health services. A further important consideration is that fewer women than men work in the profession until retirement age. They are more inclined to leave early for a variety of reasons, often to do with family. None of this denigrates women doctors, but merely highlights a dilemma that occurs when large numbers of the work force have entirely legitimate reasons for putting in fewer hours than was once the case. It would be irresponsible not to acknowledge the problem and doing so does not criticise or point the finger in any particular direction. Only an idiot would think that it did.

Vaccination

(First published on 16/08/2013)

Edward Jenner, 1749-1823, born in Gloucestershire, UK, was apprenticed to a local surgeon at the age of 14 and obtained a medical degree from the University of St Andrews. He noticed that milkmaids were generally immune to smallpox, a very common ailment in his time. Lady Mary Wortley Montagu, wife of a British ambassador, had observed the practice of variolation while in Turkey, in which the pus from smallpox vesicles was scarified into the skin of others in an attempt to promote immunity to the disease. The process carried a 60% infection rate and a 20% mortality rate among those so treated. She imported it into Great Britain in 1721, several years before Jenner's birth, where it became standard practice. Jenner introduced the practice of vaccination, using pus from cowpox vesicles instead. Cowpox, a relatively minor illness, is caused by a virus similar to that responsible for smallpox and was a common affliction of milkmaids. Vaccination proved to be very effective against smallpox and much safer[1]. Jenner first tried his technique on James Phipps, a young boy. Phipps became mildly ill. When he was subsequently variolated, he suffered no ill effects. From these humble beginnings the science and practice of immunology developed and Jenner can claim to have saved more lives than any other practitioner before or since!

In 1979, the World Health Organisation declared that smallpox had been eradicated and that only two samples of the smallpox virus remained extant: in laboratories in the USA and in Russia. Improved public health measures around the globe and the widespread use of vaccination had for the first time succeeded in removing a human scourge.

I have some personal experience of dealing with smallpox outbreaks for they used to occur regularly in Northern Nigeria. The method of handling such epidemics was to isolate victims in settlements consisting of temporary grass huts on the edge of population centres, vaccinate every other living soul in town and then to set fire to the huts when the outbreak burned itself out. Limited, supportive treatment was provided for the patients during their sickness. Health workers, caring for them, would often be vaccinated several times during their careers.

Other infectious diseases have been tackled during the last hundred years or so and are no longer the scourge they once were. The main weapons against these diseases have been the widespread employment of various vaccinations and improvements in the level of public health. Illnesses such as measles, mumps, whooping cough and rubella no longer cause the problems they once did. Widespread campaigns to immunise those most likely to succumb to these infections have been carried out in most of the developed world. Previously, these illnesses carried substantial death rates and caused much morbidity. Less than 1% of people under the age of thirty suffer from measles where immunisation is widely practised. In 1998, Dr Andrew Wakefield published an infamous paper in the Lancet in which he linked the use of measles-mumps-rubella (MMR) vaccine to autism. He suggested that thiomersal, a mercury containing preservative used in the MMR vaccine, was responsible. (MMR, or triple vaccine is used to protect against measles, mumps and rubella and is administered in two doses: one in infancy and the other just before school age.) His paper provoked widespread panic among parents. Before its publication, 92% of all children in the UK were routinely vaccinated, 'herd immunity' was high and rates of infection low. Afterwards, rates dropped to 80% and cases of measles increased from a handful each year to nearly 1500. Much the same happened in other developed countries.

The General Medical Council of Great Britain subsequently found that Wakefield's work was dishonest and struck him off the medical register. The Lancet fully retracted the original paper. The British Medical Association declared that the work was fraudulent and the Centre for Disease Control and Prevention, the UK National Health Service and the Cochrane Review all declared that there was no connection between MMR vaccination and autism. But the damage had been done and many parents became reluctant to subject their children to vaccination, citing fear of possible long-term harm. As well, modern parenting styles seek to shield children from all or any discomfort and some vaccinations are given by injection!

Public health attempts to educate the public about the actual and not imagined complications of the childhood fevers and the preventative vaccines have not yet been able to overcome the irrational apprehension of many parents, provoked by Wakefield's shonky research. It is all very well to cite risk rates and Cochrane reviews but many mothers and fathers point out that vaccinations are not entirely free of complications and they prefer to take the chance that their offspring will not catch one of these infections. The wretched Andrew Wakefield has much to answer for. Afflictions such as measles can give rise to encephalitis, pneumonia, serious eye infections, long delayed degenerative neurological diseases and much acute illness. Rubella or German measles can cause serious damage to the unborn child if mothers pick it up during the first few weeks of pregnancy: deafness, visual impairment and intellectual problems. Vaccinations have rare unwanted side effects: mild fever, local soreness, rashes and allergic reactions. Overall, however, their benefits greatly outweigh any disadvantages.

I saw the harm that can be caused by the childhood exanthemata during my time working in Jerusalem during the 1960s. When travelling on a bus that stopped outside a school for the blind, I observed a file of some dozen adolescent girls get onboard. Each one was blind from dense, central, bilateral, corneal opacities resulting from poorly managed external eye infections brought about by chicken pox or measles and, as such, entirely preventable.

Two schools of alternative health practice continue to cause a great deal of trouble by stoking the fear of vaccinations in the general public. Some chiropractors hold that vaccination is unnecessary if bodily health is maximally maintained by ensuring that spinal subluxations are treated promptly. According to this view, removal of spinal abnormalities allows the autoimmune system of the body to function optimally. Conventional medical theory is not at all certain, that the subluxations causing so much excitement among chiropractors, actually exist. It is worth remembering that chiropraxy was invented by D. D. Palmer, one time proprietor of a grocers' shop, who dabbled in magnetic healing and spiritualism. Homeopaths administer so-called homeopathic vaccines as preventatives. They follow the doctrine of like healing like and they give drugs in such great dilutions that no active principle remains in the prescribed medicines. They believe that the weaker the solution, the more powerful the effect. Perhaps, chiropractic and homeopathy should not be the first port of call for reliable information about immunology and preventative medicine.

Sixty years ago, infantile paralysis or poliomyelitis was a dreaded scourge which often left many children permanently disabled or condemned to lives in 'iron lungs' — primitive breathing machines. Jonas Salk developed an intramuscular vaccine against this disease. A few years later, Albert Bruce Sabin produced an oral vaccine. These vaccines have been so successful that polio is on the verge of being declared the second human disease eliminated from the world. Unfortunately, certain fundamentalist, Muslim clerics in Pakistan, Afghanistan and Northern Nigeria, the last places where pockets of the disease still occur, inveigh against their use, claiming them to be part of a Western plot designed to emasculate good Muslim boys. Several indigenous health workers have been slaughtered while carrying out the work of distributing the vaccines. Consequently, the incidence of this unpleasant disease is rising again and spreading across international boundaries to infect more enlightened folk. Allahu Akbar!

An article of this sort cannot cover in detail the field of vaccination about which vast libraries exist. It has been an anecdotal attempt to sketch the history of vaccination and to explain what great benefits have been derived from Edward Jenner's early observation and work and to show how public health measures frequently handle disease in effective and cost efficient ways. The price of shots is much less than the cost of a few days in a hospital treating complications. It is truly sad when conspiracy theories and irrational fears impede the good work going on to eliminate infectious diseases, the cause of so much morbidity and suffering, in both the enlightened West and a few benighted Muslim countries.

Post script. Vaccination levels continue to drop in several western countries and outbreaks of measles are on the increase. Some people are apparently unconcerned that their unvaccinated children may spread measles and the like to other children, who may be more prone to developing complications from such diseases.

1 (Variolation is derived from the Latin name for smallpox, variola and vaccination is derived from the Latin vaccam, a cow.)

Residential health care for the elderly

(First published on 12/05/2014)

BBC television conducted an enquiry into aged care facilities in the UK last month and broadcast its findings on Panorama, a long-running investigative journalism programme. They were disturbing and gave rise to considerable public disquiet and excuse making by the healthcare authorities. It turns out that the level of care experienced in many old folks homes is substandard, often callous and sometimes downright abusive. Many of the staff employed in such facilities are poorly trained, poorly paid and lacking in basic empathy for their charges. There was one distressing scene shown of an elderly, bedridden woman calling out innumerable times for help to get out of bed on to a commode as she wished to open her bowels. She was seen banging a spoon on a plate and calling out to attract attention. She was repeatedly ignored. When at last someone entered her room, she was asked if she was wearing an incontinence pad and, if so, to do her business into the pad and wait to be cleaned up afterwards!

Various relatives of other residents were interviewed and some said that they had felt obliged to resort to installing hidden video cameras in the bedrooms in order to check on the care given by the staff. The footage obtained often revealed staff members behaving abusively and even taunting helpless, old people. Scenes where staff members were seen slapping residents were captured. Panorama showed some of this footage to independent aged care nursing consultants, who agreed that some of the staff behaviour recorded amounted to common assault.

In England, there are approximately 376,000 old people living in more than 10,000 aged care homes. Four out of ten of these residents suffer from dementia. All of these homes are supposed to be supervised by the Quality Control Commission. The basic qualifications for a care worker appear to be minimal. It is desirable to have had some experience with working with older people, to be pleasant and have a clean, background, police check. The starting wage is £12,000 per annum ($20,000US), which translates into £7.50 per hour ($12.60US), just £1.20 ($2.00US) more than the minimum wage. The work is arduous and involves lifting helpless individuals, then feeding, bathing and toileting them. Residents who are demented can become aggressive towards their careers and may lash out. The Panorama programme claimed that as many as 7% of all homes or 700 institutions are substandard.

A disturbing development in the old people's care industry is takeover by investors, who have noticed that homes provide a steady source of income from fees and government allowances. The real estate that harbours the residence is expensive but certain to increase in value. Such institutions can be nice little earners: assured income stream and capital appreciation. Investors pay attention to the bottom line and the return on their investment. They do not invest because of charitable inclinations. To enhance their returns, they have two options: maximise the number of residents or cut costs. There is no shortage of customers for more people are surviving to extreme old age. On the other hand, little is done to ensure that adequate staff levels are maintained and the quality of catering and other facilities remain high.

Medical technology is able to keep people alive for longer and the resulting increased numbers of elderly people will place an increasing burden on national exchequers. The ratio of elderly and non-productive people to those who are working and paying taxes will move unfavourably and the task of funding health care will become more onerous. The UK, Canada and Australia already devote between 8-12% of gross national product to health care and their health care systems are already showing signs of strain. In none of these countries is a frank and honest discussion taking place laying out the problems posed by the increasing number of elderly citizens. Demographers expect that 50% of those born today will live to see their one-hundredth birthdays. The pressure upon resources will be difficult to bear. 'Efficiencies' can only go so far.

No government likes to propose large tax increases and so discussions about the looming problem are actively avoided. The public plays along because it has an intrinsic squeamishness about death and extreme old age.

If care, in homes for the elderly, is already proving to be problematical and unsatisfactory, what is it likely to be when numbers requiring it go up substantially? Already, many consider that such homes are little more than warehouses. What term will be used once the demand doubles in a few short years? Many frail elderly folk are often fed up with life. Being confined to bed, unable to feed oneself and look after one's own personal hygiene is not much fun. The prospect of hanging on, indefinitely, under those circumstances, is a daunting prospect. Talk about assisted suicide, for example, is frowned upon and discouraged. Obviously, assisted suicide cannot be the sole remedy for the problems caused by the increasing numbers of so many really elderly folk, but surely it should be on the table for discussion. There are many whose lives have become burdensome to them and who see that spending large sums to keep them living in a state of great discomfort helps no one save the doctrinaire who consider that life is a gift from God, whose course must run until He deems otherwise. A prominent oncologist in the United Kingdom has recently questioned the sense of administering very expensive anti-cancer drugs to those who are old and frail and suffering from other fatal medical conditions. His musings have been howled down and he has been accused of ageism!

Obviously there are costs associated with housing the elderly, which will rise inexorably. Many of them own houses whose value has greatly increased since they were purchased. Perhaps a good deal of the cost of care could be paid for out of the proceeds of house sales, but there is a good deal of community resistance to that idea. The elderly often feel that they should leave something for their offspring who, in turn, are only too ready to benefit from inheritances. In the popular mind, the fact that all will die sooner or later is too awful to contemplate. Those, who insist that every possible intervention be employed to postpone death at any cost, often regardless of the wishes of the sick person, are living in dreamland. It is permissible to talk about any topic in modern society save death –the last obscenity. Perhaps this will change when the bills become totally impossible to pay.

I have written about the situation in the United Kingdom but it is mirrored by experiences in similar countries. No great enthusiasm for grappling with the geriatric time bomb is apparent in either Canada or Australia.

Health care for all...
but who pays?

(First published on 08/05/2006)

A baby has just been delivered here in Coffs Harbour suffering from multiple congenital defects. The baby will have to spend the next two years in hospital undergoing treatment and complicated surgery to remedy the defects. His mother has complained how hard it will be for her to forgo all the normal pleasures of motherhood: cuddling, washing, caring and so on. She says it will be very hard for her to bond naturally with her baby while he is hooked up to all kinds of machines and tucked away in an incubator.

We, in the wealthy West, think nothing of arranging for a prolonged period of medical care, such that this little mite is going to require. Nor do we stop to consider that such children are likely to require pretty much full time attention for the rest of their lives. We can do all the medical tricks and we can arrange for the care, so let's go for it. And it is natural to be sympathetic towards the parents who are crying out for these things to be done but there is another side to the story.

Two years full time hospital care at $500 per day will cost $36500 and that is a very conservative estimate. One paper I read, calculated that paediatric intensive care could cost as much as $3750 per day. Daily after hospital care is likely to cost at least $200 per day, which amounts to another four million dollars over a sixty year life – a total going on for five million dollars. And there is no guarantee that the baby will live a normal life after all the treatment and surgery he is going to need.

When this sad story appeared in the local paper, ways and means of contributing towards his and his family's welfare and costs were outlined and it likely that the local community will give generously. Today's media are full of appeals for funds to provide clean water for children living in poverty stricken villages in Africa. Requests for money to provide treatment for malaria or diarrhoea are common. We are told that very few dollars a month can make an enormous difference to otherwise healthy children. A quick Google search reveals that about a third of all children born in parts of southern Africa are born with HIV/AIDS and that some governments in that part of the world have about thirty cents per head per annum to spend on medications. Thus, the outlook for many of these children is quite wretched.

So, we live in a world in which almost limitless sums of money can be found for one child with multiple birth defects but virtually none for thousands of others who face all kinds of infections and illnesses that could be controlled or even eradicated very cheaply.

Now, I am not suggesting that our little Coffs Harbour baby be left to die from his abnormalities and that the money saved by not providing his treatment be diverted to Africa. I am merely trying to point out the huge disparities in the distribution of the world's goods and suggesting that we all think about these matters to try and come up with some answers. It might be that solutions to such problems might lessen the rage and disregard that is directed towards the West by so many people in the less fortunate parts of the world. I am giving a tutorial to some sixth year Australian medical students in a few days and I shall put this matter to them to find out what they think could be done. Who knows but the idealism of youth may illuminate the matter?

A tale of two Naomis

(First published on 27/09/2008)

I have been exceptionally privileged to attend lectures, here in out of the way Lethbridge, during the last few days, given by two exceptional women called Naomi. Naomi Wolf of 'The Beauty Myth' fame delivered the first of these. She has moved on! Her lecture was entitled, 'The End of America' and was based on her book of the same name. The thesis of the lecture is that America is changing in very sinister ways. She drew eerie parallels with the end of the Weimar Republic and the accession to power of Adolph Hitler and the events that followed that awful event. She maintains that the so-called War on Terror, declared by George W. Bush has given his administration the opening to do many things that were first tried by the Fascists in Italy and then Germany in the 1930s.

Hitler came to power through legitimate means and then almost immediately started to dismantle or ignore several provisions of the

German constitution. His administration arrested people without warning and then held them incommunicado. He employed torture to force confessions. He opened and censored private mail. He set up concentration camps. He controlled the press and rounded up pesky journalists who questioned his right to act in these ways. He interfered with private bank accounts. He prevented the free movement of German citizens or made them pay extortionate sums for permission to leave the country. He demonised certain groups of people: Jews, Gypsies and homosexuals. He staged a mock attack on the Reichstag – the German parliament – and then blamed it on the communists. He made great use of extra legal paramilitary forces.

Sound familiar? Many of the games that George W. Bush's administration has played since the attack on the World Trade Centre eight years ago bear a sinister resemblance to the way events unfolded in the Germany of the 1930s. For concentration camps read Guantanamo Bay. For the use of torture read Abu Ghraib prison. For unlawful arrests refer to

David Hicks and Mohammed Khader. For paramilitaries read Blackwater. (Blackwater has opened up two bases in the USA and operates more or less beyond the law. It is hard to discover to whom they were answerable in Iraq.) Many investigative journalists in the States tell horror stories about being thrown into the pokey for refusing to reveal their sources. Naomi Wolf, herself, claims that her mail is regularly opened and searched. Mail from her daughter never arrived from the summer camp that the girl attended last year. She has had money disappear from bank accounts and her various email accounts shut down. And the list goes on and on.

I put it to her that nasty men like Hitler, Stalin, Pinochet and Mugabe were anything but fools. Bush is a fool and so who is behind all of this? She claims that it is not at all uncommon for powerful cabals to construct a straw figure as the front man and for the real power behind the throne to remain concealed. Her best guess is that the devils in the woodpile are Dick Cheney, Carl Rove and Donald Rumsfeld along with the military industrial complex. Her arguments are very chilling and persuasive.

Naomi Klein, a Canadian born writer, journalist and filmmaker, gave the second lecture. Her talk was given against the background of the mayhem presently going on in Wall Street and was entitled, 'The Shock Doctrine.' She exposed the excesses that have gone on in the name of free markets and the lunacies that follow when the creed of Milton Friedman of the Chicago Business School are followed to the bitter end. The present financial crisis affecting World stock markets provides an excellent example of the use of shock. The ordinary man and woman in the street can see their life savings going down the gurgler as they watch; many face repossession of their homes; others cannot withdraw their savings because of bank failures. Those in charge then announce that the end of the World as we know it is just around the corner and that the only way to save things is for the central government to bail out the very people who caused the problem. So we see arguments going on in Washington in favour of the Treasury coughing up $700 billion dollars to buy up 'toxic assets' from Wall Street in order to restore stability to the market. The proponents of this scheme are led by one Hank Paulson, formerly chairman of Lehman Brothers, a merchant bank that has just gone into receivership because of dodgy financial practices. Surely, Mr Paulson must bear some responsibility for that and yet he is the Treasury Secretary and the leader of those holding out a giant begging bowl! How's that for chutzpah?

Klein's thesis is that there is so much fear of total financial collapse, that the public will go along with any scheme because it is in shock. She claimed that Bush and his boys were able to introduce all kinds of doubtful legislation, much of which was unconstitutional, in the aftermath of 9/11, because the public was also in shock. The American homeland had been attacked and there were devils at the gates. OK, let's arrest people and hold them without charge; let's start opening up mail and blocking back accounts; let's demonise certain groups and so on. Strike while the ordinary men and women in the street are off balance. Once you have passed toxic legislation under such circumstances, reversing it is often impossible.

Naomi Wolf thinks that the upcoming presidential election is crucial. She is afraid that a win for the Republicans would ensure that there would never again be another free and fair election in the USA. Naomi Klein suggests that a win for the Democrats would be more or less the same as the last many years – a repeat of Reagan, Bush Senior, Clinton and George W. Bush. She considers that a win for Barack Obama would be a poisoned chalice for he would inherit such a mess that the necessary measures to put things right, if taken, would ensure that he remained in power for no more than one term. Now, there was an element of Chicken Little in all of this, 'The sky is falling'. But listening to these articulate and passionate women was very frightening! I thought that it was Cassandra, not Naomi, who was supposed to scare the pants off us.

Africa

(First published on 30/06/2008)

Were the proverbial man from Mars pay us on Earth a visit and take a quick look round the planet, he would notice that things in Africa are just a little dicey. He would observe that the largely white Western nations were living pretty high on the hog and that huge chunks of Asia were making great efforts to follow the example of the West. But when he came to examine and report on Africa, he would have a very different story to tell. Why, he would ask, are so many wars going on there? Why is there such widespread famine? Why are there so many dictators? Why is there so much disease? Why does Africa appear to be the AIDS capital of the World? Why is religion apparently so important there?

These might be interesting questions for us to try and answer. As to wars, Africa consists of mainly of countries in which tribal considerations are paramount. Africa emerged about fifty years ago from a colonial past and the former colonial masters were not very thoughtful when they drew up the boundaries between the countries. Although many African leaders would point to the anomalies, few or none are prepared to revise their boundaries to ease some of the tribal tensions. During the past twenty years or so, there have been many ghastly civil wars: Sierra Leone, Liberia, Rwanda, Congo, Sudan, Angola and now Zimbabwe. Common features in these wars have been the remorseless slaughter, mutilation and rape carried out by the protagonists against each other. Naked attempts at ethnic cleansing have been characteristic of the fighting. Today, large numbers of people in Darfur, an area of Sudan, are being systematically driven out of their homes and starved to death. Various African organisations have tried, rather half-heartedly to intervene but without much success. So today, militias backed by the central government run riot and do more or less whatever they want. Our Martian observer would tell us that the war in Darfur is being run on racial lines: Arabs are shafting blacks. The recent wars in Liberia and Sierra Leone involved warring groups of blacks that were fighting about the control of the very rich diamond mines in Sierra Leone. Peace has now been restored but thousands of casualties have been left whose limbs were hacked off by militiamen. One important leader is undergoing trial at The Hague.

In Rwanda, the majority Hutus tried to slaughter the minority Tutsis. Much mayhem went on unimpeded before the World community as a whole stirred itself to action. Rwanda's neighbours did very little in the way of intervention on the grounds that it is not seemly to interfere in the affairs of your neighbours even if they are carrying out unspeakable crimes. Several years on, few ringleaders have been properly tried and punished. A civil war has smouldered on in the Congo ever since that unhappy place attained independence from its former Belgian masters.

Zimbabwe escaped from the colonial yoke of Great Britain about thirty years ago. Much of the credit for this is due to Robert Mugabe who has ruled the country ever since. Zimbabwe has been a pretence democracy and elections have been held every few years. Latterly, the policies of Mugabe and his clique have brought the country to the verge of collapse. The currency is worthless. Eighty per cent of the population is unemployed. Large numbers rely on imported, donated food aid for survival. A recent election resulted in the defeat of Mugabe but he declined to go quietly. The results of the election were almost certainly fudged and a run off election between him and the opposition leader was called. The interval between the two polls has allowed Mugabe and his thugs to beat shit out of his opponents, to set up torture camps and to deprive natives of donated food if they were shown to have voted for the opposition first time round. What was one of the most successful and wealthiest countries in Southern Africa is now a tip. The West has watched all of this going on and has reacted with predictable shock. Mugabe has thumbed his nose at Britain, the US and the UN. Zimbabwe's neighbours have stood on the sidelines and remonstrated mildly with him and suggested politely that he was letting the side down. However, he is seen as a hero of the African liberation struggle and, as such, not a man to criticise too openly or strongly, in spite of the fact that he and his thugs have been behaving like hoodlums and terrorising fellow blacks.

African solidarity trumps such considerations. Various distinguished African leaders have sat watched what was going on but have said very little. Most guilty has been the South African president, Thabo Mbeki, who appears to be entirely under the thumb of Robert Mugabe. During the past couple of days, the final act of this drawn out 'election' farce has been played out. The opposition withdrew from the race and Mugabe has announced a landslide victory and had himself sworn in as president for another term. It is noteworthy that the results of this phase of the election were published within a few hours of the closing of the polls, whereas those of the first round did not come to light for nearly a month. Perhaps Mr Mugabe has taught his tame election officials how to count.

Much of the African continent is very fertile. Zimbabwe used to export foodstuffs to its neighbours. Large quantities of raw materials are all around for exploitation. Were African leaders able to stop fighting each other and their own citizens, the continent could be very prosperous. Instead we see a place wracked with turmoil, disease and poverty.

Side by side with all of these disasters, a very thriving religious culture exists. Islam makes great strides in the North East and in large parts of West Africa. There are probably more active Christians in Africa than anywhere else in the World outside South America. It is interesting to note that while the Zimbabwean farce was being played out, several of the African prelates were attending a conference in Jerusalem devoted to rescuing the Anglican Church from what they describe as disaster. These African bishops are worried about other branches of their church ordaining women as priests and also allowing openly gay men to be appointed as bishops. Not one word did they have to say about the mayhem that passes for normal on their native continent. The excesses of Mugabe, for example, are small beer to these worthies compared with the notion that a female should be a priest.

The much revered Nelson Mandela has retired from politics and devotes his declining years to his foundation set up to combat AIDS. He describes this disease as a genocide that is ripping the heart out of Africa. He is right. There are several countries in the south of the continent where most of the children are orphans. Their parents died of AIDS. In Malawi, one-third of all newborns are infected with AIDS. Why should this be? Might it have something to do with the sexual proclivities of African men? The situation has not been helped by a Roman Catholic cardinal spreading the lie that condoms had no part to play in the prevention of the spreading of HIV. Mr Mbeki, president of South Africa, is on record in saying that HIV-AIDS is not a virus disease but has more to do with low standards of living. It is truly depressing to go on with this litany of disaster.

Presently it is very hard to discover any success stories. Tribalism, ignorance, ethnic hatred and overweening respect for chiefs and others in authority all play their part. It is rather feeble for Africans to blame the colonial legacy after all of this time. Perhaps a willingness to interfere in the affairs of leaders who are seen to be acting tyrannically towards their subjects might be a good starting point for reform. The present course looks unhopeful. The record of the colonial West was by no means spotless but the way in which so many Africans treat each other is hardly inspiring. It is a little rich for the likes of Mr Mugabe to point the racist finger at anyone when his own behaviour is so appalling.

Global Warming

(First published on 17/01/2010)

Representatives from nearly two hundred countries assembled in Copenhagen just before Christmas to chew the fat about global warming, climate change and the possible contributions made to these phenomena by human activity.

Climate scientists are almost unanimous in claiming that the planet is undergoing significant climate change and that, overall, temperatures are rising. They are able to predict what the likely effects such warming will have on the Earth and the people who inhabit it. Moreover, they hold that a rise of two degrees will cause sea levels to rise by x metres and that one to four degrees will produce a rise of y metres and so on. They also predict that acidification of the oceans will result in great loss of species and that overall warming will result in declining rainfall amounts with disastrous effects on food production. Nobody who has been conscious during the last few years can have escaped these predictions and there is no need to rehearse all of the Cassandra like possibilities. What is not so clear is how much human activity has played a part in these changes.

There have been warming periods interspersed with ice ages in the past. There is good evidence for such changes having occurred but no one is quite sure why they took place. Sunspot activity has been cited. Tremendous volcanic activity has also been suggested: clouds of ash blocking the Sun's rays for many years. On the face of it, it does seem plausible that the widespread burning of fossil fuels that has occurred during the past two or three hundred years allied to the enormous increase in global population could have played a part. Combustion produces carbon dioxide, water vapour and methane, all of which are efficient 'greenhouse gasses'. The climate scientists are nearly unanimous in claiming that the large population, allied to its industrial activities, is the main cause of the changes that are evident today.

Unfortunately, we don't really know and that is the beauty of science. Postulations lead to more questions and it is often hard to be quite clear about causes of naturally occurring phenomena. The best scientists can do is to present their case to the politicians and the public and ask them to make up their minds and to take any action deemed necessary. Of course, that puts the politicians in a very difficult spot! Should they take draconian action to reduce industrial output and growth levels? Ought they to impose uncomfortable restrictions upon the voters, they depend upon for re-election, in an effort to reduce greenhouse gas emissions, without being absolutely certain that human activity plays any part in the current changes? Is it reasonable for the prosperous, fat West to insist that the developing countries, such as India and China, restrict their activities to save the planet when patently they have not been the main engines for greenhouse gas emission, caused climate change?

If a global population of one billion in 1800 and six and a half billion in 2000 has wrought the damage the scientists are claiming, what will a population of nine and a half billion, due by 2040, do to the environment? Are there leaders powerful enough to engineer a huge reduction in population? Do methods to secure this aim exist? Imagine the outcry from religious groups and the most vocal proponents of human rights!

Futurists have suggested that the globe cannot sustain a Western life style for all those seeking to attain it. If every last person in India and China hopes to live like everyone in the USA and Europe, resources will run out. Suggestions have been made that all should seek to adopt the life style of Great Britain in the nineteen sixties. It was not so bad! There was universal health care; free education from primary school through university; single family dwellings were the norm; good public transport – more than one vehicle per household was the exception. Law and order reigned and most respected the police; stores were adequately stocked and seasons were respected, so those who yearned for strawberries in winter were out of luck; electronic gadgets had not arrived and most either listened to the radio or watched black and white television. Divorce was rare and families consisted of two parents and a number of children. Most people were in employment. Drug and alcohol abuse was unusual. This is not to paint a picture of a golden age but merely to suggest that such a life style was far from intolerable.

The modern world is predicated on a notion of endless growth. After the recent financial crash – brought about by runaway growth – the central bankers of the developed world were suggesting that it was necessary to grow ones way out of the mess caused by excessive growth. This is a little like suggesting that good treatment for concussion caused by a hammer blow to the skull would be another tap on the brain box with the same hammer. Presumably, a planet with finite resources cannot allow endless growth. Common sense would dictate that stuff eventually runs out.

The deliberations at Copenhagen were inconclusive. No targets were agreed to. Each of the major polluters kept a close eye on the others to see who would blink first. The West had no desire to hobble its economy and allow the major developing countries free rein. There was much pious talk about the need to reduce overall greenhouse emissions to 1990 levels by the end of the next decade or two but no actual commitment to do so. Some hard choices have to be made if emissions levels are to be brought under control: for example, swingeing taxes on motor vehicle use; speed limits of 80 kph on rural roads; laws mandating the installation of solar panels on all private dwellings where practicable; domestic water rationing; huge taxes on meat products to discourage the continuing use of arable land and forests for cattle farming; power supply rationing; substantial increases on air fares to discourage idle tourism; widespread use of nuclear energy; the rapid phasing out of coal burning; ways and means to control or preferably reduce population and economies that shrink rather than grow until they reach sustainable levels and zero growth. The politician who presented such a bleak set of proposals to an electorate would not prosper. Citizens of the First World are living high on the hog and probably enjoy it that way. The idea of regressing rather than progressing would not be attractive.

Yet, if the climate scientists have got it right when they suggest that human activity is slowly but surely poisoning the planet that is home to humanity, then mankind can either just go on as before and stand by as ecosystems fail catastrophically, or it can take action which is more directed to the future and not merely the merry present.

It is hard to be hopeful. Prudence and forethought and concern for subsequent generations have not so far been a hallmark of homo sapiens. 'Eat, drink and be merry, for tomorrow we die,' has been the universal motto. What will bring about the change and will it be too late? Is the hope for some technological marvel to enable the species to avoid the abyss just too far fetched? If the doomsayers are right, there will not be too long to wait to find out.

Politics and the Media

(First published in July 2010)

A fine old scandal has hit the headlines in the United Kingdom in the last week or so. It seems that the News of the World (NOTW), a celebrated, muckraking Sunday newspaper, has overstepped the mark. Its owners, the media empire run by the odious Richard Murdoch, have shut it down, effective Sunday July 10. So, a press institution that was founded more than one hundred and sixty years ago has come to a sudden and ignominious end. The NOTW became celebrated for its stories uncovering the derelictions of British celebrities. It organised various sting operations and entrapped prominent people in embarrassing situations and made them look very foolish. An inebriated Sarah, Duchess of York, fell for one of these. The poor woman claimed that she was willing and able to arrange access to her former husband, Prince Andrew, Trade Representative for the United Kingdom. She was heard boasting that the Prince could put the supplicant in the way of all kinds of sweet deals. Sarah was filmed accepting a package of bank notes. David Beckham, former international soccer player, was led into confessing his dalliances with a number of mistresses. No one came to any particular harm through this sort of thing. Sarah and David ended up with egg on their faces, but who cares?

The NOTW regularly ran all sorts of scoops and gained something of a reputation for investigative journalism and became the biggest selling newspaper in the English-speaking world. But, this was not enough. In the early 2000s it began to engage in phone hacking. Practising the dark arts, it revealed several personal messages in the voice mail of aides to members of the Royal Family and other prominent members of the establishment. Again embarrassment all round. However, when it hacked into the phones of families who had lost relatives in the Afghanistan and Iraq wars, a line was crossed. Not content with that, it hacked the phone of the family of a missing teenaged girl, who was subsequently found to have been murdered. For some weeks, the family of the girl harboured hopes that she was merely missing and that she would turn up unharmed.

It seems that NOTW managed to break into the private affairs of former UK Prime Minister, Gordon Brown, and revealed that Brown's son suffered from cystic fibrosis. In 2007, its royal affairs reporter, Clive Goodman, was jailed for hacking the phones of employees of the Royal Family. Glenn Mulcaire, the house special investigator, was sent to jail for aiding and abetting former editor, Andy Coulson, who was forced to resign when he accepted responsibility for the activities of these rogue employees. David Cameron, then leader of the opposition, subsequently employed him, (Coulson), as his communications director, remarking at the time, that Andy had screwed up and deserved a second chance! He brought him along when he, Cameron, became prime minister in 2010. Thus a media man who had been very much at the helm of NOWT, found himself occupying an important and extremely sensitive post at the very heart of UK government power. That David Cameron did not realise the implications of hanging on to this rogue shows him to be a fool and unfit for office.

The NOTW was able to wield enormous political influence during the past twenty odd years. When papers in the Murdoch Group supported a particular party in a general election campaign, that party always won. Consequently, political leaders went to enormous lengths to curry favour with Rupert Murdoch, who in turn obliged the various arms of his media empire to smile benignly on the anointed party. Tony Blair and New Labour won in 2000 and ended a very long spell of Conservative Party dominance. Gordon Brown got the nod after Tony Blair resigned. The tide turned after a few months of Brown's leadership and the Murdoch blessing was confirmed upon David Cameron, leader of the Conservatives. The Labour Party lost in 2010 to be replaced by a coalition led by David Cameron and Nick Clegg of the Liberal Democrats.

Now, it seems that the party is over. As more and more details emerge about the nefarious activities of the Murdoch media empire, more and more people in high places are being implicated. It is alleged that senior police officers in Scotland Yard have been accepting bribes to turn a blind eye to phone hacking. Policemen responsible for royal protection duties are alleged to have taken money in exchange for lists of personal details, including telephone numbers, of the royal household staff. Ian Edmonson, recent editor and Neil Thurlbeck, chief reporter, have been arrested and released on bail. Rebekah Brooks, now chief executive of News International, one time editor of the Sun, another Murdock paper, and former editor of NOWT has been arrested and subjected to twelve hours of questioning. She is the tenth Murdoch employee to be arrested as this mess unfolds. It is likely that James Murdoch, son of Rupert, is to be hauled in for questioning.

Events are now moving thick very quickly. Sir Paul Stephenson, chief Commissioner of Police at Scotland Yard, 'Britain's top cop,' has just announced his resignation, accepting responsibility for his many corrupt police officers. John Yates, assistant commissioner of police in charge of the terrorism unit, is on the brink of suspension. He has been involved with another crook, owned by the Murdoch empire. The British prime minister has boasted that he has set up an enquiry headed up by a senior judge, with powers of summoning witnesses who must testify under oath. He has promised to undertake a wide ranging enquiry into the affairs of British media and to ensure that it will no longer be self-regulating. Parliament was due to begin its long summer recess this week but that has been postponed so that it can be ready and able to deal with the ever-widening scandals surrounding the NOWT affair.

David Cameron, Rebekah Brooks and others involved in this nasty muddle are all personal friends inhabiting a toney area in the Cotswolds. It is hard to imagine that local dinner table gossip did not touch on the malign influence and power of the media in general and the NOTW group in particular. Cameron has stepped forward to claim that such a tangle cannot happen again and that he intends to clean up the Augean stables represented by the British tabloid media. He is putting himself forward as the knight in shining armour who is going to sort it out. This pose is unconvincing in that he has unwittingly had a hand in it through his misguided relationship with both Andy Coulson and Rebekah Brooks. After all, one is known by the company one keeps, and Mr Cameron has been rather indiscreet with his choice of mates. It is hard to forecast where it will all end but the story has legs and is likely to occupy those in power for weeks to come. As the Western World teeters on the edge of a new and even more serious financial crash, it is unsettling to learn that the British leader is embroiled in a sordid media scandal, which may bring him down. Far better that he be able to keep his eye on the important financial ball and not be preoccupied with watching his back.

Sarah Palin – Sarah who?

(First published on 11/09/2008)

We have just finished the Party Convention season in the balls achingly, long American Election process. It feels as if nothing much else in the World has gone on for more than two years. But, take heart, the actual election takes place in two months and then we get a short break before they go at it all over again. The Democratic Party held its convention in Denver and it appeared to go well. Barrack Obama accepted the Democratic nomination and at the same time seemed to heal the many rifts within that notoriously fissiparous mob. It looked as if the Democrats would depart from Denver with an added spring in their heels. Their Republican opponents had to come up with something fast to titillate the American public's notoriously short attention span and so they chose Sarah Palin to be John McCain's running mate.

'Who the hell is she?' came the resounding response. It turns out that Ms Palin has been the governor of Alaska for a couple of years. Before that she was the mayor of a tiny town in that state and before that a city councillor in the same two-bit burg. In her acceptance speech she proudly claimed to be a hockey mom, a mother of five children, a gun lover, an anti-abortionist, a flat earther, a creationist and a climate change denier. She is also anti-gay marriage and school sex education. The highest education level achieved by Ms Palin was high school graduation. All that can be concluded from that is she knows how to read and sign her name. There is no guarantee that she has any knowledge of history, geography, science and the arts. In fact it is almost certain that she does not. Incidentally, she was a high school beauty queen. It is not uncommon for young North American women who go in for such activities to be more interested in their bust-waist-hip ratios than their IQs.

Her views on abortion are positively scary! She holds that no woman, even one who is pregnant following rape by an HIV positive uncle, should be allowed to terminate her pregnancy. This is pro-life to a lunatic extent. She has won personal acclaim for giving birth to her fifth child earlier this year knowing that it had Down's syndrome. My question is what did she think she was doing getting pregnant aged forty-four, having already had four children? How responsible is that on this already overcrowded planet?

She maintains that everyone should be allowed to buy, hold and have guns of all kinds without let or hindrance. What more needs to be said? She is a long time member of the National Rifle Association. She proudly claims that her freezer is stuffed to the gunnels with game she has gone out and shot. Ms Palin believes that drilling for oil should take place in hitherto protected areas of Alaska regardless of any environmental or ecological consequences. Apparently she has no truck with those who consider that global warming might possibly be related to human activity. She considers that primitive creationism should be taught in schools. She is on record as being less than content with current health care policies in the US. Apparently the indigent sick should bear more of the cost of treatment on the grounds that their own fecklessness put them in the situation of requiring medical attention.

She is not in favour of providing benefits to gay couples. The notion that there could be some sort of system of acknowledging gay unions to make it easier for the partners in these unions to give consent for treatment and to inherit insurance benefits is anathema to this woman.

So, we have a politician whose slogans are, 'Guns, babies and Jesus!' (Rush Limbaugh) I do not know this lady personally. I am sure she does her job as hockey mom to perfection. She probably bakes a mean cookie and is kind to animals – all those that she does not go out and shoot. But are these sufficient qualifications for someone who could be voted in as vice-president of the United States of America? She is the running mate of a seventy-two year old potential president and so there is more than a sporting chance that she could occupy the Oval Office by default during the next four years and almost a racing certainty that she would, were

McCain to be re-elected. He is a man with considerable medical history, who would be rising eighty by the time he was completing his second term.

Presidents of the USA are, faute de mieux, leaders of the Western World, That is, your leader and my leader, whether we like it or not. We, who are not Americans, have no say in this matter. That is why we have been lumped with a man most would not have put in charge of a whelk stall on Hampstead Heath on a Bank Holiday Monday, during the past eight years and one, moreover, who has turned out to be an embarrassment to most Americans. Should the unthinkable happen and Ms Palin assume the style and title of Vice-President, we would be saddled with someone who would have no idea where Darfur, South Ossetia or Abkasia are on the map, would have no idea who is the president of Russia, China or France or what language is spoken in South America. Should someone mention that there was trouble in Georgia she would likely remark that she was on the phone yesterday to Atlanta and no one said that anything amiss. By the way she can't pronounce the word 'nuclear' and that is always very telling. Listen to George W trying.

Clearly the Republicans are desperate. They are burdened with the most unpopular president in years. The economy is tanking. They are mired in two very unpopular wars. The signs are that they are about to be turfed out of office in a big way. The Democrats have just gone through a very tough primary campaign in which the first woman likely to head up a major party ticket lost out to the first black man to do so. Several female supporters of Hillary Clinton seemed to be pissed off at the outcome. Perhaps the Republicans considered that a woman, any woman, even this Neanderthal, would attract the disaffected female vote. I find it difficult to fathom why any other woman would vote for her for, clearly, she subscribes to the women as cattle school of sociology. The motto of this faction is, 'Keep them barefoot and pregnant' or more elegantly, 'Kinder, kücke, kirke.'

Her views on abortion are positively frightening. I have dealt with the vile after effects of illegal abortion gone wrong. You only need to see that once to be willing to subscribe to any means to prevent it happening. Women will sometimes be driven to take desperate measures to rid themselves of unwanted pregnancies. No sane individual regards abortion as something to be celebrated but those same persons recognise that it is sometimes necessary. During my career, I have had to deal with members of religious factions who strove might and main to prevent women having access to legal abortion services. It is understandable that membership of certain religious cults or sects precludes abortion under any circumstances. But why should those deluded fatheads, who belong to such sects, be able to wield such power over those who do not subscribe to their delusions?

Ms Palin considers that sex education in schools is wrong. She feels that kids should be shown the virtues of chastity and abstinence. It is now pretty well recognised that reliance on these methods does not reduce teen pregnancy rates nor do they cut down the incidence of sexually transmitted disease. A new vaccine is available that prevents girl catching the herpes virus. Infection with this virus leads many women to suffer from cervical cancer from which a fair number die. Gardasil, the new drug, effectively prevents this. Persons of Ms Palin's ilk dislike the use of such vaccines, because in their view, they encourage promiscuity. In other words, they would prefer to employ the real threat of death by cervical cancer to keep their young women 'pure' than to treat them so as to avoid the risk of getting this nasty cancer almost entirely. It is a view common among the evangelicals, who have a positive terror of sex. The egregious Dr Reginald Finger, another figure on the far right fringe of the Republican party, is on record holding that were there to be a safe and effective vaccine against HIV-AIDS he would oppose its use. The threat of AIDS, in his view, is a legitimate tool in the quest for female purity. He will have his view fully endorsed by the new, Republican VP candidate.

The prospect of Ms Palin wielding any substantial power is too frightening to contemplate. She is a know-nothing, been-nowhere, redneck. She is thoroughly in bed with John McCain, who is tacitly endorsing most of the worst policies of Wee Georgie – a spectacularly unpopular, ham fisted president. Imagine Ms Palin in the same ring as Vladimir Putin or Hu Jintao. They would turn up to the meeting with knives and forks and bibs! Ms Palin is a demagogue and is capable of giving an effective rabble rousing speech as she did when she accepted the VP nomination a few days ago. In the few days since the Republican convention, that party has drawn ahead in the polls. Is the great American public so blinkered that they can see no further than their wallets, locality and next week? How anyone with half a functioning neurone in his head can be hoodwinked by the sort of guff uttered by Ms Palin and her cohorts is a total mystery to me.

Life under President Palin does not bear thinking about.

September 11 2001

(First published on 11/09/2011)

Ten years ago today, a group of Islamists high jacked four commercial airliners and drove them calmly and deliberately into the Twin Towers in New York and the Pentagon in Washington. One plane destined to crash into the White House crashed into a field in Pennsylvania when the passengers and crew managed to regain control of it from the hijackers. All up, just over three thousand people died as the result of these attacks, the majority of them in New York. The destruction of the Twin Towers resulted in the release of all sorts of toxic materials which poisoned many of the rescue workers and others in the neighbourhood at the time and, consequently there has thus been an additional death toll of up to five hundred persons.

Since that day, these attacks have been extensively parsed and various hyperbolic titles have been dreamt up to describe them. 'The event that changed history.' 'The world can never be the same after this.' That kind of thing has been fairly typical of the reaction around the world. The lead up to the tenth anniversary of September 11 has seen the world's media picking over the entrails of the day and replaying over and over again footage of the impact of the planes as they flew into the Twin Towers. The anniversary itself has been the major story in many important newspapers displacing significant events that are actually going on right now, such as the overthrow of the Libyan dictator and the impending rerun of the global financial crisis.

Maudlin accounts from relatives who perished in the attacks are to be found on most news broadcasts as the events of the day are relived. Memorial ceremonies at the site of the Twin Towers, the Pentagon and the field in Pennsylvania will be attended by the current and former presidents of the United States. A solemn roll call of those who died will be read out to the accompaniment of tolling bells. There will be much talk of closure.

American reaction to this attack appears to take two forms. The first is astonishment that any group would seek to attack such a benevolent country that does so many good works around the World. 'How could anyone want to hurt us so gravely? We are such nice guys.' The second is outrage. That a group of fundamentalist fanatics could bring off such a coup really disturbs American sensibilities. 'We are not going to allow a bunch a rag heads get away with this! We shall set about punishing all those who may be or not be connected to them. We shall go to extraordinary lengths to get revenge.' The sense of lèse-majesty is palpable.

The events of September 11, 2001, spawned the War on Terror that lasts until this day. America and its allies invaded Iraq and toppled Saddam Hussein. This was followed by the involvement in Afghanistan. At home, security was beefed up to astonishing levels and that has made travel all around the world very, very tedious with intrusive searches and painful delays. The rule of law and human rights, about which the US was rightly so proud, has been subverted. Several hundred unfortunates, who have been scooped up in various forays, have been tossed into prison camps and subjected to torture and indefinite detention without charge. Many of these persons look likely to remain locked up forever. The technique known as extraordinary rendition has been invented. This term conceals a nasty practice in which suspects are captured and flown around the world to secret camps where foreign nationals are employed to behave vilely to the prisoners. An entire industry, that has grown up to service the practice and the presence of secret Central Intelligence Agency camps, comes to light on a regular basis. The war on terror has provided an excuse for the Western Allies to behave as cruelly and nastily as those who are regarded as the enemy.

Ten years on, this so called war shows no sign of coming to an end. Indeed the terrorists are winning. They no longer need to bring off spectacular attacks. Merely the threat is enough to send the security authorities of the USA and the UK into a frenzy. Ostensibly, credible intelligence has been revealed this very weekend that 'terrorists' are planning another attack on the USA during the memorial ceremonies. Consequently New York is ankle deep in squads of heavily armed police done up in body armour and sporting formidable guns. Literally hundreds of police vehicles have been seen cruising up and down the main streets of Manhattan with lights flashing and sirens blaring. If those who have authored this 'credible intelligence' possess a sense of humour, they must be splitting their sides with mirth.

Obviously, people who lost friends and family ten years ago deserve sympathy. The US has not experienced a direct attack on its soil since the British sacked Washington and burnt down the White House in the War of 1812. Countries that have led so charmed an existence for so long will naturally be rather sensitive to such perceived outrages. Whether the US, like Shakespeare's Queen Gertrude, doth protest too much is an open question. Many a land has been raped over and over again and its population has dusted itself down and got on with life. Much of Europe torn apart during World War II has not groaned and claimed that its destruction was an epoch making event. The British, subjected to remorseless bombing during the same war, have recovered their sense of proportion and put the events behind them. The US, the only country that has ever used nuclear weapons upon an enemy, when they managed over the course of two or three days, to kill hundreds of thousands of civilians and during the subsequent years many more from delayed effects of radiation, wears its sense of outrage and hurt unreasonably. Americans may regard themselves as exceptional and their country as blessed. These are not sentiments shared by the rest of the World, which sees that sees them as a source of death, destruction and just plain viciousness in so many ways.

No one would seek to mock a country trying to come to terms with an outrage in which very many people were killed. They may wish to suggest that that same country tries to regain some sense of proportion, for the US is by no means the only place where shit happens!

Syria

(First published in 2011)

Syria continues its steady descent into turmoil and chaos while the rest of the World looks on impotently. Important figures like Hilary Clinton, Secretary of State, Ban Ki Moon, Secretary-General of the United Nations and Kofi Annan, Special United Nations and Arab League representative, stand on the side lines imploring both sides of the conflict to behave themselves. Neither takes a blind bit of notice. Meanwhile, the regime led by Bashar al Assad, employs huge numbers of sophisticated modern weapons and well trained soldiers to shell, bomb and smash several towns and cities. The opposition, the Free Syrian Army (FSA), vastly outmanned and outgunned, manages to tie down the Regime's armed forces by clever use of guerrilla tactics. Kofi Annan has become so frustrated in his rôle that he has thrown in the towel and declared his intention to leave when his current term runs out in September. He has spoken darkly of dissent and finger pointing among the ranks of the influential in the Security Council.

Lately, the FSA has obtained more powerful weapons and has shown a degree of coordination and is managing to put up a better show. Two weeks ago, they brought off a massive coup by smuggling a powerful bomb into a planning meeting of the top echelons of the regime and killing a handful of the top dogs. The Western media continues to forecast that Assad is about to topple. 'He can only last another few weeks.' These few weeks appear to be very elastic. Independent reporters are not allowed to enter the country and the few that have smuggled themselves in have done so at great personal risk. The video clips that are shown daily on the BBC and Al Jazeera are all unverified and so it is very hard for outsiders to know exactly what is going on.

Resolutions have been introduced into the Security Council of the United Nations, condemning the actions of the Syrian government and calling for the president, Bashar Al Assad, to step down. These resolutions have been regularly defeated by Russia and China, who have chosen to exercise their power of veto. Both countries have been deaf to the pleas of other nations. That their intransigence enables the slaughter and mayhem to continue does not seem to register with them. It is interesting to speculate why China and Russia have adopted this hardline attitude. Syria remains Russia's only ally in the Middle East and a certain amount of commerce goes on between them. China also has some commercial interests. But, both China and Russia are fully paid-up members of the dictator's club and do not wish to be seen encouraging interference in internal affairs by outsiders. Perhaps they envisage the day when violent revolution breaks out inside their own borders and the last thing they would like, under such circumstances, is outside, armed interference in their business.

Appeals for the setting up of a no-fly zone by NATO, à la Libya, have come to nothing. The Western powers realise that the situation in Syria is very different from that which obtained in Libya last year. There is no doubt that NATO air power played a decisive role in toppling Gaddafi. Syria is a much more densely populated country than Libya and it is hard to see how or where a useful no-fly zone could be established. Moreover, the West is reluctant to be seen throwing its weight around in the Middle East yet again. The Arab league has been impotent and unwilling to play a public rôle in bringing this ghastly conflict to an end. There has not been the slightest willingness on its part to mount a coordinated military intervention to protect brother and sister Arabs. Publicly, at least, the other Arab nations have demonstrated indifference to the plight of the Syrian population: just another bunch of Arabs beating all kinds of shit out of each other?

Saudi Arabia and Qatar are now shipping arms to the Syrian opposition. Some qualified observers consider that a kind of proxy war is going on between Saudi Arabia, a largely Sunni nation, and Iran, largely Shi'ite. Most Syrians are Sunni but there are substantial Shi'ite and Christian minorities. The ruling clique in Syria are members of the Alawite sect, an offshoot of Shi'ism. So what started out as a desire by the Syrian street to unseat Assad's clique and his

Ba'ath party is turning into a sectarian war. Those are often the worst kind.

The fighting and slaughter has been going on for more than 18 months. It is estimated that around 20,000 people have lost their lives. Huge numbers have been forced to flee and become refugees. The central government controls Damascus and other large cities but the countryside is largely controlled by the opposition. More and more high-level officials of the government are defecting. Most recently, the Prime Minister, appointed by Assad only two months ago, has defected. The Syrian army is well equipped and powerful but only the Republican Guard is totally reliable. Its members are drawn from Alawites ranks and, therefore, blindly loyal to Assad. Several massacres have been attributed to government forces, which have employed irregular militias to go in, after the regulars, and slaughter dissenters. The FSA is now thought to be responsible for a few massacres of its own. 'Crimes against humanity' are no longer the exclusive province of the central authorities.

It seems certain that Assad's days are coming to a close and that some sort of regime change will take place. It is also likely that revenge and retribution will continue once he has gone. There are also fears that the conflict might spill over into neighbouring countries. Syria is known to possess large numbers of chemical weapons and Israel, for example, would not wish to see these fall into the hands of hostile, militant groups. Syria has become a messy and confused situation. It is hard to see how it will end. The United States, which is in the middle of an election year, has as good as said that it cannot be bothered to interfere until after the election. Other major powers, such as Russia and China, will likewise stay out of the mess. So, the next few months will see much of the same with many innocent civilians being slaughtered and displaced, while the rest of the World looks on with horror.

Whither America?

(First published in early 2012)

Barack Obama has been re-elected pretty handily after a prolonged election campaign, which seems to have started about a week after his first inauguration. Somehow he managed to overcome the 'uppity nigger factor'*, that must have worked heavily against him in the minds in the minds of the more crazed conservatives. He resumes control of a country that faces many grave problems. It is beset by enormous debt. It continues to be sucked into a war in the Middle East from which there appears to be no escape with any degree of honour. Its political system is gridlocked. There is a Democrat as president and a slender, fragile control of the Senate by the same party. The Republican opposition has a substantial majority in the lower house. The economy bumps along with high unemployment, a slack housing market, a declining manufacturing sector and a general lack of optimism, although there are recent signs of improvement.

Obama wants to tackle the national deficit and suggests that the government needs more revenue. He proposes tax increases. His opponents regard such notions akin to treachery and consider that the government is already far too big and that any treatment of the deficit must come from slashing expenditure. However, they refuse to countenance any cut to military spending. The USA spends more on defence than the rest of the world put together! It does seem, therefore, that compromise is necessary but there has been little sign of that during the first four years of Obama's reign and much of the rhetoric coming out of Republican mouths does not sound hopeful for a change of heart during the next four years. The current account deficit amounts to fifteen trillion dollars, a sum that is eye-wateringly hard to comprehend. In spite of this, trillions are spent annually on the military. The justification for this is the war on terror that began after the nine-eleven outrage more than a decade ago. Hawks in Washington denounce President Obama for not taking a more active role in the Libyan conflict that ousted Gaddafi. They have also called for more involvement in the Syrian civil war. And this after more than ten years of battle in Iraq and Afghanistan! Neither of those wars, one over and one due to end in the next couple of years, can be described as successes. Iraq remains a dangerous mess beset by sectarian conflict and Afghanistan is likely to fall back into the hands of the Taliban very shortly after American forces withdraw. Thousands of American lives have been lost in these theatres for very little benefit.

Against that background, it is easy to understand Barack Obama's reluctance to plunge into yet another conflict far away and of little interest to the American population at large. By far the most unsettled region of the World today is the Middle East, defined as that area stretching from the Mediterranean coast to the Indo-Pakistani border. The causes of this unrest are many and include the problem of Israel, conflict between Shia and Sunni Muslims, the recent overthrow of a handful of long standing dictatorships, Iranian intransigence regarding its nuclear programme, burgeoning religious fundamentalism and oil supplies for the Western world. Added to this mix, is a widespread resentment on the Arab street against Western imperialism and colonialism. American and NATO heavy handedness in Iraq and Afghanistan during the last ten years has not done much to make the West more popular. That the West, led by the USA, has propped up unsavoury regimes in Saudi Arabia, Egypt, Libya, the Yemen and earlier, Iran, has likewise not endeared it to the Arabs. The unconditional support for Israel over the aspirations of the Palestinians is another strike against Western interests.

The recent so-called Arab Spring has introduced a new dynamic into this region. The dictators, who had been regarded as crucial for Western interests, have been overthrown but, rather than being replaced by those who sought more democratic regimes, it now looks increasingly likely that Islamist and theocratic regimes, led by the Muslim Brotherhood, will become established instead. Democracy, as understood in the West, is inimical to the faithful who believe that society should be ruled according to the divinely inspired precepts of Sharia. Western style democracy runs counter to those ideas and is therefore blasphemous.

The involvement of the West, led by the USA, in this turbulent region, has been largely motivated by self interest summed up in the one word: oil. While the House of Saud reigns over the largest oil exporting country and can act as a counter to Iranian threats to cut off western supplies by blocking the strategic Straits of Hormuz, then oil, vital to the economy of the West, continues to flow. However, there are straws in the wind that indicate that this geopolitical reality is about to change. The major, American oil companies have discovered ways of producing huge amounts of cheap, useful fuel from hitherto unknown sources right in the USA itself. The trick is something called fracking: a process that allows huge quantities of shale gas to be harvested from subterranean rocks. There are ample deposits of suitable rocks in many parts of the Continental USA. So happy are these companies that they suggest that the USA will be a net exporter of fossil fuel within a very few years and the crippling dependence on oil from the Middle East will be at an end. If this proves to be true, then the implications for the region will be very considerable.

Saudi Arabia, Iraq, Iran and the Gulf States will lose overnight their major customer and with that their ability to shape world events. It is possible that they will be able to find other markets but these are likely to be far less sensitive to their quirks and desires. Such new customers will not have to keep looking over their shoulders to calibrate the effects that their deals will have on the fate of the Jewish state. The loss of revenue that is likely to ensue will greatly reduce the ability of elements in the Muslim and Arab Worlds to fund and export terrorism. A more robust posture towards Iranian nuclear adventurism will be possible. Once the West can free itself from its dependence upon Middle Eastern oil and gas, it can concentrate on ensuring the survival of Israel and leave the rest of the region to sort itself out and attempt to come to terms with modernity and abandon its religiously derived notion that life should still be lived according to the dictates of one who lived in the Arabian desert 1400 years ago.

So, the USA, which today looks like a has-been may well once again become the giant it has been used to being for the past 100 years. No one could have foreseen this turn of events even five years ago.

*Uppity nigger factor or, 'We ain't going to have our White House in the hands of no uppity nigger!'

Chapter Four – People

Quackery

(First published in March 2012)

About four hundred prominent, Australian, medical scientists and practitioners have formed the Friends of Science in Medicine Group. Their principal aim is to decry the teaching of pseudo-scientific health subjects in Australian universities. They maintain that a degree granting body offering courses in such topics as chiropractic, homeopathy, reflexology and herbal medicine casts doubt upon all university teaching of the health sciences. As well, they seek to ban payment by the government health care scheme to practitioners of these doubtful disciplines. Furthermore, the group holds that there is no such thing as alternative medicine: there is good medicine and bad medicine. They have no objection to employing any treatment modality if it is helpful. Bearing in mind the power of the placebo effect, almost anything done to a susceptible person will have some sort of effect.

At this point in is worth looking at some of the 'pseudo-scientific' modalities that have raised the ire of the Friends of Science in Medicine. Chiropractic holds that a life force travels down the spinal column and controls the health and well being of the body. If the passage of this force is disturbed by 'subluxations' then the patient will suffer illness. Subluxations are minor alterations in the integrity of spinal joints and those, that exercise chiropractors are very hard to identify and little, if any, scientific evidence for their existence can be reliably demonstrated. More extreme chiropractors claim to be able to treat many systemic conditions, whose relation to minor disturbances of spinal anatomy are hard to discern. Furthermore, chiropractic manipulation of the neck is positively dangerous and can lead to permanent spinal cord damage and rupture of major blood vessels in the neck. Conditions that chiropractors claim to be able to cure include colic in infants, pancreatitis, irritable bowel syndrome, autism, fibromyalgia, childhood asthma and strabismus.

Homeopathy has as its foundational doctrine the notion that like cures like. Its practitioners maintain that illness can be treated by giving a person tiny doses of noxious agents of the kind that caused the upset in the first place. They take an active ingredient and serially dilute and shake it many times so that the solution finally administered to the patient is unlikely to contain a single molecule of the original ingredient. (The shaking is dignified by the term succussion.) Practitioners of this strange art hold that the absence of any of the original, active ingredient is not important because the water, used for these dilutions, retains a memory of the original substance and that it is this memory that effects the cure. Some even claim that the spirit of the original substance haunts the final product! Not one shred of evidence exists for these bizarre ideas.

Homeopathists conveniently forget that any body of water will have contained dozens of other substances during its existence. Perhaps those are remembered as well? In effect, homeopathic products sold in chemists' shops are nothing more than pure water or sugar pills. The packaging of these commodities incorporates elaborate labelling. Recent cases of homeopathic excess have revealed that enthusiastic practitioners have taken their wares to the underdeveloped world and persuaded poor, unschooled populations to rely on sugar pills rather than orthodox vaccinations and treatment for such conditions as malaria. Consequently, many a child has developed serious illness that could have been prevented. Such behaviour by health care workers is truly shocking.

Reflexologists project an imaginary chart on to the sole of the feet and arbitrarily attribute areas of the sole to various organs of the body. Thus, they hold that stimulation of the 'kidney area of the foot' will ginger up the kidneys or that pressing or tickling the 'liver area' will sort out the ailing liver. There is absolutely no evidence for any of this.

Herbal medicine suggests that administration of various herbs can be curative. Many modern drugs were derived from plants: digitalis from foxglove: aspirin from the willow tree; tamoxifen from the Pacific yew, are examples. Modern science has managed to identify and manufacture these active substances. A molecule of salicylic acid from the factory is identical to one boiled out of willow bark. Herbs are likely to contain many impurities. Control of dosages is difficult when raw materials are used. All drugs that are produced by reputable pharmaceutical manufacturers will have been subject to rigorous testing processes and their effects relatively easy to measure and compare with other similar compounds.

Many other fanciful treatments are readily available from 'alternative practitioners'. Iridology resembles reflexology in that its practitioners project an imaginary chart, rather like a dartboard, on to the coloured part of the eye. They then claim to be able to examine various discrete areas of the iris and diagnose illness in remote organs. Reiki practitioners hold their hands a few centimetres from the surface of the body and manipulate so called energy fields that they claim to be able to detect. Shiatsu practitioners assert that they can apply pressure to certain parts of the body and influence 'energy channels', thereby altering the health of target organs. No one has isolated these channels. Acupuncturists make similar claims and even go so far as suggesting that they can rid a smoker of his tobacco addiction by sticking fine needles into his earlobes.

All of these practices share the same defect: there is no scientific evidence exists for their efficacy, but it is possible to study them in some Australian universities and be granted a diploma.

The human frame is heir to many disturbances. Symptoms such as severe belly ache, passage of blood in the stools or the urine, sudden weakness in a limb, coughing up blood, the discovery of a lump, all warrant proper and prompt attention for they are probably harbingers of serious underlying conditions. A competent, orthodox practitioner will take a full history, perform a thorough examination, order appropriate tests, seek specialist advice and propose a course of management. In the majority of instances a diagnosis will be made and treatment commenced. Not all treatment will be successful. There may well be associated problems such as pain, nausea and generalised lack of well being. The orthodox medical practitioner has a duty to address those issues as well. Some of the associated symptoms may be helped by unorthodox measures. Patients might well gain some symptomatic relief from alternative modes of treatment. No sensible doctor ought to deny that comfort to patients as long as they are fully informed.

Apart from these major medical problems, humans can also suffer from a host of minor ailments: scattered aches and pains, mild abdominal discomfort, feeling out of sorts, for example. Almost all of these are self-limiting and will clear up in a few days with or without treatment. The person, who has pain in the shoulder or mild swelling around the eyes and, who consults a homeopathist, will receive treatment in the form of a pill or some drops which contain no active ingredient whatsoever, but which will be labelled aconite, one part in several millions, or bee venom, one part in even more millions. It is quite likely that after paying for the consultation and the 'drug' he will feel better and attribute his 'cure' to the 'medication'. It will not occur to him that he would probably have got better anyway. Patients will recount the story of their elderly aunt who was treated by the application of a plaster cast for weeks for a joint disorder and who did not get better. The moment she removed the cast and went to see the Reiki practitioner, she improved. Again, the chances that all of this was coincidence are very high. The likelihood that the Reiki treatment had any fundamental effect is close to zero.

Orthodox medicine does not have all the answers. There are many who have not prospered in its hands. Maybe this was because they were suffering from incurable disease or because of a wrong diagnosis. However, medical regimens are subject to continuous review and testing. Treatments are constantly being refined. New modalities are not introduced before undergoing rigorous trials. Even then, drugs that appeared to be promising, turn out to have serious and unwanted effects. Vioxx and Rosiglitasone are glaring examples of this kind of thing. Both were thoroughly tested before release.

Alternative therapies are not subject to this same kind of rigour. No body of literature exists in which these modalities are reported on, compared and criticised. Any good they achieve comes through the placebo effect, which can be very powerful. Alternative practitioners rely heavily on the laying on of hands. More often than not they spend lots of time on each case. Both activities are known to be comforting but neither can be scientifically tested. The Friends of Science in Medicine do not seek to ban them. They merely hope that the public understands what it is up to when it buys homeopathic remedies, attends a Reiki session and the like. The public should have this right but it should not expect others to pay for such eccentricity through publicly funded health care schemes.

Why are Americans such a sickly lot?

(First published in 2012)

Some possible answers to this question are to be found in a magisterial survey: *'US Health in international perspective – Shorter Lives and Poorer Health'* produced for the National Academy of Sciences by Stephen H. Woolf and Landon Aron.

Their principal findings are that the USA spends more on health than any other comparable country but its citizens die sooner and suffer more illness. In short, the paradox is that great wealth and high spending result in huge expense, poor health status and lower life expectancy. The comparator countries are Australia, Austria, Canada, Denmark, Finland, France, Germany, Italy, Japan, Norway, Portugal, Sweden, Switzerland, the Netherlands and the UK. Each of these countries has embraced the idea of some kind of National Health Service. The United States, on the other hand, regards such a service as anathema — even evil.

Quoting freely from the report summary, it turns out that Americans have a shorter life expectancy than people in the comparator countries. For example, American males live 3.7 years fewer than Swiss males and American women live 5.2 years fewer than Japanese women. These gaps are increasing especially among females. The US experiences the highest infant mortality rates and its children are less likely to reach the age of 5 years than others. American infants have lower birth weights. Deaths from motor vehicle accidents, non-transportation injuries and random violence are more common in the US. It leads the developed world in adolescent pregnancy rates and sexually transmitted diseases. It has the second highest prevalence of HIV infection and the highest incidence of AIDS. More years of life are lost in the US to alcohol and other drugs than in the comparator countries.

Obesity and diabetes rates are highest in the US. High prevalence rates are present in US children and in all later age groups. From age twenty and up, diabetes and high plasma glucose levels exceed those of the other countries. The US rate of death from heart disease is the second highest among the peer countries. Americans reach age fifty with less favourable cardiovascular risk profiles and are more likely to die of heart disease than older adults in the peer countries. Lung disease is more prevalent and comes with a higher mortality in the US than in the other countries. Americans, in general, are more disabled by arthritis than their peers. Deaths that occur before age fifty, account for two-thirds of the difference in life expectancy of Americans compared with others. Americans have the first or second lowest probability of achieving age fifty among the nationals of the peer group of countries. As would be expected, most of these health disadvantages are more pronounced among the socio-economically deprived groups but even those who are not so deprived, generally fare worse than similar people in the United Kingdom and elsewhere. Oddly enough,

United States survival rates for those over seventy-five are better than those in the peer countries and rates for cancer screening, blood pressure, cholesterol control and lower stroke mortality exceed the peer countries. Health among recent immigrants to the US is better than that of the native born.

An endless recital of statistics, prevalences and comparisons does not make for engaging reading and enough has been quoted already to highlight the health problems of the United States.   Reasons for the American health problems are many and intriguing and the rest of this piece will speculate on their causes. Whereas smoking rates and alcohol abuse are lower in the States, abuse of illicit and prescription drugs is very common. Americans are less likely to wear seat belts; they have more car accidents as their cities are built around motor vehicle use. Public transport is not as available as in most European countries. Provision for walking and cycling is not regarded as important. Firearm ownership and use is very high in the US and death and injury from gun shot wounds more common than in the comparator countries. American adolescents become sexually active earlier than teenagers in comparator countries; are more promiscuous and less likely to practise safe sex. Americans consume more calories per capita than Europeans, Japanese or Australians. A trip to a family restaurant in the United States is eye opening: portion sizes are immense and a meal is regularly accompanied by large amounts of bread, fries and calorie dense relishes. The American economy is huge but there is a wider incidence of poverty and income inequality than in other countries. Childhood poverty, in particular, is more widespread in the United States than in the other countries. Lastly, Americans have less access to health and social safety nets than do the citizens of the peer countries. Over 50 million Americans have no health insurance! * (That number is equal to the combined populations of Australia and Canada.) Needless to say, this uninsured cohort contains the poor, the uneducated and the illiterate. Patently, such a large number of people, who share this plight, greatly skew health and medical statistics coming out of the United States.

Those who have obscure and complex diseases can find solutions in America, providing money is no object. The very best medical institutions and hospitals in the United States are without equal anywhere in the World. A person, who requires complex surgery, the latest and most expensive drugs and the newest procedures, will find them all in America – at a price! Public Health as a discipline, on the other hand, does not flourish. Health care in the States is fragmented. Campaigns promoting vaccinations, for example, are regarded with suspicion. City and State ordinances that seem to interfere with citizens' freedoms are frowned upon. Look at the negative impact that the Mayor of New York's attempt to limit the size of fizzy drinks servings produced. He wanted to ban the sale of the so-called 'Big Gulp' portions of colas that contained a mere 48 ounces. It is possible to purchase a giant hamburger that weighs in at 9000 calories, the Intensive Care Special. Such a monstrosity is inconceivable anywhere else in the civilised World. Attempts to place some limits on gun ownership are greeted with shock, horror and misplaced references to the Constitution. Sex education programmes have been denied Federal funding for obscure religious prejudices.

The notion that there is a place for nationalised health care strikes the rich and powerful in the States as being akin to communism and there is no greater criticism of any plan or idea than that. Communism or socialism are considered to be Un-American and thus beyond the pale. (Odd in a country that professes to be so Christian. Jesus Christ could be thought of as the first socialist.) There appears to be a visceral fear of anything that is set up by government for the public good. Ideas about charity and giving and trickle down economics are much more kindly looked upon. And yet, health care for all and especially public health education dealing with such matters as seat belt wear, safe sex, avoidance of illicit drugs, sensible eating, promotion of exercise, sex education (untrammelled by religious prejudice and such silly notions as abstinence), regular and free cancer screening do not find ready acceptance in American society.

It has been estimated that curative medicine, which provides hospitals, surgery, drugs and complex procedures, accounts for only about 10-15% of health benefits in any society. Public health measures, on the other hand, account for the rest. Public health is not sexy. It is prosaic, bland, simple, straightforward, not newsworthy, not eye catching, even nerdy and yet it plays a huge part in achieving good health outcomes. Most of the peer countries listed above invest a great deal of effort ensuring that such measures are in place and the results are obvious. Hugely expensive treatments for individuals with rhabdomyosarcoma, multiple gun shot wounds, 90% full thickness burns, loss of limbs, retinal implants for senile macular degeneration, for example, are exciting and heart warming but they only help individuals and their families. Campaigns to do away with smoking, unsafe sex, illicit drug use for example, that affect whole populations very positively, have nothing to do with 'communism'. They are just common sense.

*Obamacare has reduced this number and has been introduced into the United States recently but faces huge opposition and is likely to be overturned as soon as the Republican party regains control of government.

Chinese Medicine

(First published 12/11/2006)

Zhang Gongyao, a provincial university professor in China, has had the temerity to question the legitimacy of traditional Chinese medicine. This latter is a sacred cow and it is foolhardy person who questions such livestock. (Don't mess with Catholics about the virgin birth or with Muslims about the purity of Mohammed's many wives!)

Poor Mr Zhang has been denounced on web sites, and subjected to scornful attacks by the Chinese government – even called a traitor. In China, traditional medicine is a national symbol; it is protected in the constitution and taught in universities. It is a very valuable industry worth several billions of dollars annually and it claims it has about 300 million clients each year. Many persons in the West have taken to using traditional Chinese remedies. Acupuncture and the use of herbs have become increasingly popular. So, it is a brave man who takes on all of these vested interests. Naughty Mr Zhang has said that

Chinese traditional medicine is '... unscientific, unreliable, dangerous, a threat to endangered species, and even fatal to some humans in some cases.' He has suggested that the government stop promoting its use and that it also remove its protection under the constitution and to stop its being used in the official medical system. He also thinks that its practitioners should be obliged to undergo orthodox medical training. 'From the viewpoint of science, Chinese traditional medicine has neither an empirical nor rational foundation,' he says. This is man who obviously feels strongly about the topic. His opposition is not impressed and he has been condemned for betraying the Chinese people and for insulting ancestors. 'Traditional medicine is an indispensable and inseparable part of the Chinese health care system and it has contributed much to the development of the nation,' opine the authorities.

Quite the hornet's nest.

It is said that large numbers of Chinese have huge faith in traditional medicine and they will go to great lengths to follow the treatment plans laid out by practitioners. I have watched some of these remedies being prepared and have even seen some being used. What I was seeing were evil smelling and vile tasting brews made of god knows what. If grandma's old dictum that 'medicine does you no good unless it tastes horrid' is true then most Chinese medicine passes the vile taste test with flying colours. It does seem likely that little or no scientific testing is done on these remedies and that the efficacy depends on blind faith. It is probable that those who use it are not particularly ill anyway and that they would have got better regardless of what they did. Acupuncture does appear to help some conditions and it probably works as a placebo or by impeding the flow of pain impulses up the spinal cord. It is hard to understand how it could do much else. Messing about with 'meridians' is unlikely to bring benefit to those suffering from nephritis or inflammatory bowel syndrome, for example! Although there are those who will seek it for similar conditions.

I am always amused how blind faith so frequently triumphs over reason. Thinking that munching on a bunch of herbs or ground up tiger claws could be of much use in any condition is wildly optimistic. True, many modern remedies were derived from plants. Aspirin from willow, digitalis from foxglove and tamoxifen from the Pacific willow come to mind. However all of these have been greatly refined and the active principals extracted and subjected to analysis and controlled trials. Western medicine does not have all the answers but it is based on a measure of scientific enquiry and proof. And even with all of those controls in place still manages some horrible boo boos! Remember thalidomide? Still, given the choice I think I'd rather take my chances with treatments that are evidence based.

Rape!

(First published in March 2013)

A regular reader was prompted by a recent essay to ask why men rape. Were there to be an easy answer to that question then presumably measures would have been put in place to ensure that they did not. A walk through some basic anthropology might throw some light on to the question. The best that can be hoped for are reasons, not excuses.

The earliest human beings were aggregated into small, nomadic, hunter-gatherer groups. It is not known whether such groups were led by men or by women. Any hierarchical arrangements that existed are unknown and there are no records of any kind that would help us know. Such a life would have been very strenuous and the individuals, consequently, very meagre. Celebrated anthropologists such as WHR Rivers, AR Radcliffe-Brown, Margaret Mead all working during the first half of the twentieth century, visited the few remaining hunter-gatherer peoples and reported on their social and cultural practices. By extrapolating from their findings, they deemed it possible to form some idea of the structure of the earliest human societies. Reinforcement of such a view comes from observations of various aboriginal societies around the globe, for it appears that those societies remained substantially unchanged for millennia before their encounters with Europeans. The Native peoples of Australia were few in number compared to the vast territory they inhabited and it is likely that there would have been little or no competition for resources and hence little impetus for change. Early hunter-gatherer groups, elsewhere, would have enjoyed similar advantages.

The human infant remains helpless for several years – some might argue permanently! – and a mother belonging to a hunter-gatherer society would be unable to cope with more than one infant at a time. Because her life was so strenuous, it is likely that she remained very lean. Such women are relatively infertile and her very activities enabled her to space her children – an absolute necessity with the life she was obliged to live.

Came the time when these groups discovered weapons and were then enabled to catch and kill large game much more easily. It is likely that certain members of the tribe, almost certainly men, became responsible for the provisioning of the entire group. The necessity to be constantly on the move declined. The coming of a more sedentary existence led to plumper women and larger families. Tribal groups became larger and more stationary. Along with such developments, the acquisition of things and territory occurred. Over time such changes allowed for the invention of agriculture and an even more settled life pattern. Labour almost certainly became divided up: men off hunting and women left to tend hearth, home, garden and children. Whereas in the nomadic days, little difference existed between the sexes for the activities of both were necessary for survival; in a settled population, hierarchies evolved with men at the top. Protection of possessions and land assumed great importance and it is likely that neighbouring settlements would go to war to protect their assets or to acquire new territory to feed growing populations. Raiding parties would seek to capture domestic animals, tools and women. Thus evolved the idea of woman as a chattel. Another consequence of settlement was increased prosperity and the ability of communities to support full-time religious officials. These were nearly always male and so was born the patriarchy.

Fast forward several thousand years and the evolution of the Abrahamic religions takes place and one common theme of all of these is the God ordained inferiority of women to men. Where women are deemed to be no more than the possessions of men, then daughters can be given away by fathers, sisters controlled by brothers for the sake of the family honour as measured by the 'purity' of the women. Great damage is done to tribes or other groupings if the womenfolk are stolen or ravaged during warfare. By the same token, useful alliances may be formed by one group exchanging women with another. The practice of dynastic alliances based upon strategic marriage of daughters lasted well into modern times.

With the passage of time, the global population increased steadily and competition for resources became more intense. This is a process that has been speeding up during the last 200 years. In 1800, the World's population was approximately one billion. It is now well on the way to seven billion. Scores of new nation states have come into being following the collapse of the European empires. Disputes over borders have arisen. Various 'isms' have not been conducive to peace and quiet. In the last one hundred years, both fascism and soviet style communism have come and gone to be replaced by Islamism – the 'ism du jour.' World wars have been replaced by vicious and nasty little neighbourhood battles. A weapon of choice in these conflicts is the use of sexual violence: raiders arrive, slaughter the men and rape the women. Families are often obliged to watch mothers being raped before they are all slaughtered. Rape is an especially horrid weapon for its psychological, as well as its physical effects, endure. Some cultures are most unsympathetic to raped women, often regarding them as responsible for their plight. Perhaps it is worth noting that men, too, are often raped in this type of conflict.

Does any of the foregoing answer the question of why men rape? It does not for there is no one answer. In most cultures around the World, women are held to be inferior. Religion is partly to blame for this. In many societies women who are out and about are regarded as fair game. Sexual harassment is common and the sight of pretty young women in summer clothes is sufficient to cause men on building sites to break out with catcalls and wolf whistles. In more rarified environments, the British Houses of Parliament, for example, unwanted groping of women appears to be routine (vide Lord Rennard)! The notion that, 'she was asking for it,' is widespread. Penalties for sexual misbehaviour are often not too harsh and very difficult to impose. The judicial process that follows rape is onerous, pitiless and embarrassing and frequently discourages victims from coming forward. The sentiment that boys will be boys is firmly embedded among many. In the West, the disappearance of low skilled labouring jobs, which absorbed large numbers of uneducated young men, results in them being pitted against women in shrinking job markets which in turn breeds resentment and hostility towards females.

Orthodox Muslims are said to consider that the sight of women's hair or curves inflames male desire and that for that reason women should be covered, hence the burka and niqab. (They do not teach that men ought to learn to control their desires!) Others, especially in Western societies, laugh at this notion. Unwanted sexual advances are common, rape is also common, both in times of calm but especially where conflict rages. Patently, there is no one magic solution to the problem. Change for the better will only come about where attitudes change and that all males learn to regard all females with respect and as their equals. It has been remarked that males possess two brains: one between the ears and the other between the thighs. When the anatomically superior one comes always to control the inferior, then rape might become less of a problem.

Patriarchy

(First published in 2012)

A pair of elderly men, whose background could not be more different, both experientially and geographically, but whose intellects have both been clouded to the point of imbecility by religious dogma and prejudice, have recently unburdened themselves of outrageous remarks about women.

The first, Richard Mourock, a senate candidate in the just completed American election, opined that a woman who got pregnant after a rape should not seek an abortion because God obviously intended her to become pregnant in that fashion and, moreover, should regard the pregnancy as a gift from God. The other, an unnamed spokesman for the Pakistani Taliban, warned the young friend of Malala Yousafzani, the 15 year old girl cold-bloodedly shot in the head by a team of goons for advocating education for girls, that she, too, would meet that same fate unless she shut up about that idea. This toe-rag went on to say that the girl had forgotten her culture. Indeed, it is hard to know what goes on in the minds of men who make such statements. Perhaps they do not have minds and that they are mere automatons actuated solely by unexamined, religious dictates. However, their observations are on the record so it is reasonable to parse their statements to try and make sense of their ideas and motives.

Richard Mourdock is a social conservative who believes passionately that abortion is sinful in all circumstances. This belief is derived from his religious views and does not allow him to make any allowances for circumstances and obliges him to insist that a 12 year old girl carry an unwanted pregnancy to term willy nilly, regardless of the disastrous effect that would have on her life, future prospects and ambitions. Only a fool considers that therapeutic abortion is a lark without possible lasting, serious physical and mental health consequences. Permitting a raped, pregnant 12 year old to take the course of abortion weighs in the balance the good of allowing a potential human life to blossom against the harm of blighting the life of young woman. Ridding the girl of a few-celled blob of tissue seems to be, by far, the lesser of two evils.

The hit squad, that shot Malala in cold blood, in front of her friends while she was in a school bus on her way home from school, hold that females should not be educated for that might give them ideas above their divinely ordained station. They leave any observer struggling to find words sufficiently potent to express his or her disgust. Needless to say, they belong to a fundamentalist branch of Islam and use for their guidance literal interpretations of the Koran, a book reputed to have been dictated to Muhammad nearly 1400 years ago by the Angel Gabriel. This book, held by the faithful to be the authentic word of God, may not be interpreted, revised, or edited to take into account the passage of time and the fact that the majority of believers no longer live in the Arabian desert. The fundamentalist view appears to be that if it is in the Koran, then that's it: accept or take the consequences.

Malala was taken to hospital in Pakistan and then flown on to the United Kingdom for specialist surgery and rehabilitation. It does seem that she might recover, at least in part. (Very recently, some slightly more cunning members of the Taliban realise that they have made a misstep with this assassination attempt and are now trying to cast it as a western, imperialist plot to discredit them!) These same heartless thugs have gone on to threaten other young women who have had the temerity to suggest that they want an education and do not wish to spend their lives tied to men they despise, bearing child after child until they expire, worn down long before their time.

These profoundly misogynist stories do not end there. Todd Aiken, another Republican senate candidate is on record as that women's bodies have a way of shutting down after 'legitimate rape' so that pregnancy does not follow. (Where does the Republican Party flush out such stars to run as its representatives?) A fourteen-year old Polish girl, pregnant following rape, has been refused an abortion by two hospitals and 'counselled' by a Roman Catholic priest to accept the pregnancy. She was harassed by pro-life groups, encouraged by the blathering of this priest. She was then hauled in for police questioning before finally being allowed to travel to the other end of the country for a termination. Tonio Berg, the Maltese minister of foreign affairs, has been nominated to become the European Commissioner for Health and Consumer Protection. He is a man who has publicly campaigned against women's rights, Lesbian, Gay, Bisexual and Transgender rights, against rights for migrants and has done his best to write a ban against abortion into the Maltese constitution.

The activities of Messrs Mourdoch and Aiken in the USA, Tonio Berg in Malta, the Roman Church in Poland and the fundamentalists in Pakistan all have in common, a fear and loathing of one half of the human race. They appear to believe that women, are inferior beings, whose rights are of lesser import than those of men, and who can be regarded as little more than brood mares, ordained to bear children, remain uneducated and to serve their masters. These deeply held views are justified by writings in the so-called sacred texts and have no regard for the fact that these texts were put together in another place and another time and often have little or no relevance to modern lives. No one discounts the enduring value of some of the moral teachings of the scriptures and their continued relevance. However, their sociological prescriptions are wildly outmoded and totally irrelevant to life in 2013 – even in the most undeveloped parts of the world. Excuses could be made for illiterate peasants in Pakistan but it is hard to work out how these same excuses can be made for prominent members of Western societies such as the Polish priest, the Maltese minister and the American senate candidates unless it is accepted that their powers of reason have been well and truly hijacked by their unquestioning religious faith.

A tale of two salons

(Date of publication not known)

Wealthy, educated circles in the seventeenth and eighteenth century Europe featured salons. These were gatherings of the literati and artists of the day in the drawing rooms of rich, often titled ladies. Ideally, the mistress of such salons would be an outstanding beauty who possessed a majestic house in London or Paris. Sometimes, the women, presiding over such affairs, were celebrated courtesans, which added a thrilling frisson of titillation to the whole business. Regular, informal meetings would take place during which poets, artists, writers or musicians could strut their stuff and perhaps attract the attention of potential wealthy patrons. Lustre would accrue to the lady for surrounding herself with the stars of the day and the struggling artist might find a pay check in the form of some young nobleman who wished to achieve celebrity by supporting the next Mozart, Pope or Gainsborough.

By the beginning of the twentieth century the classical salon had ceased to exist but two assemblies of writers, artists and thinkers coalesced on opposite sides of the Atlantic, both of which could be considered to have been latter day salons. In Bloomsbury, the district close to the University of London, the celebrated Bloomsbury Group came into being. It lasted until the mid-fifties and was formed around the two Stephens daughters: Virginia (Woolf) and Vanessa (Bell), who purchased a house in Gordon Square along with their two brothers, after the death of their father. The Gordon Square house was the unofficial headquarters of the Bloomsbury Set. Sir Leslie Stephens served for several years as the Editor of the Dictionary of National Biography. Virginia Woolf was a celebrated novelist and one of the pioneers of the stream of consciousness school of writing. Her best known works include *To the Lighthouse*, *Mrs Dalloway*, *A Room of One's Own* and *Orlando*. The contrast between her novels and those of the late Victorians is startling. She deals much more with the interior of her characters rather than the more usual recital of external events. Vanessa Bell was a competent painter whose works include *Studland Beach* and several portraits of her more famous sister, Virginia.

The male members of the group were almost all educated at Cambridge and moved to London to prosecute their careers. They were introduced to the Stephens women by their brothers, Thoby and Stephen, who had attended the same university. Indeed, the Bloomsbury Group or Set was often termed, Cambridge in London. At its height, it included John Maynard Keynes, E. M. Forster, Lady Ottoline Morrell, Lytton Strachey, Roger Fry, Clive Bell, Leonard Woolf as well as several other less well-known members. Clive Bell had helped Roger Fry organise the Post Impressionist Exhibition of 1910 in London, which was held to mark a turning point in the appreciation of fine art. Several critics at the time felt that it constituted a breakaway from the art of the Victorian era. Bell and Fry propounded the theory of significant form in pictorial art. Some went so far as to suggest that this exhibition was the actual the beginning of the twentieth century.

E. M. Forster's contribution to English letters was profound although his output was small. It includes *A Passage to India*, *Howard's End* and *Maurice,* a frankly homosexual tale. He spent most of his life as a don at Cambridge and was a revered figure there. Lytton Strachey wrote *Eminent Victorians* as well as a good deal of criticism. John Maynard Keynes' theories of economic practice are still influential. He overturned older ideas that free markets would and could provide full employment as long as workers did not demand high wages. Instead he encouraged the use of fiscal stimulus during periods of recession. His influence wained in the latter part of the 20th. Century but the recent financial crises have obliged governments to revisit them. He has been considered by some to be one of the most influential people of the twentieth century.

As a whole, the Bloomsbury set held an abiding belief in the importance of the arts and they had a great influence on literature, aesthetics, criticism, feminism, pacifism and sexuality. Vanessa Bell had an 'open marriage' with Clive. Virginia was a sometime lover of Lady Vita Sackville-West. Lady Ottoline Morrell, one of the first people to be famous for being famous, was the mistress of Bertrand Russell, the philosopher. Perhaps it was she who came nearest to presiding over a salon, in the old formal sense, in her house in Bedford Square, Bloomsbury. Many members of the set were homosexual at a time when such practices were illegal and could be punished by long terms of jail. The majority of the male members of the Bloomsbury Set had been members of an exclusive secret society at Cambridge known as the Apostles. A few years later this society achieved great notoriety when it was discovered that Burgess, Maclean, Philby and Blunt, all notorious spies, had belonged to it. More than a faint whiff of queerness was associated with them.

Virginia and Leonard Woolf founded the Hogarth Press and used it to publish several controversial books including several dealing with psychoanalysis. Some of Virginia's own works were published by Hogarth.

In summary, the Bloomsbury Set were a remarkable body of men and women whose influence on the arts, society and ideas about feminism and sexuality was profound. Almost all of them came from an upper middle class background and several had private means and so were freed from the burden of going out to work. This good fortune is well summed up by Virginia Woolf's observation that for a woman to be able to practise her art, she requires a room of her own and money to pay for it.

The other 'salon' evolved in New York and gathered for lunch on a daily basis at the Algonquin Hotel and became known as the Round Table – or among its detractors, as the Vicious Circle. It lasted roughly from 1919 until 1929. Its most prominent members included Dorothy Parker, one time writer for Vanity Fair and later the theatre critic for the New Yorker, Robert Benchley, humorist and actor, Ruth Hale, writer and women's right activist, George S. Kaufman, playwright and director, Roberts E. Sherwood, author and playwright, Alexander Woollcott, critic and journalist and Harold Ross, the editor of the New Yorker. Occasional members included Talulah Bankhead, Harpo Marx, James Thurber and HL Menken. They met regularly to discuss the issues of the day and to play silly games. Their meetings were characterised by exchanges of witty sallies and less elevated wisecracks.

James Thurber became disenchanted with them and considered them, 'Too consumed by their own cleverness'. HL Menken was more dismissive and wrote that, 'their ideals were those of an inordinately trashy vaudeville actor!' The group staged a review in New York in 1922 called *No Sirree*, which ran for one night only. The members of the inner circle gradually moved away from New York to pursue other career opportunities. When Edna Ferber turned up at the hotel in 1932, she found the famous round table occupied by a family from Kansas. Many of them remained friends long after the Round Table as such, had ceased to exist. As several of them were working journalists, their views were widespread and influential. A few of them won Pulitzer Prizes for journalism and so their contributions to letters could not be seen as negligible. However, the literary lions of the day: Scott Fitzgerald, William Faulkner and Ernest Hemingway stayed well clear.

It seems, therefore that the Bloomsbury Group made a more significant contribution to the arts and philosophy than the more light hearted lot that met at the Algonquin. Although New York was not so very far from London by the 20's, there was never any cross fertilisation and both groups did their thing largely unaware of each other.

'Twere better they kept their trousers on

(First published on 09/08/2013)

This is a tale of three prominent men who could not keep their pants on and the consequent troubles that ensued.

The first hero is one Anthony Weiner, former US congressman and latterly running for the job of Mayor of New York City. Mr Weiner was elected to Congress in 1998 and resigned in 2011 after the publication of sexually explicit photos of himself, accompanied by lewd messages that he sent to several young women. Apparently, this gent assumed that the ladies would enjoy and approve of pictures of his private parts turning up in their inboxes. The shame of the scandal becoming general knowledge was enough for him to promise to withdraw from public life and mend his ways. Mr Weiner married Huma Abedin in 2010. She had been an important member of Hilary Clinton's entourage for several years before marriage. Nobly, she announced that she was going to stand by her man, in spite of his asinine behaviour. Early this year, Weiner announced that he proposed to run for the post of Mayor New York City. Unfortunately for him, further revelations were made public to the effect that he has continued to send photos of his private parts to sundry young women, but this time under the pseudonym of Carlos Danger! (Carlos Danger! Incredible!) So far, he has refused calls to withdraw from the mayoral race. It is hard to know what Weiner's motives for this singular behaviour can be, but it does suggest that he is not quite all there and perhaps not the ideal person to assume the role as Mayor of New York City, one of the most important public offices outside the Federal Government. Of course, it is entirely a matter of taste, but one can argue that certain parts of the nude male body can be described as beautiful: the upper torso, a noble brow, a fine profile, in some cases, the hands. But, few would consider the external genitalia to have much in the way of beauty. Few would relish finding photos of them in the e-mail or on the others forms of social media. It is hard to know what Mr Weiner hoped to achieve by dispersing such pictures.

The second prominent man, who has had difficulty with continence is M. Dominic Strauss-Kahn. Born in 1949 to wealthy parents and the beneficiary of an expensive private education, he became an economist, lawyer and politician He was a former professor of economics and managing director of the International Monetary Fund and a leading candidate for the French Socialist party's nomination in the last presidential race. DSK, as he likes to call himself, has been married several times and has three daughters. His last wife, Anne Sinclair, is a very wealthy heiress. On the 14 May, 2011, a 32-year old maid, working at the Sofitel Hotel in New York, complained that DSK sexually assaulted her when she came to his room to clean. He was arrested, arraigned, released on $1 million bail and ordered to stay in New York. The case was dropped because of the unreliability of the victim's evidence, in spite of positive DNA testing. DSK was allowed to return to France whereupon he resigned from the IMF and withdrew his candidacy in the French presidential election. On July 26 this year, he was charged by the French authorities with aggravated pimping. It is alleged that he was a leader in a prostitution ring operating out of Lille.

What motivates M. Strauss-Kahn? He is rich, privileged, educated and able to hold down very important posts in the international scene. Since his fall from grace, he has been offered posts as consultant by organisations in Serbia and Russia. The conventional view of French public life has always held, somewhat romantically, that prominent men installed mistresses in expensive apartments that they visited for dalliance, on their way home from the office. Furthermore, such activities were held to be unremarkable as long as they were discreet. DSK has been anything but discreet and seemed to prefer rough trade. His appetites have led him astray and he now looks like an elderly figure of fun.

The last member of the trio is Silvio Berlusconi, former prime minister of Italy. His career has turned into a serial dog and pony show. Recently, he has been sentenced to jail time for tax fraud. He faces several other trials but seems to escape the consequences of his behaviour because of the labyrinthine nature of the Italian legal system. Berlusconi, aged seventy-six, has been a successful property developer, owner of a large media empire, proprietor of AC Milan, founder of the Forza Italia Party and prime minister of Italy three times. His first marriage fell apart in 1985 and he re-married in 1990. The second came to an end in 2009, when his wife accused him of 'frequenting minors'. In 2011, he took up with Karima El Mahroug, a seventeen-year old nightclub dancer, aka Ruby the Heart Stealer. He threw 'bunga bunga' parties for her and several other young women. At these he claimed that elegant dinners were taken and polite conversation ensued. Ruby is a spectacularly endowed young woman, who denied ever having sex with Berlusconi.

In 2012, he was sentenced to four years jail for tax fraud and a year later to a further seven years for abuse of office and buying sex from a minor. Recently, the sentence for tax fraud was upheld. Bizarrely, Berlusconi took part in the general election in 2013 and won sufficient seats to permit him to be part of the negotiations to form a new government. Like Dominic Strauss-Kahn, Berlusconi has morphed from capable businessman and prominent politician into randy old goat.

This piece is not intended to slight elderly men who form relationships with much younger women. There are many instances when such have proven to be very successful – the long lasting marriage between Charlie and Oona Chaplin, for example. The intention is to draw attention to the louche and tawdry conduct of some of those who seek and hold high office. Weiner, Strauss-Kahn and Berlusconi have all behaved like wanton fools and it is starling that they have found sufficient numbers of supporters to put them into the positions they came to hold. It is unlikely that these gentlemen would appeal greatly to the female half of any electorate and so their support must come mainly from the males, who are prepared to overlook the foibles of such goons. Perhaps those, that vote for the likes of this three, harbour secret fantasies of taking part in bunga bunga parties with the polite conversation and elegant dinners entailed. Men forget that the sight of themselves with their trousers down: shirttails, reedy shanks and socks revealed and their struggle to get their pants over their shoes is a comical and not a noble sight. Women are able to doff their duds in a far more alluring way. Fortunately, the ladies are able to suppress their giggles and so preserve the amour proper of their lovers, thereby allowing matters to proceed. Presumably, Ruby and her sisters took solace in the dinners and the fat checks that were cut before the parties concluded. It seems unlikely that they found their hosts all that admirable.

Cheating

(First published on 19/01/2008)

The plight of Marion Jones, African-American sprinter, has prompted this essay. She was so talented that she would have achieved great things anyway, but instead sought to obtain an unfair advantage over her fellows by cheating. And look where that has got her: six months in the pokey, eight hundred hours of community service and two years of probation as well as the universal approbation of her fellow athletes and the general public.

Marion Jones appeared to win a slew of gold medals at the Olympic Games in Sydney in 2000: she crossed the line ahead of the others in five events. That was the first time that any woman had picked up five gold medals during the course of one Games. She was subjected to many, many drug tests before, during and after the games and apparently she passed them all. However, she was once married to CJ Hunter, World champion shot putter. In 1999, he was found to be a drug cheat and stripped of his record. The next man in her life was Tim Montgomery, Olympic Gold Medalist in the Sydney Games of 2000 in the four by one hundred metres relay and one hundred metres world record holder in 2002. He, too, fell foul of the drug police and had long bans imposed upon him. Meanwhile, Marion was able to carry on competing and setting records and passing drugs tests! Eventually, it became obvious that she had been involved with a rather dodgy, dietary supplement laboratory on the West Coast of the USA. Several of its customers fell under suspicion and one by one, they were found to be in breach of the drugs regulations. Finally, Ms Jones turned herself in and confessed her sins. The Olympic and the athletics authorities stripped her of her records and required that she hand back her medals. Various court cases ensued during some of which she lied. This lying under oath is what has led her to jail and ultimate disgrace. She has now announced her retirement from track and field, a sport that she claims to have loved. The whole saga is very sad. A talented individual has managed to screw up her life and her place in sporting history through greed and the desire to seem even better than she undoubtedly was. She made a great deal of money during her sporting career and I expect she retained much of it. All of that is her tragedy.

There is much greater tragedy caused by the antics of Marion Jones and other drugs cheats. Firstly, she denied the real winners of events of their moments of glory: being on the podium, receiving their medals to the sound of applause and their national anthems. Even if these real winners are subsequently given their rightful medals, they are likely to turn up in the mail and that is not quite the same. Secondly, the cheats make everyone very suspicious about any new records or outstanding achievements in the future. So if some exceptionally fleet-of-foot girl from Harlem starts to chip time off world records, we will ask what's she on. Lastly, many of the most notable cheats have been African Americans starting with Ben Johnson back in 1988 and including runners, baseball players and field events stars. Cynics who are told about the latest black speedster from the USA are likely to be highly sceptical that his results are legitimate. All new, outstanding athletes are going to be tarred with the same brush and who have they to blame: Marion Jones and her crew?

The bodies that control the Olympics and athletics strive mightily to ensure that events are clean and that competitors are performing without the aid of drugs. The pharmacological industry appears to be able to stay one jump ahead of the testers with more and more sophisticated products that are harder and harder to detect. The Drugs Police are forever playing catch up. Perhaps the time will come when any attempt to ensure that events are drug free will be abandoned and future games will be thrown open to anyone regardless of what they are taking. So the person that wins the one hundred metres event will be the one who crosses the line ahead of all the others and no one will care what possible long term harm they have done to their bodies by fostering a desire to win a medal by any means possible. At least, the rest of us would be certain that everyone was competing on even terms.

Post script: Ms Jones turns out to have been the veriest amateur in the drugs cheating game. The erstwhile, sainted Lance Armstrong, apparent winner of a staggering total of seven Tours de France has been rumbled. He had been tested a squillion times, during events, afterwards, and at random. Every time, he appeared to come up clean. However, he was eventually found to have been using drugs and blood doping all along. He ran the most sophisticated system to avoid detection. He has been stripped of his titles and sent into eternal perdition. Of course, those who really won the events have not been rewarded in his place. In a very recent interview, he claimed that he would have behaved in the same way if he could have his time over again.

Days after the interview, he was involved in a drink-driving car accident and tried to blame it on his girlfriend and to get her to claim to the police that she was driving at the time. Seems that Lance Armstrong lost something else besides one ball when he had surgery for testicle cancer many years ago.

Naughty children

(First published on 13/04/2008)

There have been some fairly startling reports about the behaviour of groups of teenagers in the past week or two. In the United Kingdom, a band of about a dozen teens have kicked to death a young woman they came across in a park. She was with her boyfriend, who was also attacked, but managed to survive. Both the girl and her friend were dressed in Goth clothing. In Sydney, New South Wales, another gang of fifteen-year old youths rampaged through a high school brandishing baseball bats and machetes. They injured a handful of other students and a teacher and did a good deal of damage to the fixtures and fittings of the school. In both cases the local police were able to capture the miscreants and prevent further damage. Some of the English kids had previous convictions for violent behaviour. One of the Australian boys was out on bail. His father had provided a $500 surety. The Australian boys made a great deal of fuss when they were transported to the local court the following day and were very offensive to onlookers. One of the English children joked around with his mother when he was in court. Neither the English nor the Australian kids appeared to show any kind of remorse for what they had done.

Newspaper editorials, op-ed pieces and correspondence columns in both the United Kingdom and Australia were full of suggestions and outrage about what can be done with such children and how should public policy deal with the problem. Opinion seems to be divided equally among those who consider that the fault lies with society and others who think that harsh physical punishment is needed. Presently, the identities of young offenders are concealed. We do not learn that it is young Bill Bloggs who has beaten up a lady schoolteacher. To publish his name would breach his human rights. Courts are anxious not to lock up young people in jails, for those institutions are breeding grounds for further antisocial behaviour. Jails in both UK and Australia are overcrowded as well.

In the UK, young thugs are given ASBOs (anti-social behaviour orders). Many youngsters seem to consider such orders as marks of distinction. It does not seem likely that a young thug who violently assaulted someone will be much moved when he is told that he has been a naughty boy and that he must do a little community service. And should he come before the court again he will told that he is an extremely naughty boy and that he must now do even more community service. The magistrates, when confronted with groups of angry, violent teenagers, like those who took part in the incidents retailed above, have limited powers. They can award community service orders or they can impose short custodial sentences. The days when a young thug would be given half a dozen strokes of the cane are long over and most unlikely to return.

Sociologists have suggested that some form of national service might be the answer. Others have mooted the idea of sending hooligans off to boot camps in remote parts of the country and forcing them to live under harsh conditions where all of their energies would be consumed in keeping warm, clean and fed. At such camps they would not have access to modern gadgetry like mobile phones or to any sort of artificial stimulants such as tobacco, alcohol or other drugs. Both national service and boot camps would be administrative nightmares and fearsomely expensive. Violent, antisocial people of any age who tangle with the law repeatedly and, who do not seem to give a tinker's cuss about the strictures placed upon them by magistrates, are obviously hard to deal with. Keeping anyone in prison is extremely costly and the question arises as to whether it is a justifiable use of public funds.

The original theory behind incarcerating miscreants was that they could be reformed. Many prison inmates are serving their third, forth or even fifth stretches. Reform does not seem to have occurred. If it is truly the case that teenagers in 2008 are behaving worse than those of earlier eras, it is instructive to ask why. The decline of the nuclear family is often cited. The need for both parents to go to full time work leaving no one at home to keep an eye on things is also blamed. Widespread moral turpitude throughout modern society is mooted. Violence in the media, rap music and other cultural fads all come in for censure. Whatever the case may be, a society in which innocent bystanders can be kicked to death because they are differently dressed or schools terrorised for no obvious reason is one with hard questions to answer. If only it was as easy as bringing back the birch!

Racism

(First published on 03/05/2008)

It is axiomatic among the chattering classes in the West that the colonial days of the past were an unmitigated disaster for the subjugated peoples of Africa and Asia. Furthermore, it is widely assumed that with liberation from the colonial yoke would come sweetness and light and that the former slaves would all turn out to be benevolent and farseeing rulers of their fellows. The white, colonial masters were all presumed to look down upon their subjects as being members of an underclass and unable to run their own affairs. Any infrastructure created by the West was deemed to be created purely to facilitate shipping the loot down to the coast for onward transport to the coffers of the Europeans. As with most generalisations, there is a grain of truth in these assertions. Undoubtedly, Britain, France, Belgium, Holland and Portugal benefited greatly from their colonial adventures and it would be foolish to deny it. However, it is worth taking a look at postcolonial Africa in the light of the ongoing farce in Zimbabwe to see how the average citizen is faring, since liberation, under the rule of his countrymen.

A glance at a map of Africa and a quick look back over the history of events of the past forty odd years is not reassuring. The Congo, the Sudan, much of West Africa but especially Sierra Leone, Rwanda, the former Portuguese possessions, most of East Africa and now Zimbabwe have all been hosts to quite ghastly civil wars and abuses of human rights. Those, who came to power, after the colonialists packed up their tents and stole away, have, in the main, treated their fellows with disdain and horrible cruelty. Groups of armed thugs roamed around in Sierra Leone hacking off the limbs of their enemies. Armed militias are still laying waste to large stretches of the Darfur region of Sudan, raping and pillaging as they go. About one million persons were casually slaughtered in Rwanda. Nigeria experienced a horrible civil war during which many Ibos were killed. Angola and Mozambique have been hosts to civil wars that have lasted for decades. And so on and so on.

The HIV-AIDS epidemic has flourished in sub-Saharan Africa like in no other place on Earth. It is often quoted that up to one-third of the population is infected. One reads of the armies of orphans left to fend for themselves because both parents have perished from the disease. Famine and pestilence are almost constant occurrences throughout the continent and huge amounts of food aid must be shipped in each year to keep populations from starving.

In short, post colonial Africa has had its problems and these show no sign of going away in the near term. Freedom, though infinitely desirable, has been no bed of roses. Zimbabwe gained its independence from Britain about thirty years ago. At the time of independence, it was prosperous, self sufficient for food and able to export grain and other foodstuffs to its neighbours. The chief architect of independence was Robert Mugabe, who was widely revered throughout black Africa as a hero. Over the past several years he has managed to bring his country to its knees. Inflation runs at astronomical levels. Two billion Zimbabwean dollars is worth about $60 US today – who knows what tomorrow? Zimbabwe no longer produces enough food to feed its remaining population. Eighty percent of the people are out of work. More than a third of the population has run away to neighbouring countries in order to survive. The place is a wreck. Robert Mugabe runs his country as a personal fiefdom.

Robert Mugabe permits elections from time to time but these are usually rigged. He has dedicated teams of thugs who go round scaring the hell out of anyone he suspects might vote against him. His regime has previously made much of its apparent electoral successes and has trumpeted the results just about as soon as they have been tallied. In late March 2008 the latest of these elections was held. It looked as if Mr Mugabe had lost. For a brief moment it seemed that he would have to shuffle off to a dictator's retirement home. Not so fast! Unfortunately, much behind the scenes duck shoving took place and the results were comprehensively massaged. A recount of the presidential election was carried out before the initial results were even published. After a delay of several weeks, Mugabe and friends have now conceded that they lost the parliamentary election to the opposition and that he did not win the presidential election either. However, the regime maintains that his opponent did not secure the necessary 50% plus one in order to win outright and so a run off is required. During the few weeks following the election Mr Mugabe has unleashed his thugs who have gone about beating, torturing and terrifying those suspected of voting against him and making it obvious that worse would follow should they dare to vote against him in the run off contest. While all of this was going on, Zimbabwe's neighbours have been wringing their hands and maintaining that there is no crisis and that everyone should wait to see how things played out. None of the leaders of Southern African countries has dared to criticise the machinations of Robert Mugabe's regime or to suggest that it had acted illegally, immorally or inhumanely. They have stood by and watched while opposition members have been rounded up and taken off to torture camps and generally roughed up. No one is quite sure how many of the opposition supporters have actually been killed.

Thabo Mbeki, president of South Africa, is a vastly influential man in the region. It is he and his government that have been mainly instrumental in keeping Zimbabwe afloat during the last few years. South Africa has been the principal destination for fleeing Zimbabweans. Mbeki and other important, black, South African leaders such as Nelson Mandela and Desmond Tutu all seem to have turned a blind eye to events in Zimbabwe. Kofi Annan, recently retired secretary general of the United Nations from Ghana, has not openly criticised the machinations of Robert Mugabe. It seems that his status as hero of independence from the former colonial masters insulates him from blame or censure. The fact that he has treated his fellow, black countrymen and women in ways that would provoke howls of anger and outrage had they been carried out by European powers, is strangely acceptable. Indeed, the depredations of post colonial rulers towards the long suffering black populations of Africa have never really excited the same level of censure as that routinely directed towards the colonialists. An eerie silence has often surrounded the most ghastly and demented behaviour of many African tyrants.

In short, an odd double standard pertains. Appalling behaviour of the powerful towards the less privileged is roundly condemned and decried. Similar actions carried out by peers against their fellows are often ignored or condoned. Moral relativism is a minefield. Contrast the patriarchal attitudes of the colonialists towards the subjugated peoples of Africa with the often shocking conduct of some African rulers towards their fellow citizens. The former is always regarded as racist, the latter merely politically expedient.

Man is vile–even black man!

Growing old

(First published on 07/02/2015)

The recent death of Mrs Ethel Lang, Britain's last Victorian; reports that children born today might live to be 150 years old; and my recent 80th birthday have made me think about growing old. Mrs Lang was born on 27/5/1900, while Queen Victoria was still on throne. During her long life, she lived under half a dozen different monarchs and more than a score of prime ministers. The notion that future generations might hit their 150th birthday reminds of me of a silly sketch in an American TV show called *'Laugh In'*. An actress dashes on to the stage and says to Goldie Hawn, 'Goldie, Goldie, have you heard, soon medical science will ensure that we shall all be able to live to one hundred and twenty?' Goldie replies, 'Gee! That's great! Little old lady for sixty years!' Today she would say, 'Little old lady for ninety years!' Not an especially enticing prospect.

My mother, Vera, died when she was 93. She spent the last five years of her life in a nursing home and was in the grip of some kind of dementia for three years or so before she died. She had lived for years with my father, who was a dedicated two to three packets-a-day man, and so, poor Vera inhaled a ton of second hand smoke. It is likely that her dementia was more of the vascular kind than straight Alzheimer's. Came to the same in the end, however. She hailed from long-lived stock. Her mother died aged ninety and her two sisters lasted well into their tenth decades.

I remember asking her about growing old and she made a few sage observations. She reckoned that during her sixties, she experienced little, if any difference in her physical and mental capabilities. During her seventies she considered that some things were getting a little harder but she claimed not to notice any real decline until she was in her mid-eighties. This was borne out by her own life. She still had a couple of part-time jobs when she was eighty-five. Most of her working life had been spent in retail and she used to serve in the Norwich Cathedral Gift shop. It was housed in part of the actual cathedral building and involved going up and down a steep spiral staircase to obtain items from the stock room. It was centuries old and the steps well worn. A twenty-first century health and safety wallah would have had kittens if he saw it. Her other post involved helping out in the Octagon, a drop in centre attached to the beautiful old church, St Peter Mancroft, situated just off the market square in the centre of the city. She had to take public transport for this job as parking is so difficult to find in Norwich. Her cathedral job came with a parking permit for the Close. She loved flashing her pass and being waved into the Close, via the St Ethelbert Gate, by the liveried attendant. Of course, these jobs were voluntary and the rewards were personal satisfaction, an invitation to the Bishop's garden party, at his palace every June, and an annual letter of thanks from some elevated church official. I am not sure how she managed to become involved in church affairs late in life for she never attended any services or demonstrated any obvious religious beliefs. Once she gave up the job in the gift shop, the managers decided that there should be an upper age limit for helpers. They had obviously been secretly dreading a serious fall by Vera, dressed, as she always was, in very high-heeled shoes.

All of us arrive in this world, helpless, unable to feed and dress ourselves and without possessions. Over time we learn to walk and talk and slowly we become independent agents and begin to acquire stuff. The end of our lives runs these processes backwards. As young persons, we move away from home and begin to travel far and wide. Some of us acquire fancy houses into which we can put our gear. Later, we may abandon our mansions and go for a small apartment in a seniors' complex. In some regards, this relieves us of endless household chores but does oblige us to take communal meals where we have to endure the company of people that, heretofore, we would have hardly passed the time of day with. One such organisation, I checked out was at pains to stress that free transport was provided so that I would be able to visit the doctor, the pharmacist, the optometrist and the physiotherapist. 'Big deal,' thought I, 'Every waking moment spent visiting some health professional or other.' No suggestion that the transport could be used to go to the movies or to a concert. Just health, health, health.

My own 80th birthday has come and gone and if I take stock of my own situation, I reflect that I do not have to take medication or make regular visits to any medical practitioner. I am able to take my dog out walking several times each day and thereby more than cover the recommended daily 10,000 steps. I gallop up and down a steep staircase several times a day. I do, however, note that the short-term memory is no longer as sharp. Frequently, I carry out some routine task and do not remember whether I completed it or not. Unconsciously, I find that I have adopted little strategies to ensure that I do not spend too much time looking for my glasses and keys. For example, I have installed a little basket just inside the back door and make sure that I empty my pockets into it. When I wonder where I have put my keys, that is the first port of call, and more often than not, there they are. Energy levels decline and remind one of the letter sent to the Times, by an old man, some years ago, who said that he had more and more difficulty doing up his shoe laces. He added that while he was down there, attending to them, he would look around to see if there was anything else he could accomplish while bent double to save himself the bother of bending double again. I have noticed that tasks requiring the manipulation of small objects become harder. The sensitivity of one's fingertips seems to decline and the hands are no longer as supple.

I have always had a sense of responsibility. If given a task, I would see to it that it was done. Most often, such tasks were self-imposed. At last, I am able to give myself permission to let them slide. 'To hell with it! I can do it tomorrow.' At my retirement party three years ago, I listed several things that I intended to prosecute, immediately afterwards. I dutifully took them all up but it did not take long to discard a few and to concentrate on the ones I felt really strongly about. I gave up the attempt to learn to knit. I resumed my futile attempts to play the piano and found that my lack of progress, dispiriting and so that has also gone by the board. Dog ownership is a delight and I still very much enjoy writing. I like to play bridge on-line, which saves me the bother of joining a club and being snorted over by a bunch of strangers and catching regular bouts of 'flu. A life governed by shoulds and oughts has, at last, changed into one governed more by perhaps and maybe and even, 'to heck with it'. But, the change has taken a long time to come. I am no longer obliged to anything I don't want to. It's fun, that way.

I find that my eating habits have changed. A beefsteak the size of a small doormat posed no problems when I was forty years old. Today, such a prospect is quite unwelcome. A lamb chop no bigger than the palm of my hand is as much as I require or can stomach. Second helpings no longer appeal. Two glasses of wine at one sitting satisfies me. Halfway through the third, I realise that taking it was unwise. Alcohol, in theory should be an aid to sleeping. For me it is the opposite. Some taken with dinner works fine but a nightcap inhibits sound sleep.

Some years ago, Pat and I made a list of places we had to visit. Gradually, we crossed several of them off the list. Trekking in Nepal was first to go followed by the visit to Machu Picchu. We half-heartedly planned to go to Havana before the USA normalised its relations with Cuba and unleashed floods of American tourists. Well, Mr Obama has begun the process just about the same time that Havana got crossed off the list as well. In any case, travel is no longer much fun and has lost its savour. This comes about by reason of declining vigour and concerns about what we might be faced with should we fall sick on the upper reaches of the Zambezi River or in the Hindu Kush. Airport security precautions are no picnic. The palaver that one has to endure at airports and the misery of being packed into the back end of the plane outweigh the possible enjoyment that the visit might bring. Getting on to the plane, nowadays, is a nightmare, requiring passport and document checks half a dozen times and intrusive searches of the person and bags. I have had a recurring nightmare that I would find myself on a 12-hour flight stuck between two vastly oversized persons whose bulk would overflow their seats and engulf me. Such a plight is my personal version of hell. Presumably, proper hell lasts for more than twelve hours.

I have always been a keen follower of sport, especially cricket, tennis and rugby. Indeed, I could be quite downcast if one of my favourite players or teams failed to do as well as expected. Nowadays, I really no longer care if Roger Federer loses in the third round of a major tournament or if England fails to live up to expectations. Why should I worry? The divine 'Rog' has made more than enough money to satisfy a team of players, let alone one man and he has enjoyed sufficient success for several careers. When England capitulates to the hungrier and more skilful Aussies, yet again, I reflect that it probably means more to them than to the English, for whom winning is not quite proper form, especially if it looks as if one is trying. Anyhow, I shed no tears either way. I must admit that the evident perplexity of the Australian Rugby team following the serial thrashings handed out to them by the rather despised Kiwis, from across the ditch, remains delicious. Also, I still enjoy American teams and athletes coming in second. I am at a loss to explain these pusillanimous emotions other than by a misplaced satisfaction on seeing those, who consider themselves to be entitled, denied.

Reading has always been one of my main pleasures and it remains fun. However, I am less forgiving. A newspaper article has no more than one sentence with which to engage me. A magazine article is given half a paragraph and a book, ten to twenty pages. If I am not gripped within those limits, I go on to the next piece. There is so much really good stuff to read and I do not have to bother with impenetrable prose, however highly recommended by people whose opinion I value.

There is a curious symmetry between life's beginnings and its conclusion. At the start, you own nothing and then spend time accruing things. You are helpless and depend upon others to feed and protect you. You do not go about alone. Your horizons are, perforce, very limited. As you wind down, you accept that you have far too much stuff and take delight in giving or throwing some of it away. It is quite elevating to realise that the discarded items were not that important, after all, and are not missed. I am not yet helpless and manage to provision the table and feed myself – but for how much longer? I go out less and less. I prefer my own quarters and company. Restaurants and places of entertainment are frequently far too noisy. As I have already remarked, the desire to see far away places has diminished. Besides, modern technology allows one to experience so much vicariously and without the need to field the indignities surrounding travel. Shakespeare knew what he was talking about when he said that one moves towards being, '...sans eyes, sans teeth, sans smell, sans everything.' I can still see very well, I have almost all my teeth. I lost my sense of smell after a vicious cold three years ago. I am sans quite a lot but by no means sans everything. Watch this space! On second thoughts, that will be a waste of time for by the time the sans everything rolls around, I won't be able to fill it.

Mabel Barltrop, Daughter of God

(First published 14/09/2006)

This is the strange and amusing tale of Mabel Barltrop, widow of an Anglican vicar and founder of the Panacea Society.

Mrs Barltrop was widowed in 1906 and was left to bring up four children. She had difficulty in coping with the loss of her place in society as the vicar's wife and for a while suffered a spiritual crisis, which caused her to dread going to church. She began to study the works of Joanna Southcott, a late 18th century, self declared prophetess at the local library where she picked up a leaflet and sent away for more information. She later founded the Panacea Society, a group of mainly comfortably off women who met regularly for prayer and reflection. This group indulged in spiritualism, séances and table rapping. Joanna Southcott believed that she would give birth to a messiah called Shiloh. Unfortunately, when she died in 1814 she was a virgin and not pregnant. Some of her followers held that she had produced a spiritual child, Shiloh, who would be incarnated at some later time. On Valentine's Day in 1919, one of Mabel's followers declared Mabel to be Shiloh, the daughter of God. Several others alleged that they too had had the same idea. Mabel changed her name to Octavia because she believed that she was the eighth prophet after Southcott.

Mabel now began to preside over religious ceremonies, including a celebration of the Eucharist at which she appeared draped in a Liberty's scarf with an embroidered handkerchief on her head. She held regular meetings with God at 5.30PM each day during which she would take notes and pass on the information to her followers. She believed that everyone should try to make themselves perfect so that they could live eternally on Earth in their own bodies. She appointed twelve female apostles, one from each sign of the Zodiac. Thus if the Libran died, she had to be replaced by another Libran. She lived at 18, Albany Road, Bedford, England and she taught that Christ would return and live in that same house among the apple orchards and that it was really the Garden of Eden. Many detractors held that the notion of Christ living in a large house in suburban Bedford was absurd, to which Panacea Society members replied that the idea of him living as the son of a carpenter in Nazareth is also pretty odd, too.

The Panacea Society is the custodian of 'the Box.' Joanna Southcott placed a number of prophecies in a sealed box before she died in 1814 and demanded that it only be opened in a time of national crisis and by no fewer than twenty-four bishops of the Church of England. It remains sealed.

Clearly many of Mrs Barlthrop's activities were provoked by her frustration at not being allowed to be a 'regular' priest because of her sex. That situation is still largely the case seventy years after her death. Joanna Southcott and the women who came after her believed that many of the World's problems would be overcome by the special qualities that only women possess. Mabel died in 1934 much to the astonishment of her followers who felt that she would live forever. After her death they kept her in her bed awaiting her resurrection but when it did not occur, they reluctantly arranged a regular funeral. The surviving members of the society are awaiting the return of Octavia and Jesus Christ and also the opening of the box. After which time, Octavia and Jesus will set up house at 18, Albany Road and all will be right with the World.

Sorcerer's Apprentices

(First published on 12/10/2008)

As everyone, who is not actually on retreat in a monastery in outer space, will know by now, we are in the midst of a shattering global financial crisis. The best efforts of the World's senior politicians seem to be totally powerless to do anything about it apart from throw gargantuan sums of tax payers' money at it, wring their hands and beg for patience. It is never clear to me how everything in the garden can be lovely on September 10, say, and that the end of the world can be announced on September 11. There is still as many mouths to feed, cars to fill, shirts to be worn and presumably someone has to produce the necessary merchandise. But what do I know? It has been well said that economics is the dismal science and so it seems to be.

During the past few years a several financial scandals have occurred, which might provide a clue as to the origins of our present debacle. In 1995, Nick Leeson, a medium level official working for Barings Bank managed to fool around with certain securities such that he ran up a debt of $1.2 billion and caused the bank to collapse. Barings was England's oldest merchant bank and had financed the Napoleonic wars, the Louisiana Purchase and the construction of the Erie Canal. It was also the Queen's bank! A copper trader working for Sumitoma Corporation in New York managed to gamble heavily in copper futures in 1996 and ran up a debt of $2.6 billion and caused great hardship for his employers. Another rogue trader working for the Allied Irish Bank pulled off a similar stunt in 2002 causing a loss of 691 million euros. In 2007, a trader working for Calyon Inc. in New York lost 250 million euros by playing the markets. This year, Jerome Kerviel lost huge sums of money for Société Générale in Paris in the same way.

All of these vast losses seemed to be caused by relatively low level operatives dabbling in various markets with huge sums of their employer's money without much or any supervision. One is reminded of the Goethe poem about the Sorcerer's Apprentice. An old magician left his young apprentice in charge of the shop while he went off about his business elsewhere. The apprentice was given some work to do but he grew bored and used magic that he did not understand to get a broomstick to fetch water for him. The broom set about the task with gusto and soon it looked as if there would be a flood. The apprentice was unable to stop the broom for he was not very skilled in magic and so he attacked the broom with an axe. He split the broom in two and to his astonishment each half turned into a complete broom and now two brooms were bringing in water. The return of the Sorcerer, in the nick of time, prevented a serious inundation.

Messrs. Leeson, Kerviel et al. seemed to have been playing the role of the apprentice and unfortunately the Sorcerer's return was unduly delayed and the damage was done. The media have been full of stories about over-caffeinated and over-testosteroned traders in red braces playing markets for all they are worth during the vigorous bull market that has been running during the last few years. These traders have earned huge bonuses for their efforts. It seems that several of them were moving money in and out of shares and stocks very quickly: taking positions and liquidating them within minutes, as prices fluctuated. Modern computerised technology permits that kind of activity. The days of investing in shares of sound companies for the long haul appear to be over, at least in the eyes of the red braces brigades.

Global financial markets have been confounded with all kinds of extremely complicated derivatives. These are mixtures of short positions, underfunded mortgages, smoke and mirrors. Even their inventors did not seem to understand them fully. But, all bubbles burst and our financial buccaneers obviously went too far with the results that we have seen during the past few weeks. In the USA, politicians are asking questions of some of the senior executives of the financial institutions about what went wrong. These same politicians were often those who were all in favour of deregulating markets and allowing a culture of anything goes. They seem to be a little miffed to find that these same executives were able to pay themselves fat bonuses shortly before their companies went down the tubes.

Richard Fuld, ex-CEO of the now defunct Lehman Brothers, seems to have got away with nearly $500 million before throwing in the towel. Traders working for this same company were paid Christmas bonuses of between two and five million dollars in 2007. It does appear that some of the activities promoted in the market during the last few years have been mighty close to fraud. But while everyone in the know was making a fortune, who was going to rock the boat? Thus, many people have lost large chunks of their retirement savings. Many others are in danger of losing their houses. Several banks seem to be on the point of collapse. Currencies are falling. Commodities are tanking because in the face of a prolonged recession who needs them to make stuff: there is no one with the money to buy it.

It is all very gloomy.

Economics does live up to its name. It is rather comical to discover that the neocons in the States, who regard any government

337

interference in the play of the markets as the purest evil, are now lining up for government bailouts. Perhaps this fragment of bittersweet comedy is all that there is to laugh at in the mess.

Repent! For the end is nigh

(First published in July 2012)

Years ago it was a common sight on the streets of England to see shabby, doleful men wandering about carrying sandwich boards bearing such exhortations as, "Repent! For the end is nigh!" These men, if approached, would hand out little pamphlets begging the recipients to mend their ways for Jesus was about to return for Judgment Day. More recently, various cult leaders announce that the end of the world is going to arrive any day soon and they lead their flocks up mountains armed, with sandwiches and soft drinks, to await the rapture. Neither the little men with their sandwich boards nor the cult leaders have a very good record at timing these millennial events. The cult leaders and their flocks come shuffling back down the mountain looking rather sheepish and admitting that they have read the tea leaves wrongly and are going back to the drawing board.

Recent news items have prompted these recollections. The first described a large group of peasants, normally resident in the uplands of Peru, who are laying waste to a huge area of the Amazonian rainforest in order to mine for gold. The second noted that the once pristine countryside between Nairobi airport and the city has been turned into a large housing settlement and that the jungle is shrinking. The third pointed out that lemurs, once present in enormous numbers in Madagascar, have recently being placed upon the endangered list. The last reported exhaustion of fish stocks from over fishing.

The Peruvian peasants normally live in poverty in their villages. They have found that a month's work in unofficial goldmines produces more money than they can earn in a year from the land. Their activities cause environmental degradation and the local authorities are trying to drive them away – but these same authorities don't have any other plans for them. Obviously the miners are choosing a practical way to improve their lot. The population in Kenya is increasing rapidly and

Masai herdsmen are finding it more and more difficult to find grazing. Their traditional way of life is threatened. There is a worldwide trend for rural populations to move towards the big cities to seek better circumstances. Several mega-cities are developing which impact adversely on surrounding countryside. Consequently, grazing and wildlife habitat are shrinking causing wild animals such, as lions, to attack the herds. The graziers respond by killing the predators. Lions, formerly plentiful in East Africa, are under threat of extinction. It is said that there are only twenty or thirty-thousand left. Similar pressures exist in Madagascar and the natural habitat of the once plentiful lemurs is being steadily reduced. Their extinction is feared. The demand for seafood is high worldwide. For poor coastal villagers, fish forms a vital part of their diet. They have no other source of food. In the developed world fish adds variety to an already adequate diet. However demand exceeds supply and marine biologists report fears that common edible species are endangered. Modern commercial fishing techniques strip the oceans of fish at an unsustainable rate.

Stories like these are common the world over. Old-growth forests in Borneo are being chopped down to produce wood for furniture. The cleared land is then used to grow palm oil trees. The soils on which the forests stood very quickly become exhausted and then it is not possible even to grow the palm oil. The Amazonian forest is being destroyed to make way for cattle. It is easy to see why all of this destruction of the natural world goes on. Who can tell the Peruvian miners to go home and starve along with their families when they know that modest riches are to be had through illegal gold mining? Who can tell the rural poor to remain on their tiny farms to scratch out a meagre existence for themselves and their families when they suspect that life would be better in the cities? People in Borneo are sitting on a modest fortune if they chop down the forest and sell the trees; consequently it makes good short-term sense to do so.

To return to the theme of the opening paragraph it is unlikely that the end is all that nigh but ways and means have to be found to distribute the earth's bounty more equitably. If illegal forest and land clearing goes on at its present rate serious problems will ensue and it will become harder to produce sufficient food for an increasing population. The land stocks remaining for potential agricultural use are of low quality with poor soils. Unfortunately, mankind doesn't have a very good record of cooperation. Selfish motives and the desire to survive trump other considerations. If those in the developing world seek to ape the standard of living of those in the developed world, the outlook for all will be quite stormy. It is difficult to see how the fortunate will be able to insist that the rest just put up with their lot. Coming to grips with these global problems is very difficult and requires complex, concerted action. The tiny targets that rich countries have set themselves to help the poorer ones are probably insufficient and even these are not being met. A fraction of one percent of GDP for a country like the USA or even Australia does not seem a lot but governments don't seem either willing or able to stump up. Beyond these meagre efforts, there is not a lot of evidence that much effort is going into the solution of the problems facing the poor of the Third World.

Telepathy?
It can't be possible, surely

(First published 01/10/2006)

There was considerable fluttering in the scientific dovecotes at the recent British Association annual fair. (The BA is an important learned society in the UK.) Several mainstream scientists took exception to a paper presented on the subject of telephone telepathy by Dr Rupert Sheldrake. They felt that such stuff had no place at a kosher scientific gathering. They made sufficient noise that the Times newspaper gave them front page cover.

Rupert Sheldrake maintains that people have telepathic powers. He instances the phenomenon whereby people claim to know who is calling them on the phone before they answer it. He decided to test this notion and he set up an experiment in which a number of subjects provided him with a list of four close friends or family members who were likely to call at any time. He contacted each person on these lists and arranged, at random, for one of them to call the subject a few minutes after he contacted them. The subjects could not know who was calling because a member of their list was chosen at random. The subjects were asked to guess who was on the phone when the calls duly arrived. They were photographed and recorded taking the calls. The results were startling. By chance, his subjects should have got the right answer 25% of the time. In fact they were right 45% of the time. 300 hundred subjects were tested and the odds of getting this sort of result by chance in a sample of that size were more than a billion to one against. Dr Sheldrake claims that similar results have been replicated at the University of Amsterdam.

So is there an explanation? Dr Sheldrake claims that the subjects and their nominated callers had to know one another well for it to work. It is not distance dependent and appeared to work as well with callers from the next street as with callers from Australia. He offers two possible theories: quantum entanglement or morphic fields. In quantum theory, two particles of the same system remain entangled even if they move apart. So where two people have interacted, their minds may retain this sort of connection so telepathy may be working through quantum effects in the brain. His preferred suggestion is that members of social groups are linked through 'morphic fields!' According to this idea, if you have been part of a group and you move away from it, you continue to be linked through these morphic fields. He admits that he does not know whether this is a just another way of talking about quantum effects.

Morphic fields remind me somewhat of theories used to explain homeopathy. Practitioners take a drug and dilute it many times so that a dose of the final preparation may not contain one molecule of the original drug. They say that the water, which is left, retains some sort of imprint of the active principle! Great, but all water has come from the sea or from rain and has dissolved an infinite number of chemicals during its existence. Why then do not those extraneous substances also leave an imprint? Homeopathy has always seemed to be stuff and nonsense to me.

But let's to return to telepathy. Perhaps Dr Sheldrake is on to something, but I think his work needs closer scrutiny. A better statistician than I may find a flaw in his methods. Before we conclude that telepathy really happens, other workers must replicate his results over and over. If not, shall we have to conclude that the paranormal is for real? What next: ghosts? astrology? little green men in UFOs? channeling? the Indian rope trick? spiritualism? Where will it all end? Shall we be asked to abandon reason and accept the existence of a creator, a supreme being?

That prospect is too awful to contemplate!

Please let someone debunk the good doctor before things get out of hand!

Australian Sporting Prowess

(First published on 06/09/2013)

Australia is a large country – almost exactly the same area as the continental United States. Its population is small: 23 million and thus on a par with the Netherlands, Belgium and the Czech Republic. One could tuck each of those countries away in Australia's vastness and never find them again.

Sport is very important to the national psyche of Australia. Successes and failures often feature on the front pages of major newspapers, taking priority over wars, natural disasters, famines and other calamities. It is also true that sporting success is valued more highly than artistic and scientific triumphs. A win over the old enemy, England, is much more likely to be reported as headline news than the award of a Nobel Prize for theoretical physics. Yet, Australia punches well above its weight in both sporting, artistic and scientific endeavour.

Some numbers will illustrate this point. Australia has won four hundred and sixty-eight Olympic medals. The UK, with three times the population has won seven hundred and fifty. Australians have secured thirteen Nobel prizes, the UK one hundred and nineteen, the US three hundred and thirty-eight and Jews of all nationalities one hundred and eighty. Australian writers have won three Man Booker prizes for fiction.

Australia has a positive win/loss record against all nations that play test match cricket. It has played seven hundred and forty-four matches so far, won three hundred and fifty of them and tied or drawn two hundred and lost one hundred and ninety-four. It has a positive win/loss record at Rugby Union against all four of the 'home' countries. It has won the Davis cup at tennis twenty-eight times, exceeded only by the USA with thirty-two victories. Australian players, both male and female have performed outstandingly well in the four major tennis slams over the years. These statistics date from the late 1800s when Australia's population measured a scant 3.7 million. By

1999, this had grown to 19 million and has recently passed the 23 million mark. These numbers merely heighten the point that Australia's success has been disproportionate to its population size. One could go on, but the case has been made.

Australian cinema scores highly among discerning reviewers. Australian writers have achieved success that is not necessarily reflected in prizes won. Australia has produced many first class actors, singers and musicians. And yet, sporting glory is what resonates most with the general public. The national broadcaster, ABC Radio National, has good claims to being the best of its type in the World – better even than the much vaunted BBC. Yet, who really cares in Australia? If the ABC is mentioned at all, in the print media, it is because it seems to have a built in, left wing bias.

There is not a single Australian who has not heard of Donald Bradman, Keith Miller, Shane Warne or Dennis Lillie – wonderful cricketers all. Bradman was likely the greatest batsman of all time and Warne, the best bowler. Yet who recognises the name of Howard Florey, the discoverer of penicillin; or Norman Mc Allister Gregg, the discoverer of congenital rubella syndrome; Terence Stamp and Geoffrey Rush outstanding actors; Germaine Greer, pioneer feminist; Elizabeth Blackburn, pioneer scientist in the field of ageing; Fiona Wood, inventor of 'spray-on skin' for the treatment of extensive burns; Fiona Stanley, public health pioneer in Aboriginal health or Lowitja O'Donoghue, Aboriginal advocate? These figures, significant on the World's stage, are not household names in the same way as the 'flannelled fools' of cricket. It is curious what makes a country tick and which of its children are seen and honoured for their achievements. Many Australians talk of the 'tall poppy syndrome', which requires that those who get above themselves be cut down to size. That philosophy does not apply to sporting gods!

There are ominous signs in the wings about continued sporting success. Australia has few tennis players in the top echelon. Also, there are few signs of any emerging greats waiting in the wings. The cricket team, which a mere five years ago was probably the best team the cricketing world had ever seen, suffered a string of retirements. The replacements have proven to be competent but not outstanding and Australia's ranking has fallen considerably. There was once a mine of excellent rugby players in the country, which has dried up. New Zealand, the outstanding rugby playing nation of all time, has a better than two to one record against Australia and has recently notched its 100th win. Australia has produced many Olympic swimming champions in the past but that stream of topnotch performers also appears to have petered out of late.

Australia's fall from sporting glory of late may turn out to be temporary but it does seem that other nations are devoting more and more resources to fostering success in these fields. Tennis, for example, is just about owned by continental European players. Several 'new' countries have taken up rugby and are achieving surprising success. Cricket is still widely played at the club level throughout

Australia but new forms of the game have been devised to satisfy television audiences and these are diluting the panel of players able and willing to play the long form of the game, namely test match cricket. In parts of the World large sums of money are available to players willing to devote themselves to shorter forms and this proves very seductive. Consequently, it becomes harder for the traditional form of the game to prosper and for countries like Australia to rebuild dominant teams.

Australia is blessed with an ideal climate for outdoor sport and so previous successes are unsurprising. The traditions in schools, that emphasised the importance of physical exercise, are waning and the young are beguiled by other avenues to achieving success. It could be that Australian sporting successes will align more closely with that expected from a country of similar population size. Over time, the importance of sport may become less and the loss of a test match series to England, for example, will be seen for what it is: a reverse at a game!

New Year 2015

(First published on 07/01/2015)

The New Year is traditionally a time for reflection. One looks back at the year just past and forward to the one about to start. Incidentally, sociologists tell us that the vast majority of New Year's resolutions are abandoned by lunchtime on January 2. All kinds of feeble articles are published in the press about how to live life henceforward. A particularly daft example popped up in the Toronto Globe and Mail: *'15 steps to better health in 2015'*. Essentially, it boiled down to take regular exercise, don't drink too much, get a good night's sleep and eat your fruit and veggies. Contributions had been sought from professors of nutrition and kinaesthesiology and the like, all to tell us what we already knew.

2014 was a hectic year. Two Malaysian outliners loaded with passengers came to grief. The first disappeared in mysterious circumstances somewhere over the Indian

Ocean. To date, absolutely no trace of it has been found: no luggage, no flotation devices, no bodies, nothing. The other was shot down over eastern Ukraine. Russia blames agents of the Ukrainian government. They, in turn, blame Russia. The ongoing, rumbling discontent in the Middle East has turned into something altogether more sinister. A bunch of Wahhabi fundamentalists, called ISIS, ISIL or Islamic State has proclaimed a caliphate in Iraq and Syria. Syria continues to be beset with a horrible Civil War. Iraq is chaotic with the Shi'ite government not really in control of much of its territory. Islamic state, Al Qaeda, Boko Haram and many other similar organisations across the entire Middle East and much of Muslim Africa are moving closer together. They are coordinating their propaganda, training and murderous activities in order to wreak as much mayhem in their own territories, as well as in the West, as possible. The United States, the United Kingdom and France have set up a coalition to clip the wings of these fundamentalists. Presently, they are using military aircraft and drones to seek out militant bases and bomb them. At the time of writing, it is not certain how successful this strategy is likely to prove.

The situation in Ukraine has become steadily worse during 2014 and gives cause for alarm for the future. Early in 2014, the Russians and their Russian speaking, Ukrainian supporters annexed the Crimean peninsula. Later on, Russia seemed to be helping insurgents in eastern Ukraine and a Civil War is in progress. The West has responded by imposing sanctions on Russia and relations between that country and the West are now as frosty as they have been for many a year. Citizens in the Baltic States and Moldova are frightened that Russia may interfere in their internal affairs. Russia's present leader, Vladimir Putin, is behaving truculently and there is much talk in the media of a new Cold War. Is he trying to re-establish the territorial spread of the defunct Soviet Union? Some of his neighbours are frightened by that possibility. His popularity remains high in Russia in spite of the turbulent economic conditions brought about by western sanctions and a halving of the value of the ruble due to the remarkable fall in oil prices. Should economic conditions in Russia become too unpleasant, Mr Putin's position might come under threat.

An epidemic of Ebola haemorraghic disease broke out in parts of West Africa and continues to rage on. There is no specific cure available. A vaccine against the virus is some way off in the future. Various western health workers have returned to their homes with the illness and a handful have died. Control measures restricting free flow of persons to and from the affected areas have been put into place. The death toll to date is unknown but is likely to be more than 10,000.

So, we start the New Year with legitimate concerns about Islamic occasioned violence in the Middle East and Africa and with fears that this violence can spread to Europe and North America through the agency of terrorists posing as refugees coming to the West or as returning jihadis, young people from western countries who have fought for Islamic State and then gone back home ready and able to cause trouble. Several senior journalists have cautioned against becoming too fearful about the threat posed by Islam. Matthew Parris, of the Times, points out that more people in the United States have died of bee stings than through terrorism since nine-eleven. I feel that attitudes like that are over complacent. Remember the hordes of angry demonstrators in streets all around the world after the publication of Salman Rushdie's book, *The Satanic Verses*, and the similar noise when a few dopey cartoons lampooning Muhammad showed up in Denmark. Angry crowds, weeping and wailing, rending their raiment and gnashing their teeth, turned out in a trice. By contrast, when a bunch of crazed thugs slaughtered one hundred and forty schoolchildren in Pakistan last month, it hardly caused a stir. I have been to lectures by Islamic seers who have maintained that the slaughter of innocents, the beheading of prisoners and the eradication of non-Islamic communities, are not true Islam. When these apologists are asked why Muslims around the world do not publicly and noisily decry such activities carried out in the name of their Prophet and God, they have no very

359

convincing answers. Militant Islam cannot be taken lightly. It is on the march.

Is Ebola a one-off? Are we correct in assuming that it will be controlled and recede into insignificance? Could it be the first such disease to cause widespread concern and harm? Remember, since 1930, we have moved into the antibiotic era and are now emerging from it. It is many years since a new class of antibiotics was developed. Our progress with antivirals has been very slow and hesitant. The control of Ebola-like illnesses is still a matter of using old-fashioned measures: quarantine of contacts, isolation of sufferers and supportive steps. Vaccines have eradicated smallpox and nearly got rid of poliomyelitis. However antivaxers: pampered middle-class Western mothers and crazy African and Pakistani clerics, are putting up stiff resistance to their use and we are once again seeing such illnesses as measles and mumps breaking out. Moreover, vaccines cannot be produced overnight as the present Ebola epidemic demonstrates.

The world community has not reached a consensus about global warming and the possible role that human activities are playing. Commercial interests are keen to extract oil, gas and minerals whether such activities are harmful or not. Climate scientists, geologists, ecologists and oceanographers are nearly unanimous in advocating caution. Capitalists, led by fossil fuel companies, are throwing doubt on the views of the scientists saying that major changes to commercial patterns and activities should not be taken unless there is absolute certainty to be had from the scientific data. Science does not work like that. Hypotheses are drawn up and tested repeatedly. If a hypothesis stands up, it is regarded as being as nearly true as it is possible to determine. Climate change deniers, urged on by powerful commercial interests, seize upon this and suggest that there always remains a scintilla of doubt.

Oddly enough geo-engineering schemes have been mooted as possible answers to the problems posed by climate change. Proposals have included sending vast numbers of mirrors suspended from helium balloons, into low Earth orbit with a view to reflecting the sun's rays back into space. Others have suggested seeding the atmosphere with sulphur dioxide to achieve the same result. The organisations that preach so vehemently against global warming are quite keen on these wild notions for they see that there is a quid to be made. In other words, go on pouring greenhouse gases into the atmosphere and hope that mirrors on balloons will ameliorate the effects. Curious, is it not, to reject the possibility of global warming, but to be so keen to benefit from madcap geo-engineering projects to deal with it!

The fourth major problem facing us at the outset of 2015 is the widespread unemployment of young people. Youth employment in southern Europe is as high as 40 to 50%. In much of the developing world, there are squadrons of idle young men, with nothing to do with little prospect of much turning up in the future. The days, when young men, with little or no schooling, but with brawny arms and broad backs, could support a family from wages derived from digging holes in the ground, are over. The need for manual labour has largely disappeared, for such tasks can be done better by machines. Mechanisation and the widespread introduction of computers have greatly reduced the size of the job pool for grunts. At the same time, 85 individuals are known to have a combined net worth that exceeds that of the poorest 3.5 billion individuals on the planet. Or in other words, one of these squillionaires has as much dosh as four million of the impoverished. Statisticians point out that income disparity is becoming steadily more apparent in the United Kingdom, the United States, Canada and Australia. Average wages render such once routine matters as house purchase more and more unaffordable in major cities like London, New York, Sydney and Vancouver. There have been times in the past when similar circumstances obtained. In 1789, for example, the have-nots stormed the Bastille with unfortunate consequences for the wealthy, most of whom lost their heads. In 1905 and 1917, things turned out badly for the Russian aristocracy, especially for the family of the Tsar. When so few have so much, the masses are inclined to be restless and I wonder if such unrest is on the horizon today.

To sum up, I suggest that the four Horsemen of the Apocalypse are saddling up but have not yet left the stable. These riders classically represent pestilence, war, famine and death. Pestilence is certainly on the cards as new diseases, especially those caused by viruses, emerge. War is already taking place in the Middle East and Africa. It will be worth keeping an eye on a resurgent Russia, Iran and Pakistan, all countries bearing grudges, with two of them possessing nuclear weapons. Famine, brought about by climate change induced crop failures, is likely to occur. The fourth rider, Death, will draw comfort from the themes I have outlined in this essay: disease, global warming, war and the potential for revolution.

There will be those who say I am far too gloomy but I see little evidence that our rulers are facing up to what seem to me very serious problems in the next ten to twenty years. They are all far too keen on scoring petty political points off one another to have time to sort out the hard stuff.

Happy New Year!

SNAFU or FUBB*

(First published on 05/05/2006)

An off duty, Australian, private soldier had died in Iraq of a gunshot wound to the head. His death occurred in barracks with other people in the room. The military/government spin machine immediately went into action and reported that the soldier had accidentally killed himself while cleaning his rifle. This statement given to the press by the Minister of Defence was very soon retracted along with howls of protest from the soldier's family who claimed that he was a gun expert to whom such a mishap could never had happened. Arrangements were then made to have the body sent back to Australia for burial. A coffin arrived in Australia but was found to contain the wrong body. The soldier's family were hastily informed and advised to go back home while the mess was sorted out.

Red faces all round.

(Don't you just love it when leaden tongued ministers of the crown are obliged to defend the indefensible and you can watch them slowly turning in the breeze as they try to obfuscate and lie their way out of the holes they have dug for themselves?)

The dead soldier's body has now been found and returned to Australia. This time, an elaborate, silver coffin, draped with the flag was solemnly carried off the aircraft by an honour party. A funeral with full military honours, attended by the Prime Minister, the Defence Minister, the Chief of the Armed Services and the Army Chief is to be held in the soldier's hometown today.

Since the initial statement about the circumstances of the soldier's death was made and then withdrawn, there has been a lot of speculation about the exact circumstances surrounding the event: suicide, murder, accident or prank. What was an experienced firearms expert doing with a loaded gun in his barracks? The mix up with the coffins has also sparked a good deal of adverse comment. It seems that the body was sent from Iraq to Kuwait and then stored in a private morgue operated by a company owned by mates of Vice-President Dick Cheney. Some flunky employed by the morgue popped the body of another unfortunate into a coffin and dispatched it to Australia where it languishes, still, in the care of the coroner.

Needless to say a number of enquiries are now underway. Coroners and the Homicide squad are looking into the circumstances surrounding the death of the soldier. A full military enquiry is taking place into the muddle in the morgue. The public has been told that these enquiries are likely to take at least six months and so definitive answers to all the questions that arise will not be available until the initial furore has died down. The Prime Minister, John Howard, has apologised to the widow and that must be a first for this Prime Minister, who is not very good at saying sorry.

Everyone will be sad for the soldier's family. What an unfortunate thing to have happened. Their grief will hardly have been made easier to bear by the events that followed.

SNAFU or FUBB?..... you decide.

*SNAFU (situation normal, all fucked up)
*FUBB (fucked up beyond belief)

Chapter Five – Protests

Abortion

(First published in 2012)

For some unfathomable reason, abortion continues to be a hot button topic in the United States and even more so during this general election year. The US is beset with major problems: wars, debt, unemployment, a gridlocked political system, an unprecedented level of partisanship are just a few of them. In spite of these weighty issues, a large amount of political time and energy is devoted to raking over the matter of abortion.

Most of those wielding the rakes are middle aged, white men who presume to know best how women should deal with their own bodies. The hard right of the Republican Party is especially wedded to the notion that abortion should not be allowed under any circumstances. A Republican candidate for the Senate, Todd Akin, has made an ass of himself during an interview, when he opined that women who were 'legitimately raped' would not get pregnant because their bodies had a means of 'shutting the whole thing down'. Such views are beyond belief and it is truly frightening to consider that a human biologist of this calibre could find himself in a position of power after the election.

Back in 1973, the Roe v Wade decision held that *"a woman, with her doctor, could choose abortion in earlier months of pregnancy without legal restriction, and with restrictions in later months, based on the right to privacy."* Unfortunately, this decision provoked the splitting of society into pro-life and pro-choice factions. The hard right continues to attempt to subvert this ruling by any means possible. Ironically, certain of the pro-lifers have not hesitated to gun down surgeons known to carry out abortions and they have often harassed women attending clinics with aggressive picketing. Pro-lifers hold the view that women who have an induced abortion are guilty of murdering their unborn child. The most extreme members of them hold that human life begins at the moment of fertilisation. These same people hold that abortion is wrong under all circumstances and make no exception in cases of rape or incest. They claim that abortion punishes the innocent. They are apparently not bothered about the wrapper in which the foetus comes: the woman!

A great deal of debate has gone on for millennia about the moment when a fertilised ovum can be considered to be a human being. For example, the late Pope John-Paul II held it to be the moment of fertilisation. Other prominent Catholic thinkers and previous holders of the office have postulated different dates. Catholics believe in ensoulment, the moment when the developing foetus is provided with an immortal soul. The timing of this event has been the subject of much argument during the history of the Christian faith with various dates being suggested. Most have settled upon the rather arbitrary number of forty days after conception. It is worth noting the number forty has several mystical connotations in Judaeo-Christian religious dogma. Especially noteworthy is the fact that most of the writers and thinkers on the topic down the ages have been male. Few women's voices have been heard.

Aristotle held that ensoulment took place for male foetuses at forty days but at eighty days for females! Hebrew theology chose forty days for both sexes. Islam suggests sixteen weeks and has a rather ghastly calculus concerning the blood money that should be paid should someone induce an abortion through assaulting the pregnant woman depending on the nature of the aborted foetus: two dinars for a clot; five for flesh and twenty for flesh and bone! This sixteen week timing was chosen by Islamic scholars for they thought that the potential for rational thought existed at that stage of development. It beggars the mind to know how these sages, Greek, Jewish and Islamic, came up with these numbers. What were they smoking?

William H. James, in a Ph.D. thesis submitted to the University of London, held that about one in three of all fertilised and implanted ova are aborted in early pregnancy. If this is true, then it poses a profound ontological problem for the religious who hold that God controls all things. It seems, then, that this God is the greatest abortionist of them all bringing to a premature end of one-third of all pregnancies whether ensouled or not!

Perhaps a thought experiment is in order at this point. Mary is an eighteen-year old girl, who has just been acknowledged as the valedictorian of her school. She intends to be a doctor and has secured a place in university. Her career is all mapped out. Fred is the dolt who lives next door. He has tried to pay court to Mary and been politely told to get lost. He has brooded about this affront to his manhood and considers that the bitch needs to be taught a lesson. One summer's evening, Mary has gone to bed early and is alone in the house. She is fast asleep with scrubbed face, tied back hair and demurely clad in a plain nightshirt and covered from ankles to throat and wrists. Fred manages to break into her room and to rape her. Mary is naturally devastated for she faces huge problems, none of which are of her own making. She may become pregnant. She might have been given one of a number of unpleasant sexually transmitted diseases. She may decide to report the rape with all of the humiliation that that entails: a visit to the local emergency room, a detailed physical examination of her most private parts, an interrogation and a possible, subsequent court appearance in which the most intimate details of her life will be trawled through in public. (In some societies, she could even face death by stoning for having sex out of wedlock.) Her planned career may have been placed out of reach. In short, through no fault of her own, everything has changed.

Mary would be well advised to take the morning-after pill but perhaps to do so would go against her conscience. It might be that she lives in a community whose pharmacists refuse to sell this product on religious grounds, as has happened recently in the UK. Perhaps she does not take this pill and does conceive. She then has to consider whether to carry the pregnancy to term or have an abortion. A community that does not sell the morning-after pill is likely to be one in which getting an abortion would be difficult. If she lived in Ireland, she would be obliged to travel abroad for the procedure. Therapeutic abortion is no stroll in the park. It involves finding a clinic that performs the operation, undergoing surgery and dealing with the psychological issues surrounding the procedure. It is associated with a range of possible complications that can play a significant role in future health. But to force Mary to carry this unwanted, enforced pregnancy to term seems to be cruelty beyond belief. Yet, many pro-lifers would insist that it be done.

The most doctrinaire opponents of abortion believe that their views should be imposed upon all. It is often the case that the most vigorous proponents of a particular religious belief seem to think that their views are or should be universal. More thoughtful folk regard such arrogance as intolerable but are prepared to concede that adherents to such beliefs have the right to insist that their co-believers cleave to the party line. For Catholics or Republican evangelicals to manipulate public policy, such that their doctrines apply to all, is unacceptable. Many bishops are known to use the power of the pulpit ruthlessly on such matters. Other religious leaders demonstrate little reluctance in forcing their views on society as a whole. Medical progress is being hampered by religious reluctance to allow certain kinds of research using human embryos. That sufferers from ghastly diseases could have their plight alleviated through such means does not seem to weigh very heavily in the calculations of the doctrinaire.

Surely, an adult woman has every right to decide whether or not she wishes to carry a pregnancy to term. Undoubtedly, abortion does bring a potential human life to an early end but as we learned above, as many as one-third are spontaneously ended by natural processes. An unwanted pregnancy can be a disaster for an adult woman and most certainly for a thirteen-year old girl impregnated by a male relative or rapist. The calculus around these matters must give weight to the person who is most greatly affected. Generally speaking, the other party to the pregnancy need hardly break stride. For the most part, therapeutic abortions are carried out very early in pregnancy when that which is being terminated amounts to a cluster of cells. Claims are made that some women chose abortion as a means of birth control and perhaps some do. In the main, coming to the decision to end a pregnancy is not taken lightheartedly. As the story of Mary shows, the consequences of unwanted pregnancy can be disastrous and life changing. A woman in this position needs understanding and support and not strident, doctrinaire views being thrust down her throat. She most certainly does not want to undergo a forced, mandated, trans-vaginal ultrasound investigation as is required in some US states. Indeed, in Texas the woman is obliged to view the images and have the findings described.

Men have sought to control the bodies of women through the ages. Where religion is taken especially seriously, this control is more strictly enforced. Religious belief appears to give men the right to exert such control. Perhaps in the West, denial of abortion under any circumstances is the equivalent of the Muslim veil — a means of exerting and clinging on to traditional power over females.

The morning after pill

(Date of first publication not known)

The United States of America is the teenage pregnancy capital of the Western World. This unfortunate fact was commented upon in the recent study: 'US Health in international perspective – Shorter Lives and Poorer Health' produced for the National Academy of Sciences by Stephen H. Woolf and Landon Aron.) Respectable organisations including the American Academy of Paediatrics and the American Medical Association have been working to ensure that the "morning after pill" be available to all women, including those under 16 years. Two years ago the United States Food and Drug Administration (FDA) approved its use without prescription for anyone who wished to purchase it. The Health Secretary, Kathleen Sebelius, overruled the FDA and she, in turn, was supported by President Obama. They felt that women under 17 years of age should only have them on prescription.

Judge Edward Korman of New York State has ruled that all restrictions be dropped, stating 'There is no coherent justification for the views of Ms Sebelius and Mr Obama.' Needless to say, the Administration has announced its intention to appeal the decision. The question will now enter the maw of the tortuous US legal system and be unlikely to emerge for years, so putting the health of some of the most marginalised young women further at risk. The judge described the restrictions as pure politics and that such actions were forbidden where drug approvals were concerned. (In passing, it is worth noting that these pills have been available to women of any age without prescription in Canada for the past eight years.)

The morning after pill has been on the market for several years. Women can use it to prevent pregnancy, if they have had unprotected sex or if a condom has ruptured during sex, providing they take it within 72 to 96 hours following intercourse. The pill contains high doses of female hormones similar to those found in regular contraceptive pills. It works by delaying or preventing ovulation. Thus, spermatozoa deposited in the lower genital tract will not encounter an ovum, while they remain viable, and pregnancy will not result. These pills are not designed for regular contraceptive purposes but more as an emergency measure that women can use when either they have neglected to take precautions or feel that the precautions they may have taken have been insufficient. Such pills are not abortifacients. Hence, they do not kill a developing embryo. That fact alone should comfort the Pro-Life Lobby. They have few side effects apart from occasional nausea and bouts of abnormal bleeding. They are fairly effective: when 1000 women have sexual intercourse without precautions, approximately eighty will become pregnant. The use of the morning after pill reduces that number to twenty.

Birth control is a contentious issue and several religious groups inveigh against its use, especially the Catholics. Their objections seem to be based on nothing other than a declaration that using birth control is contrary to their beliefs and so should not be available to anyone. This is an intolerably arrogant position. It is one thing to insist that members of a particular tribe toe the party line but quite another to insist that such views be imposed universally. In the States, members of the Religious Right along with Catholics and Southern Baptists seem to harbour fears about female sexuality. The notion that women want to control their bodies and decide when and if they wish to have children is anathema to them. The arguments against the free, untrammelled availability of the morning after pill are flimsy and based on fears that it would lead to promiscuity — for which there is no evidence — as well as their overarching distaste for contraception.

Teenage pregnancy is a curse for it results in babies giving birth to babies. Its highest incidence is among those at the bottom of the socio-economic heap. The denizens of this group are the least well educated people in the United States. There is a good deal of evidence suggesting that young single mothers give birth to children, who then go on to repeat the cycle. Hence a ghastly treadmill of poverty and ignorance results. Public health is low on the list of health priorities in the United States and any simple measure that can contribute positively towards ending or, at least, controlling a scourge, is to be welcomed. Pious appeals encouraging chastity before marriage do not seem to have had much effect. Poor, ignorant, young women who have sufficient initiative to want to avoid pregnancy should be encouraged to adopt simple measures that could help them. Sound contraceptive advice is a start and where that might have failed, the morning after pill seems like a very handy backup device. Asking a poor, marginalised, 15 year old to joust with the United States medical system, to obtain these pills on prescription, is to place great barriers in her way. Raising the cash to buy them at the local pharmacy will be hard enough. For President Obama's administration to get in the way of their provision for political reasons, aimed at pandering to certain religious and conservative groups, is shameful. No sops offered to such groups will ever satisfy them for they are motivated by faith and gut reactions, not reason.

Solitary

(First published on 11/10/2013)

A poor wretch has just been released from jail where he spent forty-one years in solitary confinement. Yes, that's right, forty-one years. How long is that? The smart answer is forty-one years or two thousand, one hundred and thirty-two weeks or four hundred and ninety-two months but metaphor makes the torment this man endured more vivid. Imagine a young woman obtaining her medical degree on her twenty-fourth birthday, the very day the poor wretch was entombed. Forty-one years later she would reach her sixty-fifth birthday and be ready to retire after a long and satisfying career. During all of that time, the prisoner would have been in solitary. Ten US presidents would have come and gone: his spell would have begun during the reign of Richard Nixon and endured through those of Gerald Ford, Jimmy Carter, Ronald Reagan, George Bush, Bill Clinton, George W. Bush and into that of Barack Obama. He would have been confined during ten Olympiads. The Summer Games would have floated from Montreal to Moscow, Los Angeles, Seoul, Barcelona, Atlanta, Sydney, Athens, Beijing and London and during all of that time our hero would have been locked up in his cell and allowed out to shower and exercise for one hour a day. By the way, his cell measured nine by six feet or fifty-four square feet. A full size snooker table covers seventy-two square feet. So, can one imagine a space about the same size as a handicap public lavatory stall and then consider spending forty-one years locked up inside and allowed out for one hour per day?

Where did this take place: North Korea, Iran, Saudi Arabia or some African hellhole? No! Right in the middle of the USA for Angola Jail is situated in Louisiana. In the country, that considers itself to be the 'light on the hill' and the 'home of the free', it is possible to find oneself banged up for more than half a lifetime in solitary. The poor wretch, the subject of this piece, Herman Wallace, a black man, entered Angola Jail in 1972 convicted of armed robbery. His accomplice Albert Woodfox was incarcerated at the same time. Along with Robert King, they formed a chapter of the Black

Panthers. During a subsequent prison riot, a guard was stabbed to death and the three of them were convicted of murder and were put into solitary confinement. They became known as the Angola Three. King was released a few years ago. Knox remains in jail. It is worth noting that at the time of the riot, all of the inmates in Angola were black and the guards all white.

Wallace was released last week because District Court Judge, Brian Jackson, ruled that he had not had a fair trial. The evidence that the Angola Three were responsible for the death of the guard is now regarded as very shaky. On the day that the judge made his ruling, his instructions arrived at the jail after the prison governor had gone home for his tea. He said that Wallace could wait until the next day to be let out. The judge, learning of this, told the governor to get his ass in gear and go straight back to the prison and finish the necessary paperwork to ensure the immediate release of the prisoner. Three days after his release, he died among his friends in New Orleans of liver cancer. His dying words are recorded as being, 'I am free, I am free, I am free.'

Immediately after his release, East Baton Rouge DA, Hillar Moore, challenged the judge's ruling and tried to have Wallace returned to jail.

It is hard to imagine any system of justice that could inflict such a punishment upon any human being regardless of the crime. Wallace managed somehow to retain his sanity by exercising using dumbbells made out of newspaper. He was something of a newshound and he kept abreast of current affairs. It is also hard to imagine what malign spirit would motivate the DA to cause him to challenge the ruling and attempt to keep a dying man in jail. Perhaps he considered that 41 years in solitary was not sufficient to expiate the crime of stabbing a white guy.

The US criminal justice system is one of few in the Western World that allows the death penalty. This archaic punishment is declining in frequency in many states of the Union but it is still enthusiastically embraced in the South, especially in Texas. In recent years, execution by means of hanging, the electric chair, firing squad and the gas chamber have fallen out of favour, to be replaced by lethal injection. There are several challenges percolating through the courts suggesting that the use of injections is a cruel and unusual punishment. A more practical problem that has emerged is that the drugs used for the process are harder and harder to purchase and several states have run out of stock. Foreign countries, in which they are made, have embargoes on their export to the States for fear that they will be used in executions. One state, realising that its stocks of poison were approaching their 'use by date' and that replacements would be impossible to find, tried to speed up the executions of those on death row. One wonders if a condemned man, on learning that the drugs that were to be used to end his life were a day or two past their 'best before date', would be concerned overmuch. Doubtless, health and safety reasons would be cited to prevent their use for they could be deemed unsafe!

A little research reveals that it is not uncommon for condemned prisoners to stay on death row for decades while the legal processes of appeals run their course. Gary Alvord spent forty years awaiting execution but died of natural causes before the State could kill him. He suffered from schizophrenia. Doctors refused to treat him citing ethical issues about treating a man so that he could be made healthy enough to be executed. During the time he was on the row, seventy-five other inmates were put to death. In general, those condemned to death can expect to languish on death row for at least ten years, while the many layered appeals process is exhausted. Some find the strain of waiting around to be put to death too awful and they decline to make further appeals. In a sense, they commit assisted suicide. It is theoretically possible to make a case for executing criminals for certain acts. The bounds of theory are stretched well past breaking point when the state incarcerates someone for a decade or two before dragging him out of his cell and killing him. Yet such is the plight of many sentenced to death in the USA.

The USA keeps some pretty unsavoury company with those countries that continue to use the death penalty. They include Afghanistan, North Korea, China, Saudi Arabia, Libya, Yemen and Zimbabwe. About one hundred and forty countries have abolished its use but about sixty still have it on the books, but in the majority of these, it has either not been used for years or is only employed very infrequently. There are over two million people locked up in US jails. Black people are greatly over represented among their ranks. The US bangs up a higher proportion of its citizenry than comparable countries. In spite of the harshness of the system, crime rates are certainly as high as similar, developed nations.

It is difficult to understand how this state of affairs is allowed to persist and it is one more quirk that distinguishes America from the rest of the developed world. It is highly unlikely that any politician would go far were he or she to run on an anti-capital punishment ticket. Slowly but surely, the death penalty is carried out less and less frequently and it is inevitable that it will eventually fall into disuse. While it does so, many, many poor wretches will rot in tiny cells on death row while the lawyers wrangle over their cases.

It is even more difficult to comprehend that the case of Herman Wallace and so many others, kept alive in tiny cells for years on end, are contemporary. They are happening in the twenty-first century in the Western World and not in some godforsaken satrapy in the twelfth.

Sex segregation
in United Kingdom universities

(First published on 13/12/2013)

Universities UK (UUK) has recently ruled that guest lecturers may demand to have their audiences segregated by sex if their religious beliefs prevent them from speaking to a mixed audience. UUK has ruled that such requests should be entertained providing the women's section is alongside the men's and not at the back of the hall. In this way, 'Both sexes are equally discriminated against'. Their stated reason for this extraordinary ruling is that they faced a 'legal minefield' if they did not oblige universities to accommodate the wishes of certain clerics, for to do otherwise would be to limit the free speech of the lecturer.

This remarkable claptrap obliged this writer to send the following missive to the Editor of Newsline, the house organ of the National Secular Society:

"Sir,

A creeping insanity seems to be affecting the UK. Firstly we have the nonsense of segregated seating at universities and then the new anti-annoyance bill, presently making its way through Parliament.

Surely, if Sheikh Muhammad bin Ali al Whotist or the Reverend Fred Bloggs have the breadth of knowledge and intellect to make it worthwhile to get them along to address a university debating society, then may we not expect them to possess sufficient savoir faire to enable them to understand and tolerate arrangements that perhaps are not entirely of their choosing? They ought to be able and willing to overlook such matters. If such an accommodation is too hard, then they are so blinkered as not to be worth listening to.

For Universities UK to go banging on about 'facing complex balances between promoting free speech and equality and discrimination' is sheer rubbish. Segregated seating in universities at the behest of some religious nutter is not the way matters are conducted. The only thing that prevents such persons from expressing themselves at a traditional public gathering is their own blinkered worldview.

Government moves to frame legislation to prevent annoying behaviour are likewise sheer lunacy.

Burkas, loud pop music, drunken, vomiting youths downtown at night, shoddy English and cultural relativism annoy the hell out of me, yet I do not want or expect legislation to prevent my being irritated by such things. I am prepared to look the other way and so should everyone else.

Craven capitulation to every whim or request from special interest groups coupled with the desire to avoid the even the slightest irritation to all, renders society gutless and lacking any self-respect. Is everyone now so thin skinned and fearful that great effort must be made to ensure that no one be offended about anything whatsoever and that everything must be done to accommodate all religious whims? Has everything to be viewed through the prism of cultural cohesion and inclusion? May no one be told that their demands are unreasonable and will not be met? Is the traditional, home culture worth nothing? Yours etc....,"

It is truly remarkable that authorities have become so frightened of upsetting religious groups that they are prepared to infringe the rights of everyone else. The truculent stance taken by Islamic groups, in particular, appears to be civilized society, especially in the United Kingdom. Criticism of Islam is held to be racist, when any schoolboy knows that Islam is not a race. In its most primitive form, it is a pernicious worldview that has no place in any society claiming, to be part of the civilized world.

Administrative lunacy in Academia

(First published on 17/01/2014)

Administrators of UK universities have egg all over their faces and worse still, they applied it themselves. In their attempts to be all things to all people and to prize inclusiveness, multiculturalism and relativism above all else they have made fools of themselves and have 'let slip the dogs of Law.' (Apologies to the Bard)

Early in September, the authorities at the London School of Economics (LSE) demanded that a pair of students change their 'Jesus and Mo' tee shirts on the grounds that these could cause offence to Christians and Muslims. The students concerned were taking part in the 'Froshers' Fair, organised each year as part of the orientation process. They were given the choice: remove the tee shirts or leave the fair. At first they refused; security guards were summoned and the hapless students were more or less frog marched off the premises. In more enlightened times, LSE was the home of radicals of all stripes. Its alumni are to be found in all corners of the World. Today, however, enlightenment is a thing of the past and has been replaced with the throttling dictates of political correctness: say or do nothing to anyone that could be construed as judgmental in the slightest degree. Better still, white males should stay mum for they are deemed to be possessed by unconscious, inherent, institutionalized racism.

The students concerned appealed to the School authorities and after exhaustive enquiries, the Director, Professor Craig Calhoun, issued a halfhearted apology to them pleading that the School staff, on the day of the fair, faced difficult circumstances!

In October 2012, Reading University managed to get itself into a similar pickle. Students running the stall representing the University Students Union Atheist Society displayed a pineapple they named Muhammad. Security staff were told to have this piece of fruit removed for it was causing offence. The students were threatened with bodily removal if they did not comply with the request. They took away their pineapple and returned later having renamed it Jesus. They maintained that they wished to provoke general discussions about religion and faith.

More recently, some students at another UK university invited a prominent cleric to address a society belonging to the Students Union. He agreed to speak if he could be assured that the sexes in the audience would be segregated. He explained that his religious sentiments prevented him from addressing an audience in which women and men were mingled freely. The students referred the matter to their school, which in turn passed the matter on to Universities UK (UUK), the body that represents the administrators of all universities in Britain. UUK consulted human rights lawyers and spent a good deal of time and effort before coming to a decision on the matter, which deemed that requests of this sort should be acceded to, lest the freedom of speech of invited lecturers be seen to be impeded. In other words, UUK were happy to go along with the idea that segregated seating by sex was entirely reasonable along as the seating allowed men to sit on one side of the room and woman on the other for in that way, 'Neither sex could be considered to be unduly disadvantaged compared to the other.' They did, however draw the line at seating arrangements that would put the men up front and the women at the back.

It seemed that UUK were more eager to allow some cleric to dictate the arrangements for his talk on religious grounds than to follow usual UK customs. They held that his self-imposed inability to give his talk, because his religious and cultural sensitivities might be offended, to be tantamount to him being muzzled. No weight was given to the historic struggles women have gone through to ensure that men and women be treated equally and that discrimination on grounds of race, sex, religion, sexual orientation and colour are no longer regarded as acceptable in the UK. The religious sensibilities of the invited speaker appeared, in their original view, to trump all other considerations. It is hardly surprising that this nonsense hit the mainstream media. Even the Prime Minister, David Cameron, was drawn into the debate. UUK evidently thought better of their position, for after a lot of bafflegab, they decided that their views were misguided and that segregation on any grounds would not be acceptable in British universities. They issued a statement to that effect.

This kind of madness has spread across the water to Canada. Just this week, the press has reported the case of a student of York University who has refused to join in class discussions because he would be obliged to interact with female students. He asked the professor running the course, Paul Grayson, for permission to absent himself. It was denied. The course was mostly presented on-line but required that students attend one face-to-face session at the university. The request for 'religious accommodation' percolated up to the Dean of the Faculty of Arts, who disagreed with Grayson and ordered him to accede to the student's wishes. Grayson declined because he did not wish to be seen as an accessory to sexism. Grayson's stance left him open to disciplinary proceedings but he firmly held his ground. This affair ultimately defused itself for the student decided to swallow his objections to working with women and to attend the required meeting. Perhaps he saw a big, fat zero looming up. The Dean of the Faculty of Arts and the other university administrators maintained that they did not reach their decisions lightly and that they consulted their lawyers and the Ontario Human rights policy manual.

All of these incidents, both in the UK and Canada, have things in common. Mainly they show university administrators to be terrified of upsetting the Muslim community and the lengths they are prepared to go in order to avoid the public mayhem, that can and does arise, when that community feels that its icons or dictates have been traduced in the smallest way. Naturally, they are unwilling to admit to this terror and prefer to mask their decision making processes behind lawyerly arguments around civil rights legislation and policies; in other words, pharisaical bullshit.

Maybe, there are good reasons for this caution. (Or should that be cowardice?) Muslim fundamentalists decry most features of the modern world but are remarkably adept in whipping up ferment using twenty-first century techniques: mobile phones, Twitter, Facebook and so on. It did not take long before the furore over a few inept cartoons, published in Denmark a few years ago, to result in demonstrations all round the Globe along with damage to public property. Similarly, a great fuss was orchestrated over Geert Wilders' movie 'Fitna'. Salman Rushdie's book, 'Satanic Verses' caused immense hoo-ha and resulted in him going into hiding for a decade for fear of being slaughtered by some outraged believer.

Western societies have been quite supine in the face of Islamic provocation. Large numbers of neo-Nazi thugs did not go round desecrating mosques after Gunner Lee Rigby had his head cut off in broad daylight in Woolwich a few months ago. Posses of vigilantes have not been to Tower Hamlets to duff up young Muslims who have proclaimed it to be a 'Muslim area' and thus subject to Sharia law. The backlash in the UK after the July'07 London Transport Bombings was muted. Young troublemakers have been quick to learn that they can get away with all manner of provocation as long as they disguise their actions in the cloak of religious sensibilities. The intellectual elites of much of the West are determined to be seen as entirely non-judgmental, inclusive and tolerant about all matters involving non-natives and non-Caucasians. A sort of self-loathing obtains in such circles over the perceived sins of empire and colonialism. Consequently they advocate collusion and cooperation with demands based on religion or cultural custom regardless of how outrageous and out of tune with local mores they may be.

One would hope and expect universities to be seats of enlightenment and places where doctrines and beliefs, handed down from late antiquity in very sketchy ways, would be analysed, parsed and questioned critically; places where the weak historiography surrounding Jesus of Nazareth and the Koran would be debated and demonstrated;

institutions in which faith, defined by Boghossian*, as 'belief without evidence' or 'pretending to know things you don't know', would be exposed as groundless. It is distressing to think that special favour is granted to students demanding preferred treatment because of some belief or other, especially when such beliefs run counter to the prevailing customs and fashions of the day. Discrimination on grounds of sex, race, colour and sexual orientation is now considered to be entirely out of order in Western countries. Apparently, however, it can be allowed when someone's religiously inspired disinclination to work with blacks, Asians, women or gays arises because of what is said to have been written one or two thousand years ago in some dusty collection of unsupported myths.

*'A manual for creating atheists' by Peter Boghossian, Pitchstone Publishing, November 2013.

Management

(First published on 22/11/2014)

A nasty disease stalks the Western World. It is called management and it comes in two strains, equally dangerous and enervating. The version spread by the Harvard Business School is the touchy feely one and it holds that efforts should be directed to the common good and not solely to the bottom line. That which comes from the Chicago Business School is rough and tough and wants markets to be given their head to do as they wish. It sounds as if the Harvard type is preferable. Do not be taken in: both are pernicious.

Approach any institution: commercial, governmental, educational or health related and you will be exposed to management. The fundamental tenet of the disease is that all are customers and that all transactions, regardless of place and type are the same. So, someone who goes to a hospital is a customer. A university student is a customer. A person applying for a new passport is also a customer

407

as is the dope, who is so silly as to ring up his bank, power supplier, car dealership or what you will. All are customers. Gone are notions about clients, patients, pupils, students or citizens needing help from a government agency. Customer-hood – or should that be customer-ship? – is the universal fate of us all. Organisations have stuff to sell and we poor suckers want to buy it. Q.E.D

Someone, who goes to the doctor, can be presumed to have something the matter and is suffering. The word patient is derived from roots meaning one who suffers. Going to the passport office or to the city hall for a dog license or permit to extend ones premises automatically puts one in the category of citizen approaching the appropriate state agency. Certainly a fee may be levied but is the citizen a mere customer? A young person attending a university or an even younger one going to school is a student or pupil. Such persons are going to school for instruction. They may also pay fees for tuition, but does that put them in the same position as one who goes to the grocer for a packet of tea or a pat of butter – mere customers? English is a rich language with many words having similar but not identical meanings. A customer is one who pays for a service or commodity. A client is one who attends a professional in order to gain advice or some specialised service. As previously mentioned, patients are sufferers from some sort of pathology and seeking remedies. To lump all into the one basket bastardises a subtle and marvellous language. To behave in that way may satisfy those who firmly believe that Jack is as good as his master and that to put a medical consultation, for example, on a higher pedestal than the sale of a jar of marmalade, is elitism. They are entitled to their view but it only satisfies those who seek the lowest common denominator in all things. Management gurus like to think that there is no essential difference between a neurological consultation, advice on drawing up a will, engaging the services of a prostitute or buying shoes. I believe that they are wrong but at the same time do not hold that the neurosurgeon is an inherently superior being to the lawyer, the tart or the shopkeeper.

In recent years, institutions of all sorts have made it more and more difficult for the public to engage directly with them. Try telephoning the bank. You will almost certainly encounter a machine that will tell you that your call is important to them but that call volumes are higher than normal and so it will take longer to speak to someone. Your ears will then be blasted with formless noise masquerading as music, interrupted frequently by recorded voices telling you that you progressing up the queue but that all the 'consultants' are busy assisting other suckers – sorry, customers. When you finally get through, you will be spoken to by Melanie, who has been to smiley-voice school and who speaks nineteen to the dozen. She will remind you that the call is being recorded for training purposes and to assure quality of service. If you tell her to turn off the recording you will learn that she can't. During the subsequent encounter, you will form the strict impression that Melanie is reading from a prepared script. She will ask you standard questions and immediately assume that she has the right to address you by your first name. If you reprove her for her presumption, she will fail to understand what you are on about. She may have the answers to your queries but it is more likely that she won't and will have to place you on hold. While you are in telephonic limbo, the 'music' will begin to play again. She may reappear, or Elizabeth, an older and wiser person, comes on the line. Incidentally, all of these persons have inflated titles. They include consultant, sales associate, personal financial adviser, front desk ambassador, or even aisle associate (this last refers to a store clerk or shop assistant.) The management imagination knows no bounds when drawing up fancy job descriptors. An unspoken corollary to title inflation is that the fancier the title the lower the pay and qualifications. No one must tolerate being called a clerk. Shop assistant, dustman and bank clerk are deemed to be demeaning titles that somehow damage the self-esteem of the person occupying such positions, and who will feel elevated by having some meaningless handle attached to his or her role. At the end of the encounter, Melanie will ask you if there is anything else she can do for you today and when being told no, will thank you for choosing Blogs Bank or whatever. The similarity of these encounters is quite sinister and I can attest to there being just about no difference when you phone a large enterprise in Canada, Australia or the UK. The gospel according to management is truly catholic.

It is evident that management gurus have determined that having batteries of people lined up to field telephone calls is harmful to the bottom line and so make communication by phone as onerous as possible. The preferred means of communication is email and the reasons for that are obvious. Most people are unable to express themselves in writing, and so rather than expose themselves to institutions, such as banks, as being functionally illiterate, choose not to take the transaction further. It is much cheaper to have a small posse of people fated to read emails and to provide standard answers than it is to employ squadrons of telephonists.

Another universal feature of management philosophy is the posting of silly mission statements on the walls of institutions. Go to the local emergency room and you will learn that their mission is to respect the human rights, the religious freedoms, and the inherent dignity of all who cross the threshold, et cetera, et cetera. Might something about provision of timely medical treatment be tacked on as an afterthought? Surely, the role of the emergency department is so blindingly obvious that a long, flowery mission statement is superfluous. Emergency departments are set up to treat the sick who rock up to the front door! End of! Similar stuff is posted on the walls of the fire stations, banks, police stations – they are universal. Fire stations exist to house trained people who go and put out fires when required, as well as releasing little boys who have trapped their heads in railings. Management philosophy deems that manifold statements of the bleeding obvious are somehow helpful.

Much more sinister is the way that management has become a larger element in the running of institutions. The number of managers seems to rise in indirect proportion to that of the front line staff. In short, the more managers, the fewer doctors and nurses, for example. More managers mean more paperwork, more meetings, more lost time for useful activities, slower decisions and greater attention to budgetary concerns. How often does one learn that budgetary considerations mandate the firing of several nurses and the closing of several beds? How often does one read that the finance department is to be closed or that some other arm of the bureaucracy has been told to get on their bikes and go?

Management techniques involve setting unrealistic targets and then obsessive checking to see that they are met, often at the expense of providing really good service. In the UK, the National Health Service, an organisation reeking of management, seeks to ensure that no one waits for longer than four hours in an emergency department before being seen and sorted. All kinds of stratagems are employed to meet this target, often at the expense of dealing properly with the actual problem. Public school systems strive hard to ensure that pupils pass state exams rather than ensuring that they are well educated.

This piece is slanted towards the health sphere for that is the one I have most knowledge of but I have learned that the observations made are applicable to institutions like banks and the post office. Banks close branches with gay abandon and oblige customers to do their banking on-line. Service provision for the public takes second place to those of convenience and profit of the institution.

I hold that persons who have actual training in health sciences are ideally placed to be in charge of health based organisations. Likewise large manufacturers of machinery would do well to have engineers among the higher echelons of the organisation. Schools and universities need those, who understand the nuances of the education process, to be in charge. Undoubtedly, professional managers have a role to fill but should that be the most important one? Should management philosophy trump all others? Don't practitioners of various disciplines deserve to be top dog in the appropriate institution? Is the holder of the MBA necessarily the best person to run the show regardless of the nature of the said show? Those in charge of the business schools of Harvard and Chicago would say that they are.

To conclude, a couple of historical views of management can throw light on the phenomenon. Antoine de Saint-Exupéry, author, pioneer aviator, minor aristocrat and snob extraordinaire, placed men into one of three classes. There were les hommes, les paysans and les fonctionnaires. (Men, peasants and functionaries) He admired les paysans as being solid, men of the soil who performed worthwhile tasks. He placed himself into the class of les hommes: masters of the universe, those in charge, leaders. He had only the greatest scorn for les fonctionnaires, whom he saw as little people running round with clip boards and plastic shirt pocket protectors. Such people, according to him, were bean counters, paper clip stewards – in short managers. The other figure I wish to cite is altogether more sinister, namely Adolph Eichmann. Nazi philosophy deemed that all Jews were a malignant poison that was rotting away the body of Germany and Europe. The Nazi ruling élite decided that the remedy was to exterminate them and while they were at it, to get rid of homosexuals and Gypsies as well. This task was placed in the able hands of the supremely managerial Eichmann. He set about the job with relish and was able to see the humans he had to dispose of as mere annoying items. He had them counted and isolated. He then arranged for trains to collect them and cart them off to death camps where they were gassed and burnt. Tragically, he made an awfully good job of his task.

Eichmann employed managerial techniques and was able to see the Jews, homosexuals and Gypsies as garbage he had to dispose of, not fellow human beings. Pointing out this ghastly episode in human history is in no way meant to suggest that all managers are homicidal maniacs, devoid of any feelings but to illustrate the way in which their techniques tend to sacrifice everything to the bottom line and thereby to commodify that and those, that have to be managed. So, when bank branches have to be closed down, the convenience of people living in smaller centres is of less importance than the shareholder dividends that will be engrossed through efficiencies. Sticking rigidly to the local health service budget is placed on a higher footing than providing a truly comprehensive health care system. In short, there is a coldness implicit in management methods which results in the welfare of the organisation being regarded as more important than that of those it is meant to serve.

You atheists
are just another bunch of
fundamentalists!

(First published on 03/08/2008)

Several authors and thinkers have recently produced books attacking religious faith. Notable among these have been Richard Dawkins, Sam Harris and Christopher Hitchens. Their books must have struck a chord because critics and apologists for religion have declared that atheist writers have just as big an axe to grind as do religious fundamentalists. In other words, some kind of equivalence has been shown between those who believe in unreason and fairy stories and those who do not. According to the faithful, an omnipotent, omniscient being called, variously, Allah, Yahweh or God caused the universe to come into being a few thousand years ago over the course of six days. Having brought about creation, this being seems to have devoted an inordinate amount of attention to the activities of those who live in what is now called the

Middle East. He adopted one little tribe called the Hebrews and told them that they were his chosen people. To them he gave the Bible, a sort of handbook for life and behaviour. He then gave the Muslims the Koran, a similar set of rules. Both books are held to be the true word of Yahweh, Allah or God. The Christians who turned up between these two revelations are an offshoot of the Jews and they adopted the Bible and added a few chapters to it.

During the next several millennia, various clerics have exhaustively parsed these books and have added countless pages of commentary and supplementary rules covering every aspect of human behaviour in minute detail: from what foods are permitted, what clothes to wear, regulations concerning butchery, menstruation, and capital punishment, to mention just a few All three groups believe that this extraordinarily powerful being takes an active interest in their thoughts and deeds and keeps exhaustive records that are consulted after the death of any person, whose eternal fate is then determined according to how well or badly he or she has kept to the rules laid down in the holy books and the additions of the clerics. Jews, Muslims and Christians live not for this world but for the next and they claim to be doing their level best to attract favourable notice from him upstairs.

It is worth mentioning that the religious have never been able to articulate very clearly what they expect of the after life. One or two primitives have suggested that the chosen will be able to gawp at the wicked, boiling in everlasting flames. The Muslim after world sounds like a celestial knocking shop in which martyrs will spend eternity rogering virgins. No word of how women who are not virgins will spend their time or what non-martyrs will get up to. For Christians, matters are not so simple. They claim that God sent his son to them as Jesus of Nazareth. He was born to Mary, a virgin. (The obsession with virginity is a recurring theme with religious groups.) Apparently, his conception was brought about by the Holy Ghost and not by the usual means of mere sexual intercourse. Jesus lived a short and hectic life spent casting out devils, walking on water, turning water into wine, feeding multitudes with a few fish and pieces of bread, curing the sick, raising people from the dead and preaching. This remarkable story goes on to tell us that he was executed by the Roman authorities that ruled Jerusalem at the time. It also holds that after his death, he was entombed but escaped from his sepulchre a day or so later and continued to wander about the countryside until his divine father took him directly to heaven. During the time between his resurrection and his bodily assumption into heaven he bumped into a few folk and passed the time of day with them.

The historicity of this figure, Jesus, is really quite scanty and depends upon four accounts written well after his death and some very cursory references by a couple of contemporary historians. So, it is quite possible that he never existed and that existing accounts represent amalgamated stories about any one of a number of charismatic preachers roaming around the Holy Land at the time. Jews acknowledge the existence of Jesus but deny that he was their Messiah, the long hoped for prophet who would restore them to their former glory. Muslims regard him as a prophet and their writings accord him considerable respect. However, they claim that Muhammad, who followed about six hundred years later, was the true prophet of God and that those who hope for salvation really need to come on board and accept this. They behave quite savagely towards any members of their faith who abandon Mohammed for Jesus. They are delighted if people move in the opposite direction.

Patently, what is written above is greatly abbreviated and rather flippant but it is hard to take any of this stuff very seriously. None of us have encountered dead people arising from the tomb – unless they were not really dead. Virgin birth or parthenogenesis is not something that happens to higher orders of the animal kingdom although it is common enough among some invertebrates. Walking on water is not something that the laws of physics permit. Casting out devils and healing the sick through the laying on of hands is more difficult to refute but there are many instances of sick folk recovering inexplicably after profound emotional experiences. Such events hardly qualify as miracles. Any run of the mill general practitioner can retail scores of recoveries from minor illness that just happened without any specific treatment. Angels do not dictate long and complex books to illiterate traders nor do they hide in burning bushes and offer engraved stone tablets to holy men. Tales about angels turning up in caves in Upper New York State and handing stainless steel tablets over to unknown con men also should be taken with a large grain of salt.

To postulate a god as a creator merely replaces one mystery with another. It is, indeed, very difficult to conceive of how the universe as we know it came to be. Several scientists have offered plausible explanations and have developed testable theories about how this could have occurred. These theories are under constant revision and refinement. Darwin's theory of evolution is also testable and has provided a very acceptable account of how life comes to be as it is. Of course, the truly faithful require none of this. For them it is enough to say that God did it. Imagine what an inexplicable being such a god must be. To settle for a god hypotheses answers merely substitutes one mystery with another. It also fails to deal with the problem of how God came to be.

A truly religious Jew, Christian or Muslim thinks that the holy books are the word of God and contain all the answers. They also give accounts of truly bizarre events that are not open to observation or replication. The Christian believes that the shadowy figure of Jesus was the son of God and that he died, rose again and went to heaven to save our souls. Implicit in this belief is that we all possess a soul, whatever that might be.

The atheist maintains that this is all nonsense and that there is absolutely no evidence that any such things ever did or could occur. The atheist asks for evidence. The atheist also affirms that if the Christian, Muslim, Hindu or any other religious person can show him evidence that such tricks ever could or did take place then it would be necessary to review matters and take another position. That, surely, is hardly a fundamentalist position. It is one of reasonableness and openness. In short, the faithful present a series of extremely improbable events and ideas and expect others to accept them hook line and sinker with no more justification than claims that they are carrying out God's commands. That is fundamentalism writ large. Atheists ask to be shown the evidence before changing their position. But they are quite willing to do so if it seems to be reasonable to rethink matters. They do not regard the religious faithful as blasphemers or apostates and worthy of earthly and eternal punishment. Atheists conclude that believers are deluded because they unquestioningly believe in the incredible.

Fundamentalism?

Hardly.

Religion: boon or curse

(Publication date not known)

It is widely accepted that attendance in churches across much of the western world is in terminal decline. Some of the so-called happy-clappy churches buck the trend but in the mainstream sects, numbers are dwindling rapidly and especially so among the young. Similarly, many nominal Catholics are no longer prepared to follow several of the Church's doctrines. For example, reproductive rates among Italian women are the lowest in Europe and lower than that necessary to sustain the population. The use of birth control in Italy must be universal unless there has been a sudden infliction of national barrenness. In the United Kingdom many churches have been put into mothballs while alternative uses for them are found. Try going to Evensong on a Sunday in the average village church. Such services, once routine, have disappeared.

The decay of religious practice is not matched in the Islamic world. Religious observance is still the norm. However, even here there are straws in the wind that suggest that all is not well. The recent Egyptian revolution has been followed by an election for president. Two candidates were available for the run-off: a party hack representing the ancien régime and someone from the Muslim Brotherhood. Many educated people in the large cities were dismayed to realise that they could end up under the control of a conservative, theocratic régime. In the Muslim heartlands, Saudi Arabia, Iran, Iraq and Yemen, Islam is doing very well and woe betide anyone who chooses to question it.

During the past half century a large, Islamic diaspora has established itself throughout Europe, North America and Australasia. Most of its members have clung firmly to their religion. Many reports suggest that Islam is the fastest growing religion in those areas. At the same time, the problem of Islamic terrorism has arisen. After the Twin Towers outrage a decade or so ago, the United States, in its infinite unwisdom, is waging an unending and probably futile war against terrorism. The causes of Islamic terrorism are many and varied. Many young, dispossessed Muslims fear that their religion is under threat and that its icons: Mohammed, Allah and the Koran are disrespected in the West. Another important cause is revenge or payback for Western imperialism. As late as 1950, almost the entire Muslim world was occupied and controlled by Western countries.

So, in 2012, the West, the seat of Christianity, a religion in sharp decline, is ranged alongside the Middle East, much of Africa and Asia where Islam holds sway. It could be said that these two major faiths are at war with one another.

The Christian establishment continues to exert great influence in spite the manifest decline among the faithful. The Vatican, whose political skills have enabled it to survive for millennia, shamelessly uses the pulpit to promulgate its views. It interferes in democratic elections by threatening its nominal adherents with excommunication if they do not toe the party line on such matters as abortion, the use of birth control, gay marriage and assisted suicide. Just this week in Australia, the Catholic pulpits were inveighing against current proposals to change marriage laws in that country. Yet, recent history reveals that that same Catholic Church has strayed from the paths of righteousness over child sex abuse, perpetrated for decades, and its unwillingness to unmask known pedophile priests, preferring to shield the good name of the Church rather than provide justice for the abused. The Vatican Bank has been an instrument for money laundering for years and only recently has allowed civil authorities to investigate its affairs. The Vatican is guilty of major tax fraud, refusing to pay tax on its purely commercial operations. Catholic cardinals, archbishops and priests are responsible for countless deaths in East Africa through their refusal to allow HIV/AIDS sufferers to protect their partners from infection by the simple use of condoms.

In the UK, twenty-six unelected, Anglican bishops occupy seats in the upper house and are thereby permitted to stick their unwanted oars into any piece of legislation that offends them.

Christian doctrine can be summed up in one word: love. Jesus enjoined his followers to love one another. Popes, past and present along with their henchmen have shown little love for their flocks, choosing instead to place their treasure, reputation and prestige far above the needs and expectations of the sheep. Two words are necessary to summarise the core Islamic philosophy: peace and justice. How far current, sanctioned practice strays from these ideals is shown by the espousal of violence against ordinary men and women on the streets in the shape of terrorist activities and by its treatment of women: veiling, inferior status in legal matters, disallowing female education and withholding the right to vote. How much peace and justice is shown towards those who are stoned to death for adultery, apostasy, disrespecting the Prophet or blasphemy? Many Muslims regard such practices as repellent but few speak out against them and so by their silence, they assent to them. Who could argue against the notion of a code of behaviour founded upon ideas of love or on peace and justice? The high priests of Christianity and Islam have lost the plot. They have taken unto themselves the right to interpret the religious doctrines they espouse and to use them to control the laity.

Lastly, there is dispute among learned circles as to the origin of the very word 'religion'. In very early societies every daily occurrence and action was assumed to be something to do with the gods and thus there was no use for a word for religion. Everything was religious. By the time of the Romans, different views prevailed and a word was coined from which the English term 'religion' arose. It seems that the word can be construed to mean placing an obligation upon or to bind. Either meaning implies control and modern practice most certainly emphasises this aspect of religious life: no contraception, no divorce, praying five times daily, adopting certain postures while praying, no female priests, castigating homosexuals, no abortion, no permission to allow the terminally ill to escape by means of assisted suicide, stoning to death

ʒation of women, genital
boys and girls, ostracising
ᴇss the rules of the sect,
ᴉe priesthood and the list
ᴉuch more about what thou
ᴉere is about love, peace and

n or curse? Out of the hands
and allowed to spread love,
ᴇ, what a boon it could be.
ᴉ by priests, mullahs and other
assorted 'holy men', it turns out to be a curse
standing in the way of those who might seek
comfort by trying to approach the unknowable.

Aggressive secularism

(First published on 28/02/2013 - revised on 01/03/2013)

Several religious leaders in Europe have complained about the menace, as they see it, of aggressive secularism. Pope Benedict XVI has been particularly outspoken on this matter. He has gone so far as to say that re-evangelisation of Europe and the West is an urgent priority. The reasons for this concern are not hard to find. The Christian brand is rapidly losing its market share and faces declining membership, an ageing priesthood and greater and greater difficulty engaging the young either as congregants or noviciates. Organisations, such as the Roman Catholic Church, that have become used to unquestioning obedience for hundreds of years, find it difficult to cope with this new situation.

Secularism implies a separation of church and state. Secularists do not wish to deny the faithful the benefit of religion but they seek to limit religious meddling in day-to-day management of public matters. Jesus of

Nazareth summed it up quite nicely when he told the Roman centurion to "Render unto Caesar the things which are Caesar's, and unto God the things that are God's" This saying can be interpreted to mean that churches should keep their noses out of matters that do not concern them. Secularists do not believe that religion is necessary as a foundation of morality. They hold that people can obey the golden rule without any reference to a deity. They also claim that people unconsciously understand the need for rules and regulations to be in place to ensure the prosperity and good order of society. Thus, stealing, lying, cheating, murder and unprovoked violence are things to be abhorred. The idea of the social contract is appealing to them for it ensures that less weighty matters can be nicely arranged for the benefit of all, as well.

Most religious doctrines take a prurient interest in sexual affairs. Catholicism and Islam have a morbid interest in such matters and seek to lay down the law with pettifogging detail on how people should conduct themselves in this regard. Secularists on the other hand are much more relaxed and liberal. They do not consider that abortion, for example, is wrong in every instance. They find great possible utility in stem cell research. They do not consider the activities of homosexual and transgendered people sinful, criminal and outrageous. They do not feel that humans have been allotted a certain span of years and should live them out regardless of the plight in which they may find themselves through injury or disease. They hold that these matters are best managed according to the precepts of the golden rule and the application of common sense. However, they acknowledge that certain religions find such matters contrary to their doctrines. Secularists do not deny the right of religious authorities to impose restrictions on their members. On the other hand, they object very strenuously when these same authorities seek to enforce their doctrines universally.

Certain Catholic prelates in the United States have threatened members of their flocks with excommunication if they chose to vote for one party rather than another. The United States Constitution makes the separation between the state and the church very clear. This constitutional provision has not inhibited bishops and cardinals from interfering in the electoral process. Secularists regard such behaviour as wrong.

Roman Catholic bishops have objected to the use of vaccinations for young women against genital herpes simplex on the grounds that it could promote promiscuity. Bishop Fred Henry of Calgary, Alberta inveighed against this useful prophylaxis, which potentially protects women from cancer of the cervix. He has recently changed his mind. A prominent Scottish Catholic bishop has recently done a deal permitting young women to have the vaccination as long as they are not given any sex education. A secularist might ask what business is it of bishops to interfere in such vital health matters. The Catholic Church strove mightily to ensure that condoms were not provided to populations in East Africa as HIV/AIDS prevention. It is uncertain how many women died because of this action. Again, a secularist would suggest that the Church and its officials had no business to impose its doctrines upon poor benighted peoples.

Religious leaders in the USA have fought against sex education in schools for fear of promoting promiscuity. Again, religious authorities have no right to force their ignorance down everyone's throat. By all means, let the uncritically faithful ensure that their daughters run the risk of contracting preventable, serious disease, if they so desire. They have to square their consciences with the consequences of their mindlessness. But, they cannot be allowed to saddle us all with such foolishness.

Orthodox Islam has no place for secular ideas for it considers that the Koran and Sharia provide rules for all conduct and behaviour. The most orthodox followers of Islam consider that humans have no business in voting or partaking otherwise in democratic procedures. Such actions, in their view, are tantamount to blasphemy, for Allah has laid down how public and private affairs should be conducted. Moslems can refer to their holy books for guidance on every facet of life. Hence, there is no place for man made laws. Those, who adhere to such a worldview, naturally find the very notion of secularism baffling and unsettling.

Orthodox Judaism takes a similar view and true believers can refer to Leviticus for guidance and instruction on just about every conceivable human question. They believe that God has outlined the law in great detail and that any quandary that might arise can be settled by close study of Scripture. For orthodox Jews, secularism can play no part in the conduct of day-to-day affairs. The law is there for all to see and to obey.

It does not occur to the faithful that God is a human construct. Primitive men and women invented the idea of higher powers to explain natural phenomena such as the seasons, tides, floods, day and night and the birth, growth and death of living things. Once societies had become sufficiently affluent to support full time priests, shamans and witch doctors, these men – they were almost always men – took on the role of interpreting the mysteries and insisted that they were the only portal through which contact with the higher powers could be made. Thus, they became inordinately powerful. Religion turned into a tool for controlling the masses. The likes of the Pope, the Chief Rabbi and the Caliph are the direct descendants of the early shamans. It should not be forgotten that the Holy Books such as the Bible, the Koran and the Torah were written thousands of years ago and heavily influenced by conditions as they then existed. Progress has been made and many of the mysteries that so baffled our forefathers have now been explained by science and reason. These two enlightening influences show no sign of exhaustion and it seems highly likely that more and more of the unanswered questions about the natural world will be made clear with the passage of time. Exhortations concerning diet, dress, sexual behaviour, along with the dictates of scripture that had such importance in the deserts of the Middle East and the Levant long, long ago, have little relevance today.

Christianity and Judaism are in decline and seem likely to fade away as populations become better educated and sources of information more easily accessible. The education of women and the means whereby they can be freed from the burden of endless child rearing are also likely to reduce the hold of religions and the frequently malign influence of their clerics. Islam is very much mired in the late Stone Age and followers of that belief system can expect to wait sometime before enlightenment breaks through, but it surely will. Clerics are not fools and they must be well aware that their positions of power and influence are on the wain. They have looked around for something to blame and secularism is a handy scapegoat. The use of the term 'aggressive secularism' merely serves to emphasise how weak they feel their position has become. Secularism does not proselytise. It does not seek converts. It does not ask that people give up their beliefs and take on other ones. There is no such thing as a secular apostate. Secularism cannot be blasphemed. It merely asks that religious authorities keep their noses out of everyone's affairs. It truly considers that Jesus was on the right path when he counselled the Roman centurion.

Faith

(Original publication date not known)

The Jesuits knew what there were doing when they said that if they were given the child before he turned seven, they could show the man he would become. They were well aware that the mind of a child is infinitely malleable and inclined to take on board any old stuff passed on by authority figures, including parents. In other words, a young child does not have well developed powers of analysis and reason. The Jesuits are not the only group who have come to this conclusion. Little Muslim boys are herded off into madrassas where they are taught to recite the Koran. In Arabic speaking countries, they have some idea of what each word means. However, Islam has spread to many places where Arabic is not spoken. The little boys are still taught to recite the Koran by teachers who also do not know how to speak Arabic. Hence, the poor little blighters are made to chant a series of sounds that are meaningless to them and to commit this stuff to memory. Little Orthodox Jewish boys are sent to Yeshivas where they study the Torah in detail. The Torah incorporates the first five books of the Hebrew Bible plus endless commentaries that have been written by holy men down the centuries. By the time these kids, both Muslim and Jewish, have reached puberty they have been brain washed into accepting the words of their teachers as being full of meaning and significance. They have certainly not been shown how to ask for evidence that any of the subject matter is anything more than myth and superstition. Furthermore, the priests, rabbis and imams devote almost all of their efforts towards indoctrinating the males. Much less energy goes towards brainwashing the girls.

It is the passing down of religious doctrine and ritual from generation to generation that ensures the survival of these various faith traditions. The leaders of the faiths have vested interests in keeping the entire enterprise going for they know full well that once the chains, forged in childhood, are broken, they are out of a job. It is worth considering a thought experiment at this point. The experiment works much better among Christians than either Muslims than Orthodox Jews, as will be explained later. Were Christian children not to be told anything about religion until they were sixteen to eighteen years old, the following scenario might arise. Fathers and mothers would summon their offspring to dinner table sessions and tell them that they had important information to impart: they were all Christians and followers of Jesus Christ. They would start by saying that there is an entity called God who is extracorporeal, outside the bounds of time and space, all powerful and all knowing, which resides in Heaven. They would also tell the young, that God cares deeply about them and watches their every move and keeps a kind of celestial score sheet, on which is tagged the good and the bad. God, they would learn, is greatly upset when anyone transgresses, so upset that he found it necessary to send his only son, Jesus, to Earth to ensure that all mended their ways. Jesus was born of a virgin through immaculate conception, or in other words, no sex act was involved. Jesus carried out a short ministry in the Jerusalem area until he fell foul of the authorities. During this time, he performed several miracles: turning water into wine, walking on water, feeding a multitude using five loaves and fishes, raising the dead, curing the crippled by means of telling them abandon their crutches and walk and lastly, curing the blind by anointing their eyes with a mixture of mud and spittle. He was tried and executed by crucifixion and buried in a convenient tomb. A few days later he was found to have disappeared and then to be seen walking around and contacting some of his former followers. Later on, he was taken up to heaven where he resides to this day. Jesus, the Son, and God, the Father, are accompanied by another entity, the Holy Spirit, and together, they make up something called the Holy Trinity and are three in one and one in three and with each being equally significant.

Furthermore, parents would explain that Christians went to church each Sunday to offer thanks and to worship this ineffable and transcendent entity. Moreover, Jesus told his immediate followers on the eve of his execution that they should remember him by means of a ceremony that became known as

Holy Communion, in which wine and bread were taken. After these comestibles were properly blessed by church officials, they actually became his actual blood and flesh through a process known as transubstantiation. Children are allowed to take part in this ceremony once they have been confirmed at another rite. And so on and so on.

The thought experiment is harder to envisage among Jewish and Muslim children because both Islam and Orthodox Judaism are incorporated into daily life through dress, diet and practice but it is still worth giving it a go. Muslim children would be told that their religion arose after the Prophet Mohammed was summoned to a cave where he was instructed to take down the word of Allah dictated to him by the Angel Gabriel. The resulting text was called the Koran and was henceforth regarded as the inerrant word of God and not to be altered or tampered with by so much as a jot or tittle. The dictation process took many years. Mohammed was illiterate but was commanded to read! Armed with the Koran, he set about converting his neighbours and later raised armies that subjugated surrounding tribes, who until that time had worshipped a multiplicity of gods. The sayings of Mohammed were collected and became known as Haditha. He instructed his followers that some things were halal – good – and others were haram – bad. A code of law followed, called Sharia, which laid down details of behaviour, domestic life, religious life, the status of women, dress, diet and just about everything else. Women would be regarded as inferior to men under Sharia. They were commanded to dress modestly, like the Prophet's wives, and that, over time over came to mean that they could not appear in public unless shrouded from head to toe. No intermingling of the sexes was to occur. Muslim children would also be told that Muhammad was the perfect man and God's last prophet and that Islam, the religion he founded, was superior to all other religions. They would be instructed that blasphemy or apostasy were both punishable by death. Furthermore, a series of extremely harsh punishments were mandated for sins such as adultery and theft. Lastly, the Koran contained several injunctions about the correct attitude towards kuffirs or non-believers. Jews and Christians were regarded by the Faithful as Children of the Book, a grudging acknowledgement that much of Islam is derived from Judaism and Christianity – both inferior to Islam, as far as true believers are concerned.

Jewish children would be told by their parents that their God was known as Yahweh. He specially chose the so-called children of Israel and had a covenant with them. Jewish males would be obliged to have their genitals ritually mutilated as a sign of their taking part in this covenant. Yahweh appeared to several of his followers in a number of guises. He commanded them to behave in certain ways and gave them have an immensely detailed set of instructions in the Book of Leviticus. These instructions covered almost every detail of daily life. Actions were kosher or not kosher. Pork and certain sea creatures are non-kosher. Wearing garments made of two kinds of fibres is non-kosher. Lighting fires on the Sabbath is sinful, even turning on an electric light. Men were supposed to study the holy books and women were meant to work. After marriage, women were to shave their heads and wear wigs so as not to attract other men. Jews were expected to await the birth of the Messiah who would restore them to their rightful place among the people of the World and end their suffering.

Christian, Muslim and Jewish parents would be obliged to point out that each of their religions was riven by sectarianism and that not only did Christians despise Jews and Muslims for example – these feelings were reciprocated – but that they despised other branches of their own religion. Catholics look down on Protestants. Both regard Mormons as weird. Sunni Muslims see Shi'as as infidels. Orthodox Jews despair of emancipated Jews. And so on and so on. Tiny points of difference take on immense significance in the world of religion. So, it would be a very unpalatable and bewildering package that parents would be handing their offspring as they came to the age of reason.

Parents would have to point out that each of their religions had its own holy book. The contents of these books would be shown to contain hair raising accounts of the doings of the faithful and that many of the contained writings contradict one another.

It is possible to imagine the blank looks of incredulity on the faces of sensible young people who had all of these ideas imparted in one hit. They would rightly wonder what their parents had been smoking. Virgin births, resurrection, Trinities, transubstantiation, illiterates meeting angels in caves and being commanded to read and take dictation, God appearing as a flaming bush and micromanaging just about every detail of daily life would all be impossible to accept with a straight face. No wonder, then, that religions rely on a steady drip feed of information during the formative years of childhood. Interesting also to reflect that representatives of various totalitarian polities, such as the Soviet Union and Nazi Germany, sought to indoctrinate the young through the Young Pioneers and the Hitler Youth movement, for they realised that their ideologies would have no chance of taking if introduced when children had minds of their own to make up.

Across much of the Christian and Jewish world, religion plays a diminishing role in the lives of a larger and larger number of people. This is especially true in prosperous areas where levels of education are high and means of communication freely available. It is even more so where girls are educated to the level of boys, a fairly recent development. Religion maintains an iron grip on much of the Islamic world but there are signs that it is losing its hold in the diaspora. Christopher Hitchens observed that there is an inverse relation between the claims that religions make and the evidence they can produce to back them up. As more and more of the mysteries of the universe are unravelled and that this information becomes available to all, the need for the transcendental and the miraculous declines. An eighteen year old faced with the precepts of religious doctrine for the first time would have a hard time swallowing them. He would point to the knowledge he had gained at school through his science classes and see how radically it clashed with the historical teachings of the faiths. This does not imply that religions do not have some moral lessons to impart but much of their thrust is blunted by their disputatiousness, internecine fighting and the appalling deeds carried out in their names in the past. Besides, much modern thought maintains that ethics and morals can be taught without reference to deities or need for religious faith.

In the near future, it looks as if the purveyors of religious ideas had better stick to what has worked in the past: get 'em young or else give up trying!

The end of the antibiotic era

(First published on 20/09/2013)

People born before 1935 emerged into a world in which antibiotics had not yet been developed. If one of them sustained a scratch from a thorn in a garden, for example, they could die of septicaemia should the wound become infected. Women who developed infection of the genital tract following childbirth –puerperal sepsis – frequently died. Cases of septic meningitis had very high mortality rates. In each of these instances, the medical profession was powerless to provide targeted treatment. Heavy metals, such as bismuth and arsenic had been found to be somewhat effective in the treatment of syphilis – an infection caused by a micro-organism–as early as 1910. Consequently, Salvarsan was introduced and was the first chemotherapeutic agent employed in Western medicine.

Sulphonamides were discovered by Heinrich Hörlein, Gerhard Domagk and Joseph Klarer working in Germany for Bayer AG. They were released as therapeutic agents in 1935. In the UK they were commonly referred to as M&B because they were made by May and Baker. American soldiers had them in their first aid packs during World War II. The story of the discovery of penicillin has passed into medical folklore. Briefly, Alexander Fleming, a Scottish scientist, noticed that the mould, penicillium rubens, extruded a substance that inhibited the growth of bacteria in petri dishes. Howard Walter Florey, an Australian doctor, developed penicillin as a medicine that was first used in Oxford in 1942 to save a sick person's life. Others had a hand in these events but the principal players were Fleming and Florey, who both received Nobel Prizes for their work.

Penicillins, termed antibiotics, were the first really effective tool for treating bacterial infections and were greeted with enthusiasm by the medical profession. They were able to treat streptococcal sore throats which were common and often led to rheumatic heart disease, acute nephritis and neurological problems: St. Vitus' Dance, an affliction of the basal ganglia of the brain that control aspects of normal movement. Rheumatic heart disease often caused permanent valvular, heart disease and premature death. Once penicillins were available these consequences of a simple sore throat became increasingly rare. I saw several cases of the complications of rheumatic heart disease during my training in the Fifties but heard of hardly any at the end of my career save in remote Aboriginal communities in Northern Australia. Likewise, pneumonias were now amenable to treatment and entire streets of people were not obliged to hold their collective breath wondering whether poor old Mrs Jones would recover after a crisis or just die. (cf. The Citadel by A.J.Cronin) A whole host of ailments, previously beyond the scope of medicine were now curable – a boon, indeed.

Following the introduction of the penicillins, several other antibiotics were discovered. During the next few decades more than 20 classes of antibiotics were introduced containing more than 150 drugs. Alarmingly, no new class of antibiotic has been introduced into practice for more than 13 years. The lipoglycopeptides, first introduced in 2009, are undergoing trials and one of them is sanctioned in some countries for certain infections.

Antibiotics work in many ways. Some inhibit bacterial cell division, others damage their cell walls and others impair reproduction of bacterial DNA and RNA. There are roughly two main categories of drug: those that kill the organisms, bactericidal drugs, and those that inhibit the growth of the organisms, bacteriostatic drugs. Depending how bacteria are classified there are about fifty that cause disease in humans.

Micro-organisms have shown an amazing ability to mutate and render themselves immune to the predations of many commonly used drugs. Shortly after the use of antibiotics became widespread, physicians became aware of the phenomenon of 'antibiotic resistance'. Some staphylococci showed signs of becoming resistant to some types of penicillin by the late 40s! This ability is yet another proof of the soundness of evolutionary theory and one in the eye for the proponents of creationism! In recent years, a worrying number of organisms appear to be beyond the reach of antibiotics. Certain strains of E. coli, clostridium difficile, gonorrhoea, golden staphylococcus and tuberculosis are the main villains. In the main, these organisms are the cause of nosocomial infections, or in other words, those picked up in hospitals. The Centre for Disease Control in the US estimates that more than two million people die world wide from antibiotic resistant bugs every year, 23,000 in the United States, alone. There is a good deal of dispute about why antibiotic resistance has become such a problem. Some point to antibiotic overuse: any child with a fever being given a prescription willy-nilly and many courses of antibiotics not completed. There has also been widespread use of these drugs in agriculture after they were found to promote growth in livestock. It is possible that widespread resistance would not have occurred so early had doctors been rather more stingy with their prescribing habits but it would have cropped up sooner or later.

It takes about ten years to discover, test and introduce a new drug into practice and costs not far short of one billion dollars.

Antibiotics are not attractive propositions for drug companies because the returns are small. Drugs to treat high blood pressure, raised cholesterol and diabetes make much better commercial sense because those, who take them, do so for the rest of their lives and a growing number of people need them. Antibiotics are usually given in short courses and most users only need them once or twice.

So, the outlook is not promising. Absence of effective antibiotic drugs will affect procedures like hip replacements, organ transplants, and the use of immune system, altering drugs employed in the treatment of cancer patients. People having such operations or those using chemotherapy must have efficient antibiotic cover lest they succumb to intercurrent infections. New approaches to the treatment of disease caused by bacteria are urgently required. The problem of antibiotic resistance will undoubtedly become more and more widespread and without new drugs or therapeutic approaches, it is likely that the medical profession will find itself in the same position as it was before 1935 and so, into and out of the antibiotic era over the compass of a lifetime.

Worrying thought.

Acknowledgements: this essay was provoked by an article appearing in the Guardian on 16/09/2013 and a broadcast from ABC Radio National's 'Big Ideas' programme on 05/09/2013.

Free speech

(First published on 31/01/2014)

The fuss about the students thrown out of the Freshers' Fair at the London School of Economics rages on. During a couple of popular TV shows in the UK, posses of outraged Muslims jumped up and down inveighing against the malevolence of those who would poke fun at the sacred cows of Islam by publishing and displaying satirical cartoons. They demanded that such rascals be muzzled. They insisted on knowing why anyone would treat a religion with disrespect. They claimed that they had been offended by the 'Jesus and Mo' cartoons and maintained that there was no place for that kind of material in public media. This episode raises important questions about free speech and the respect, if any, due to religious beliefs. Firstly, is it possible to offend a religion? Secondly, should one be prevented from offending a group or an individual? Thirdly, and much more generally, should there be any limits on freedom of speech?

A religion is a set of beliefs adhered to by a group of people, founded entirely on faith and unsupported by a shred of evidence. Religions may also be looked upon as a set of myths that help some people make sense of the world they find themselves in. Many people take them very seriously and look upon them as absolute truths. This group is likely to be very touchy about criticism or pointed questions. The monotheisms originated in the distant past and come with sacred scriptures and include revered figures. The historian of Islam, for example, must conclude that its sacred figure was delusional, afflicted by satryrism, practised paedophilia and spread his doctrines by means of violence. Such conclusions will receive a very frosty reception from adherents of that faith. The same historian, who researches Christianity and declares that the evidence for the actual existence of Jesus of Nazareth is scanty and that the central tenet of that faith, the resurrection, makes no sense, will be unpopular with Christians. Scriptural accounts of Jesus demanding that his first recruits simply abandon their wives and families to follow him make uncomfortable reading in the twenty-first century.

Because suggestions of this nature are upsetting to true believers, their proponents may well encounter physical violence rather than invitations to partake in sober debate. Religion has held such unquestioned sway over ideas for so long, that even non-believers or the uncommitted can be discomforted by views which appear to be disrespectful of it. Why should this be so? After all, the historian has merely looked at what evidence exists and arrived at a set of conclusions. In most other fields of endeavour, such behaviour would be considered admirable. It is also worth noting that similar sensitivity is not the sole preserve of religious faiths. Certain political ideologies have demonstrated antipathy to questioning, when in power. Those who ran Nazism or Stalinism did not permit any straying from the path of permitted thought or from their 'scriptures': Mein Kampf or Das Kapital!

The students, who displayed Jesus and Mo cartoons, faced noisy opposition on the TV shows mentioned above and were told that such cartoons should not be published for they are offensive to Muslims. The objectors seemed to be fully prepared to muzzle those who are not in agreement with their worldview. They are not satisfied with the right to express their views. They also demand the right to impose their ideas on others and forbid them the right to express a critical and contrary point of view. Opinions at odds with the received orthodoxy are categorised as blasphemy, which is some parts of the World is deemed so serious as to attract the death penalty.

The second question about the right to offend or the countervailing right not to be offended is complex. In an environment in which rights take precedence over responsibilities, certain individuals and groups maintain that no one should make comments about others that are potentially upsetting. Political correctness holds that talking about fat people, coloured people, mad people, lazy people, Muslims, Jews, drug takers, drunkards and so on, is offensive and that special circumlocutions must be used in order not to categorise anyone in negative terms. It becomes increasingly hard to speak about any particular group without using special language and so those, who are not articulate, are effectively shut up. For example, there is widespread concern about the large numbers of people who are overweight. Brushing aside for the minute whether such concerns have any basis in fact, a person who is 1.7 metres tall and who weighs 135 kgms must be described as obese or outside normal weight and height limits. To speak of them as fat is unacceptable. To suggest that much recent urban violence has been carried out by radical Muslim groups will result in accusations of stereotyping. It is not clear whether concerns of this nature originate in genuine consideration for the persons under discussion or fear of the consequences of speaking plainly. Authorities have shown that they are cautious about challenging Islamic precepts and very frightened of for provoking violence. Regardless, freedom of speech is inhibited.

Lastly, what limits, if any, should be placed upon free speech? The old chestnut tells of the mischief maker who yells out, 'Fire,' in a crowded theatre, when fully aware that panic will ensue and that people are likely to be harmed by being trampled on. In that his intention is malign, laws treating malicious behaviour ought to be sufficient to deal with him, rather than those designed to prevent certain utterances under special circumstances. The individual who attends a public debate about religion and who speaks critically about revered, historical figures may well provoke a noisy and even violent disturbance. Should such talk be banned? Does the individual not have the right to make such observations? If a riot ensues, is he responsible for damage and physical harm that could follow? There are certain topics that are held to be inviolable. Those who deny the holocaust face jail in many countries. It is easy to imagine how annoyed and saddened people, whose families perished in Nazi death camps, would feel when they learn that such views are openly spoken about. That these notions are totally without foundation is not sufficient balm for hurt feelings. Does society do itself any good by forbidding controversial utterances? Is it not preferable to allow the purveyors of such arrant nonsense to be exposed as the idiots and poltroons they really are? Some individuals hold that human induced global warming is a myth put about by groups who wish to inhibit the operations of contemporary capitalism. The fact that the overwhelming majority of respectable climate scientists are in accord on the matter is of no moment to them. Rather than trying to silence climate deniers, it must to be preferable to allow them space to express their views and thereby make fools of themselves.

Governments around the World insist that tobacco and alcohol advertising should be limited in scope. They forbid promoters of sporting events to accept sponsorship from the tobacco and alcohol industry. Recently, some authorities have mandated plain packaging for cigarettes. Now, there are good public health reasons for these actions but there can be no denying that the freedom of speech of the companies concerned has been limited. It is no longer permitted to advertise certain products on TV during the hours children are likely to be watching. Good public health reasons can be adduced for such bans but again, they can only exist by limiting free speech. Perhaps a better line of attack would be to hand over to parents the entire responsibility for controlling what their children are allowed to watch. Similarly, would not control of tobacco and alcohol promotion be better achieved through public education rather than what amounts to censorship? Governments are likely to admit that parents cannot be expected to control their children and that the public is immune even to the best public health education. If that is true, it demonstrates a very poor state of affairs.

Does it, however, justify state sponsored censorship?

It is not so very long ago, that the Lord Chamberlain had the right to read every play and every book that was to be performed or published. He also had the right to forbid their appearance. James Joyce's *Ulysses* and DH Lawrence's *Lady Chatterley's Lover* were banned by him for years until a celebrated court case showed how silly such bans really were. Even today, examples of state censorship of works of art continue to crop up occasionally. The affair of the 'Piss Christ' comes to mind. Material deemed offensive because it deals with sex or violence in unpleasant ways should not be withheld, for no one is forced to read it. Is society well served by regulating pornographic material found on the Internet? Merely making it harder and harder for people to gain access to it does not address the real problem, which is the state of mind of those who make it and those who get their kicks from watching it. Doubtless, material of this sort will be harmful for children to see and this potential harm again raises the question of whose task is it to protect children: the state or the parents.

It could also be argued that unfettered free speech would allow anyone to divulge confidential information: state secrets, medical records or details of personal affairs. Such claims would be disingenuous for there are other laws that cover such matters and those who broadcast or divulge confidential material are likely to find themselves in very hot water.

Most humans apply self-censorship to their utterances in the interest of peace and quiet. The remorselessly honest person who speaks his or her mind about any topic under discussion is likely to have few friends. The visitor who goes to a friend's new house and remarks how ugly it is, may well be speaking the truth, but is certain offend his host. The husband, when asked by his wife about a new dress, and says that he has seldom seen her in a less attractive outfit, will hurt his wife's feelings and achieve little or no good. 'White lies' seem to be the necessary social lubricant that enable harmonious, interpersonal relationships. White lies or tact, although a kind of censorship, are quite different matters from limits imposed by governments or other official authorities, but are nonetheless, morally dubious.

Unfortunately, an idea such as free speech cannot be qualified. If any one thing is forbidden, then speech is not free. However worthy the motives behind limiting tobacco and alcohol advertising may be, muzzling the companies who wish to sell legal products, is censorship. Censorship and freedom of speech cannot co-exist. Voltaire is quoted as remarking, 'I disapprove of what you say, but I will defend to the death your right to say it.' Perhaps this is a very good maxim to use when considering what limits, if any, should be imposed upon the utterances of individuals and groups.

Phonics

(First published on 23/03/2008)

The long running argument about how best to teach children to read has resurfaced in the Australian media. From time to time figures are released that suggest that about a quarter of all children leave school unable to read and write fluently and unable to perform simple arithmetical procedures. There are those who blame parents for not spending sufficient time with their children and reading them bedtime stories so that the kids can read by the time they start school. Others claim that such expectations place unreasonable demands upon already over stressed parents who are struggling to pay off the mortgage and the instalments on the latest SUV. A year or two back, most Canadian universities were running remedial reading classes for their freshmen because the latter were arriving in class with very poor literacy skills. The Universities criticised the schools for not doing a good job of educating kids and the schools responded by saying that it was not their job to prepare students for university.

However, there is not much argument about the usefulness of being able to read, write and count. Those who can, tend to prosper in every way more than those who cannot. A good deal of debate has taken place about the best way to teach children to read and write. Some consider that children should be exposed to texts and then they will somehow learn reading skills by osmosis. In other words they will join up words with meaning. This is the whole language approach. Others claim that it is more helpful to teach children to break up words into their individual sounds or in other words to teach them to spell out the word. This is the phonic method. Many children seem to acquire the ability to read almost by magic. They acquire the skill very easily. It does not much matter what you do with this group. Others struggle and need more help. Children whose homes are filled with reading material tend to do better than those who come from homes where there is none. Obviously, children, who are having difficulty learning to read, need help and the question arises which sort of help is best.

The English language does not have a highly inflected structure like Russian or German. This renders it easier to learn in some ways. However, its spelling and pronunciation are quite chaotic with no rules. Just consider the words that end in 'ough.' Why are tough and enough pronounced 'tuff' and 'enuff' whereas 'though' is pronounced 'tho' and 'through' pronounced 'throo?' There are scores of similar bits of craziness. The old fashioned way to teach English reading and writing was the so-called phonics method. 'C-A-T' spells cat and so on. The whole language approach is relatively recent and it is very fashionable in certain educational circles.

During the last thirty or forty years, university departments of education have sprung up all over the place. A person can now become a credentialed educationalist with bachelors, masters or doctorate degrees. These experts purport to teach others how to teach. A quick Google search for university departments of education comes back with millions of hits. These departments support large numbers of peer reviewed journals. All of these departments produce immense amounts of research to fill up these journals.

Much effort has gone into investigating the efficacy of whole language teaching in contrast to the phonics approach. It appears that the old tried and trusted method of phonics has it over whole language. And yet, many teacher training colleges continue to turn out advocates of whole language. Consequently many children are exposed to this approach and many of them emerge from twelve years of schooling unable to read and write proficiently. Perhaps it has always been the case that a large proportion of school leavers were functionally illiterate. Can we use that as an excuse today when so much money and so many resources are poured into education? If it is true that the whole language approach has been discredited by educational research, it is hard to understand why it is still used.

A medical model demonstrates that once approved but now discredited methods of treatment are discarded and that practitioners who insist on using obsolete methods will find themselves hauled up in front of the licensing body to justify their choice of treatment. Ailments are no longer treated with bleeding or cupping and woe betide the doctor who tries to do so! Teachers are licensed by state and national bodies and presumably have to answer for their actions. To justify the use of an outmoded method of teaching as being an article of faith should not really cut it. The education of the young is surely more important than clinging to doctrine however sincerely it is believed in. Either whole language is justified or it is not. Surely all of these departments of education can settle the matter. If not, one sincerely wonders what they are all for.

Proper Use of Prepositions Society (PUPS)

(First published 23/09/2006)

Annual address from the President.

Ladies and Gentlemen,

Thank you for coming along this afternoon. We at PUPS all know what a preposition is, how to use them and when to use them. There may be a few new members who are not familiar with this useful little part of speech and so at the risk of boring long standing members I shall provide a short definition.

A preposition is a word that links nouns, pronouns and phrases to other words or part of the sentence. The common ones are: by, at, of, to, from, upon, with and without. The word or phrase introduced by the preposition is called the object of the preposition. Already you see that these little words are vital for they tell us where things are situated and when they occur. It is hard to imagine the language without them. Being so useful you would imagine that no one would want to mess about with them but, alas, that is exactly what is happening in much of today's spoken and written English.

In my view, and the in the view of PUPS executive, some of the more egregious examples of misuse attend the verbs to talk and speak. Commonly one hears the following, 'I have spoken with Jim' or 'We are going to talk with Susie.' Speaking and talking are not unlike singing and so if we write, 'I have sung with Jim' or 'We are going to sing with Susie' we mean that we shall pairing up as some kind of ensemble and that we shall all sing together. Obviously, when we say, 'My mother used to sing to us' we do not imply that we sung together, although perhaps later we may have joined in.

When I say that 'I must speak with Michael' do I mean that he and I are going to speak simultaneously? Surely, the more accurate usage is to say, 'I must speak or talk to Michael.' In other words, there is information that I need to give to or obtain from Michael.

I guess that in these days when it is necessary to bend over backwards to avoid giving offence or to make it seem that we are all good mates and that there is no question of being in a hierarchical relationship, then the notion of talking to someone is a little too brusque. Of course, there was a time when ones parents or schoolmasters would give one a 'good talking to' and that equated to having a flea put in the ear. But, I do not see how Jim can possibly take offence if I say, 'Jim, I'd like to talk to you about the new curriculum for the fourth year students.' If the aforesaid Jim is such a tender little flower as to be upset by such a verbal approach, I suggest he needs to get out more often.

Let us now turn to the verb meet. How often do you hear, 'I met with Jane this morning' or 'Let us meet with the board.' The verb to meet is transitive and so takes a direct object. What is wrong then with saying, 'I will meet Jim tomorrow' or 'The new director wishes to meet the staff.' Is this another instance of seeming a little too direct?

Prepositions are being murdered in other ways. It is distressingly common to hear, 'He entered into the building' or 'They regressed back to the beginning.' Surely any literate person knows that to enter means to go in and thus the word into is redundant; that same person knows that to regress implies going backwards and so the word back is likewise redundant. Commonly we hear people saying, 'They continued on with their work.' Presumably the users of this ugly verbal construction do not understand that the notion of continuing implies an ongoing process and so the addition of on is unnecessary. Other horrors include, 'Outside of the church' and 'It fell off of the shelf.'

I could go on ad nauseam and I fear that may already have done so, but, dear Members, you take my point. I expect all of you can think of other similar examples of sloppy speech. We at PUPS must do all that we can to fight this insidious disease that is infecting our marvellous native tongue. When your children bring work home, in which these solecisms appear and have not been underscored in red, write to the teacher to complain but be prepared to learn that he or she has not the slightest idea what you are talking about. When you hear or read this kind of stuff at work, point out the ghastliness of the usage to the sinners.

Thank you.

Passports and penny pinching

(First published 08/05/2006)

My passport was lost between the Department of Immigration in Sydney and Coffs Harbour. In spite of best efforts all round it has not turned up.

So, I was obliged to obtain a new one from the British High Commission in Canberra. It is possible to download the necessary forms via the internet and the Commission's web site contains much useful information – as well as a couple of spelling errors. However, after a careful search through the site I was left with two unanswered questions and so I thought I would phone. Imagine my surprise when I learnt that you have to pay to speak to a Commission employee on the phone and there are a number of tariffs you can choose. I decided to go for the $7.10 item, which would allow me an unlimited chat.

The employee who answered the phone was able to answer my queries efficiently and after doing so prepared to ring off. 'Not so fast,' said I, 'I've paid for this and I want my money's worth.' I grumbled about the need to pay to speak to a High Commission clerk and argued that many have to phone because they are in a jam and need major help from those who are in Embassies and paid to provide it. I was told that the British Government was no longer prepared to provide such services free of charge. Patently, my correspondent could do more than spew out the party line and so I ended the call and decided to write a letter of complaint to the High Commissioner.

In my letter I grumbled about the cheese paring nature of the telephone answering policy. I suggested it might help further to defray costs if cups of water given out to visitors to the High Commission were charged so much a glassful and that penny-in-the-slot machines should be screwed on to any public toilet facilities on the premises. I supplied a stamped addressed envelope to defray the expense of the reply.

A few days later I received a letter from a functionary who told me that the High Commission in Canberra processed more than 68,000 passports a year and that this made it essential to charge for telephone advice. But hold on, that does not add up. The fee for passport renewal is $170 and so the annual income to the British authorities comes to a shade under eleven million dollars. Assuming that High Commission staff work a 200 days year and a 7.5 hour day, and that they employ a dozen clerks to deal with passport renewals, then each one has to process about 3.75 passports an hour. If each clerk is paid $50,000 p.a. then wages amount to $600,000. If each blank passport costs $10, then that adds another $680,000 for a total of $1,280,000 a year. This is a far cry from the gross income of eleven big ones and even if I have underestimated expenses by a factor of three, it is still a nice little earner and should leave plenty over to staff a few phones.

Patently the British Government has employed some bean counters who advised it on how to gouge money from those who perhaps no longer live in the UK or who are travelling overseas and are, therefore, out of sight. It would be good if others, who find this meanness as offensive as I do, would write letters of protest to their MPs or local papers.

Sheer, daylight robbery!

The Pope and the Chief Rabbi...

(First published on 30/04/2006)

The Chief Rabbi decided that it was high time that he paid a courtesy call on the Pope and so he made an appointment. He was duly shown into the Pope's office and saw that the Holy Father was seated behind an ornate desk on which was placed a magnificent telephone made out of solid gold and encrusted with precious stones.

After the usual exchange of pleasantries, the Chief Rabbi mentioned the phone and asked why it was so elaborate. The Pope told him that it had been recently installed and it was the instrument used when he wanted to chat with God. The Chief Rabbi's interest was well and truly piqued and he confessed that he had been somewhat delinquent of late and that he had not called into headquarters for some little time.

'If we paid for the call, would it be all right for me to use this marvellous phone. It is high time that I reported to himself,' he said. 'Go right ahead,' replied the Pope. The Chief Rabbi made his call and instructed his secretary to settle the bill.

A few weeks later, the Pope felt that he ought to return the Chief Rabbi's visit. When he was shown into the Chief Rabbi's study he noticed that there was a similar phone to his own on the desk. The Chief Rabbi told him that he had it installed after his visit to the Vatican. The Pope then admitted that he was well overdue making his usual reports to Heaven.

'Would you mind if I made a call upstairs?' he asked, 'Fear not, we shall pay for it.'

'Don't bother yourself with such trifles,' answered the Chief Rabbi, 'It is only a local call from here!'

....and the **Grand Mufti**

(First published on 02/05/2006)

A little later, the Pope and the Chief Rabbi decided that they should pay a courtesy call on the Grand Mufti and tell him about their new IT arrangements and offer him some advice. They made an appointment and were duly shown into his study. The first thing they noticed was that there was no solid gold, jewel encrusted phone on the desk.

'Grand Mufti,' said the Pope, 'The Chief Rabbi and I have obtained special phones that let us talk to the Almighty at very reasonable rates any time we want to. We notice that you do not have such a phone.'

'Quite unnecessary,' replied the Grand Mufti, 'Allah drops in here all the time, and it just so happens, he's in the back parlour having his tea!'

THE END

41077027R00277

Made in the USA
Charleston, SC
22 April 2015